An Insider's Guide to Academic Writing

Academic Writing

A Brief Rhetoric

D1572896

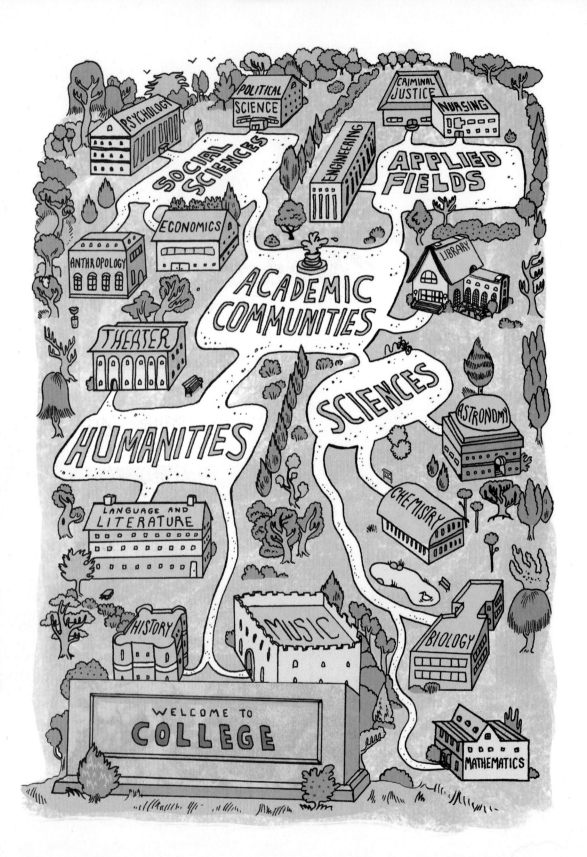

Third Edition

An Insider's Guide to Academic Writing

A Brief Rhetoric

Susan Miller-Cochran

University of Arizona

Roy Stamper

North Carolina State University

Stacey Cochran

University of Arizona

bedford/st.martin's
Macmillan Learning
Boston | New York

For Bedford/St. Martin's

Vice President, Humanities: Leasa Burton
Program Director, English: Stacey Purviance
Senior Program Manager: Laura Arcari
Director of Content Development: Jane Knetzger
Senior Development Editor: Cynthia Ward
Editorial Assistant: Bill Yin
Director of Media Editorial: Adam Whitehurst
Media Editor: Dan Johnson
Marketing Manager: Vivian Garcia
Senior Director, Content Management Enhancement: Tracey Kuehn
Senior Managing Editor: Michael Granger
Senior Digital Content Project Manager: Ryan Sullivan
Senior Workflow Project Manager: Lisa McDowell
Production Supervisors: Robin Besofsky, Robert Cherry
Director of Design, Content Management: Diana Blume
Interior Design: Claire Seng-Niemoeller
Cover Design: William Boardman
Director of Rights and Permissions: Hilary Newman
Permissions Editor: Allison Ziebka-Viering
Text Permissions Researcher: Elaine Kosta, Lumina Datamatics, Inc.
Photo Researcher: Cheryl Dubois, Lumina Datamatics, Inc.
Director of Digital Production: Keri deManigold
Media Project Manager: Elizabeth Dziubela
Project Management: Lumina Datamatics, Inc.
Project Manager: Nagalakshmi Karunanithi
Editorial Services: Lumina Datamatics, Inc.
Copyeditor: Angela Morrison, Lumina Datamatics, Inc.
Indexer: Christine Hoskin, Lumina Datamatics, Inc.
Composition: Lumina Datamatics, Inc.
Cover and Title Page Image: Andrea Tsurumi
Printing and Binding: LSC Communications

Library of Congress Control Number: 2021942629
ISBN: 978-1-319-34612-6 (Paperback Edition)
ISBN: 978-1-319-42132-8 (Loose-leaf Edition)

Printed in the United States of America.
1 2 3 4 5 6   26 25 24 23 22 21

Acknowledgments

Text acknowledgments and copyrights appear at the back of the book on page 317, which constitutes an extension of the copyright page. Art acknowledgments and copyrights appear on the same page as the art selections they cover.

Preface for Instructors

We undertook the third edition of *An Insider's Guide to Academic Writing* during extraordinary times for higher education. During a global pandemic that, in many instances, caused educational institutions to make sudden and dramatic changes to their course offerings and instructional methods, we found ourselves reconsidering many of our assumptions about teaching writing. We thought about how to connect with students in meaningful ways from a distance and how to address our students' and our own well-being during a time of uncertainty. In addition to the challenges of the pandemic, we were also writing while our nation experienced much political unrest even as we experienced an important inflection point in the ongoing struggle for racial equality. These trials of the past year have underscored the importance of facts and truth in both our civic and our academic engagements, and they've reminded us of the importance of making every effort to stem the tide of racial prejudice and discrimination in all of its forms, both implicit and explicit.

The circumstances of the last year have informed decisions related to the development of the latest edition of *An Insider's Guide*. Our primary goal remains to help college students, new to the world of higher education, learn the territory, language, skills, codes, and secrets of academic writing in disciplinary contexts. At the same time, we've endeavored in the new edition to incorporate what we've learned about student engagement and online education from the dramatic instructional shifts stemming from the global pandemic, and we've made numerous changes to the text as part of our effort to affirm our commitment to social justice in a more equitable world.

Core Features of *An Insider's Guide*

An Insider's Guide to Academic Writing continues to offer a unique set of resources for helping students develop rhetorical skills that are transferable from first-year composition to other courses and writing contexts. Through the study of writing in academic disciplines, students are also introduced to the kinds of questions explored by different academic communities.

Building Rhetorical Skills through the Study of Academic Writing

We wrote *An Insider's Guide to Academic Writing* out of a need for a text that would effectively prepare students to navigate the reading and writing expectations of academic discourse communities across the curriculum. We recognized that no single book, or course, or teacher could train all students in all the details of scholarly writing in all disciplines. What we aimed to do instead was offer students rhetorical principles that are fundamental to the understanding of texts and then show those principles at work in various domains of academic inquiry, including the humanities, the social sciences, the natural sciences, and the applied fields.

We set out with three key goals: (1) introduce students to rhetorical lenses through which they can view the genres and conventions they will be expected to read and produce in other courses, (2) provide examples of those genres and conventions to analyze and discuss, and (3) include carefully scaffolded writing activities and projects designed to help students explore and guide their production of those genres. Part One lays the groundwork for this disciplinary approach, introducing students to the fundamentals of writing processes and reflection, rhetorical analysis, argument, and research. Part Two provides unique discipline-specific chapters, and if you are using the comprehensive version of the text, Part Three offers readings from each discipline area on high-interest themes.

An Insider's Guide is as flexible as it is comprehensive. Some faculty, for instance, use this approach to support themed courses; they examine how a particular topic or issue is explored by scholars across a range of disciplines. Other faculty situate principles of argument at the center of their course designs and explore disciplinary perspectives and writing in light of those principles. Still others organize their courses as step-by-step journeys through academic domains while attending to the similarities and distinctions in writing practices (rhetorical conventions and genres) of various fields.

Engaging Students with Class-Tested Pedagogy

We designed *An Insider's Guide to Academic Writing* to provide all the resources we wanted when we transitioned the first-year writing program at North Carolina State University to a writing-in-the-disciplines (WID) approach:

- **Writing Projects**—one or more per chapter—offer detailed prompts and guidance for students to practice the skills and moves taught in the chapters. These include literacy narratives, rhetorical analyses, genre analyses, arguments supported by research, and annotated bibliographies, as well as such common academic genres as textual interpretations (humanities); theory response papers, literature reviews, and poster presentations (social sciences); and lab reports and research proposals (natural sciences).

- **"Insider Example" essays** show how students and academics have responded to different writing projects. Annotations point out key features and moves that students can consider for their own writing.

- **"Insider's View" boxes** feature scholars and students from a range of disciplines, discussing their experiences with academic writing. Several of these boxes are excerpted from video interviews that complement the instruction in this book. These videos are available for viewing in the digital platform Achieve.

- **"Connect" activities** prompt students to reflect on what they have learned and practice applying these new insights and techniques. (These were called "Inside Work" in previous editions.)
- **Tip Sheets** summarize key lessons of the chapters.

In addition to chapters with the above features, the comprehensive edition of *An Insider's Guide* offers **a thematic reader with popular and scholarly essays** that can serve as springboards for writing and discussion as well as models of rhetorical moves and disciplinary genres and conventions. The scholarly essays are organized as **case studies**; each case study includes readings from the humanities, social sciences, natural sciences, and applied fields. Through these unabridged essays, students can contrast the form and content of writing across the curriculum, while also getting practice in tackling academic reading. Annotations, headnotes, and post-reading questions provide support.

What's New

We have substantially revised the third edition to improve the online experience, while also adding new content to reflect the diversity of writing and writers. We listened to teachers using the book to learn what works in their classes and how we could do better. Here are the revision highlights:

- **For the first time, *An Insider's Guide to Academic Writing* is available within the Achieve platform.** Achieve with *An Insider's Guide to Academic Writing* offers a dedicated composition space that guides students through drafting, peer review, Source Check, reflection, and revision. Developed to support best practices in commenting on student drafts, Achieve is a flexible, integrated suite of tools for designing and facilitating writing assignments, paired with actionable insights that make students' progress toward outcomes clear and measurable—all in a single powerful, easy-to-use platform that works for face-to-face, remote, and hybrid learning scenarios. Achieve includes the complete e-book and fully editable and assignable pre-built assignments that support key assignments in the book. For details, visit **macmillanlearning.com/college/us/achieve/english**.
- Readings, boxes, examples, and photos have been revised so that **students with a diverse range of identities and experiences** can see that they too belong as "insiders" in academic communities. In the comprehensive edition, more than half of the readings in Part Three are new, bringing in a more contemporary and diverse range of writers and perspectives on matters of identity and writing, love, food, and criminal justice.

- **New Insider Examples** give students models for every writing project in the book. The new examples include an argument analysis, an annotated bibliography, a genre analysis, a poster presentation, a PowerPoint presentation, an IT paper, and a genre analysis in the applied fields. All of the Insider Examples are now annotated to highlight the writer's rhetorical moves.

- **New "Insider's View" boxes** add to the range of disciplines and research areas represented: Dev Bose, Disability Writing Studies scholar, on accessible design; historian Matthew Sakiestewa Gilbert on research in American Indian Studies; Cristina Ramirez, Writing Studies scholar, on genres and styles in the humanities; and vice chancellor Bruce Moses on writing as an administrator.

- **"Inside Work" activities have been renamed "Connect"** to make explicit their purpose of providing opportunities for students to put their learning into action. These activities have been streamlined so that many of them can be completed in a single sitting, either independently or as group work.

- **Added coverage of multimodal writing** can be found in new discussions and examples of poster presentations (Chapter 8) and PowerPoint slides (Chapter 10). A new reading (Jia Tolentino's "The I in Internet") in Chapter 11 of the comprehensive edition offers a writer's account of growing up in multimodal digital spaces.

- Chapters 7 to 9 offer **a fuller treatment of academic genres**. Each genre is structured to include the rhetorical context of and strategies for writing the genre, followed by a Writing Project and Insider Example.

Acknowledgments

We are grateful to the students who were willing to try this approach and, in many cases, share their writing in this book. Their examples provide essential scaffolding for the book's approach, and their honest feedback helped us refine our explanation of various genres and disciplines.

We are also grateful to our colleagues in the First-Year Writing Program at North Carolina State University and the Writing Program at the University of Arizona, who have shared their expertise and ideas about teaching writing in and about disciplines over the years. Without their support and their innovation, we would not have been able to complete this project.

We are indebted to the many skilled and thoughtful instructors who have used and offered feedback on the book. We are truly grateful to you for supporting, through your engaging advice and encouraging criticism, our efforts to make this book the best it can possibly be. For this third edition, we wish to recognize Jessie Blackburn, Appalachian State University; Virginia Crisco, California State University, Fresno; Lourdes Fernandez, George Mason University; Penny Jacobs, Fayetteville Technical Community College;

Debra Knutson, Shawnee State University; Robin Latham, Nash Community College; Will Mayer, Longwood Community College; Jessica Saxon, Craven Community College; and Terri Van Sickle, Craven Community College.

Our thanks also go to the incredible support from our team at Macmillan. First and foremost among that team is Cynthia Ward, our development editor, who has helped us see this revision through to completion and provided insightful suggestions that guided our approach. We are also indebted to Leasa Burton, vice president of humanities at Macmillan, who understood our goals and championed this project from the beginning. We have also received outstanding support and guidance from Stacey Purviance, program director for English, and Laura Arcari, senior program manager. We are also grateful for the work of Ryan Sullivan, who guided the book through the production process with great care. We thank Claire Seng-Niemoeller for creating the superb design of the book, William Boardman for the book cover design, and Vivian Garcia for her marketing and market development efforts. Additionally, we extend our thanks to Daniel Johnson, media editor for the Achieve platform; Bill Yin, editorial assistant; and Hilary Newman, director of rights and permissions. We thank the other contributors who helped in so many ways behind the scenes.

As always, we remain indebted to our friends and families, who provided a great deal of support as we worked on this edition of the book.

Susan Miller-Cochran
Roy Stamper
Stacey Cochran

Bedford/St. Martin's Puts You First

From day one, our goal has been simple: to provide inspiring resources that are grounded in best practices for teaching reading and writing. For more than 40 years, Bedford/St. Martin's has partnered with the field, listening to teachers, scholars, and students about the support writers need. No matter the moment or teaching context, we are committed to helping every writing instructor make the most of our resources—resources designed to engage every student.

How We Can Help *You*

- Our editors can align our resources to your outcomes through correlation and transition guides for your syllabus. Just ask us.
- Our sales representatives specialize in helping you find the right materials to support your course goals.
- Our learning solutions and product specialists help you make the most of the digital resources you choose for your course.
- Our *Bits* blog on the Bedford/St. Martin's English Community (**community.macmillan.com**) publishes fresh teaching ideas regularly. You'll also find easily downloadable professional resources and links to author webinars on our community site.

Contact your Bedford/St. Martin's sales representative or visit **macmillanlearning.com** to learn more.

Digital and Print Options for *An Insider's Guide to Academic Writing*

Choose the format that works best for your course, and ask about our packaging options that offer savings for students.

Digital

- **Achieve with *An Insider's Guide to Academic Writing*.** Achieve puts student writing at the center of your course and keeps revision at the core, with a dedicated composition space that guides students through drafting, peer review, Source Check, reflection, and revision. Developed to support best practices in commenting on student drafts, Achieve is a flexible, integrated suite of tools for designing and facilitating writing assignments, paired with actionable insights that make students' progress toward outcomes clear and measurable. Fully editable pre-built assignments support the book's approach and an e-book is included. To order Achieve with *An Insider's Guide to Academic Writing*, use ISBN 978-1-319-42370-4. For details, visit **macmillanlearning.com/college/us/achieve/english**.

- **Popular e-book formats.** For details about our e-book partners, visit **macmillanlearning.com/ebooks**.

- **Inclusive Access.** Enable every student to receive their course materials through your LMS on the first day of class. Macmillan Learning's Inclusive Access program is the easiest, most affordable way to ensure all students have access to quality educational resources. Find out more at **macmillanlearning.com/inclusiveaccess**.

Print

- **Paperback.** *An Insider's Guide to Academic Writing* is available in paperback in two versions.
  - To order the paperback **comprehensive edition** (subtitle, "A Rhetoric and Reader"), use ISBN 978-1-319-33492-5. To order the paperback comprehensive edition packaged with Achieve, use ISBN 978-1-319-44587-4.
  - To order the paperback **brief edition** that does not have the four-chapter reader (subtitle, "A Brief Rhetoric"), use ISBN 978-1-319-34612-6. To order the paperback brief edition packaged with Achieve, use ISBN 978-1-319-44740-3.

- **Loose-leaf.** This format does not have a traditional binding; its pages are loose and hole-punched to provide flexibility and a lower price to students. It can be packaged with Achieve for additional savings.
  - To order the loose-leaf **comprehensive edition** (subtitle, "A Rhetoric and Reader"), use ISBN 978-1-319-42130-4. To order the loose-leaf comprehensive edition packaged with Achieve, use ISBN 978-1-319-44631-4.
  - To order the loose-leaf **brief edition** that does not have the four-chapter reader (subtitle, "A Brief Rhetoric"), use ISBN 978-1-319-42132-8. To order the loose-leaf brief edition packaged with Achieve, use ISBN 978-1-319-44744-1.

Your Course, Your Way

No two writing programs or classrooms are exactly alike. Our Curriculum Solutions team works with you to design custom options that provide the resources your students need. (Options below require enrollment minimums.)

- **ForeWords for English.** Customize any print resource to fit the focus of your course or program by choosing from a range of prepared topics, such as Sentence Guides for Academic Writers.

- **Macmillan Author Program (MAP).** Add excerpts or package acclaimed works from Macmillan's trade imprints to connect students with prominent authors and public conversations. A list of popular examples or academic themes is available upon request.

- **Mix and Match.** With our simplest solution, you can add up to 50 pages of curated content to your Bedford/St. Martin's text. Contact your sales representative for additional details.

Instructor Resources

You have a lot to do in your course. We want to make it easy for you to find the support you need — and to get it quickly.

- *Resources for Teaching An Insider's Guide to Academic Writing* is available as a PDF that can be downloaded from **macmillanlearning.com** and is also available in Achieve. In addition to chapter overviews and teaching tips, this instructor's manual includes sample syllabi, correlations to the Council of Writing Program Administrators' Outcomes Statement, and classroom activities.

- *Resources for Teaching North Carolina English 112 with An Insider's Guide to Academic Writing* is also available as a PDF that can be downloaded from the Bedford/St. Martin's online catalog at **macmillanlearning.com**. This brief resource complements *Resources for Teaching An Insider's Guide to Academic Writing*, with teaching attention to specific course outcomes and transfer requirements articulated in the 2014 Comprehensive Articulation Agreement between the University of North Carolina and the North Carolina Community College System.

Contents

PART ONE A Guide to College and College Writing 1

Part One introduces you to the kinds of writing expectations you will face in college and equips you with core principles and strategies that you can apply to all types of writing. You'll build your skills by practicing strategies for giving and receiving feedback, reflecting on your writing processes, making supported arguments, and engaging in academic research.

3 Reading and Writing Rhetorically 33

4 Developing Arguments 48

5 Academic Research 67

In Part Two you'll look at how writing works in each of the major academic areas. You'll learn how the conventions and genres of different disciplines represent a discipline's shared values. Throughout these chapters, you'll be practicing skills of rhetorical analysis that you can transfer to your future courses and careers.

7 | Reading and Writing in the Humanities   122

Annotated Readings and Insider Examples

An Insider's Guide to Academic Writing

A Brief Rhetoric

ANDREA TSURUMI

PART ONE

A Guide to College and College Writing

Part One introduces you to the kinds of writing expectations you will face in college and equips you with core principles and strategies that you can apply to all types of writing. You'll build your skills by practicing strategies for giving and receiving feedback, reflecting on your writing processes, making supported arguments, and engaging in academic research.

An Introduction to Academic Writing

This book introduces expectations about writing you'll likely encounter in college and helps you develop a set of tools to complete writing tasks successfully. A main aim of this book is to help you find connections between what you are learning about writing and how that knowledge can help you achieve your personal, professional, and academic goals. To accomplish that aim, we first introduce you to how and why colleges and universities are structured into academic disciplines. We'll explore how your other writing experiences in high school, college, and work might compare to what you will write in college, and we will also discuss what expectations about writing you might encounter in different classes.

Teachers and researchers who study writing have found that students who are effective writers develop strategies for using what they learn in their writing classes in other classes and contexts. Most importantly, they learn how to *adapt* what they have learned about writing to those new contexts, paying attention to the expectations about writing in each unique situation.

As you read through the chapters in this book, certain recurring features will help you build these strategies as you expand your knowledge of college writing:

- *Insider's View* boxes feature scholars and students discussing academic writing. Several of these are gleaned from video interviews that complement the instruction in this book. The videos, which are available for viewing in the digital platform Achieve, offer further insights into the processes and productions of academic writers.

- *Connect* activities prompt you to reflect on what you have learned while trying out new insights and techniques.

- *Writing Projects* offer sequences of activities that will help you develop your own compositions.

  - *Insider Examples* show how writers have responded to different academic writing situations. Annotations point out key features and moves that you can consider for your own writing.

  - *Tip Sheets* summarize key lessons of the chapters.

ANDREA TSURUMI

Your Goals and Your School's Mission

As we get started on this journey, we'd like you to reflect on your goals: academic, professional, personal, or other. What brought you to college? People's reasons for pursuing an undergraduate degree can differ, depending on their interests and what motivates them. Different schools offer different opportunities as well. Some schools and degree programs focus on preparing students for particular careers that they can pursue directly after graduation. Others focus more broadly on developing graduates in a range of different areas who will be active in their communities regardless of which careers they pursue. Still others emphasize different, and sometimes quite specific, outcomes for their graduates. If you have never done so, consider taking a look at the mission or values statements for your university, college, or department. What do the faculty members and administrators value? What are their expectations of you as a student?

For example, the mission statement of Texas A&M University begins by stating:

> Texas A&M University is dedicated to the discovery, development, communication, and application of knowledge in a wide range of academic and professional fields.

This statement shows a broad commitment to a range of academic interests and professions; therefore, students at Texas A&M can expect to find a wide range of majors represented at the university. The mission statement also emphasizes that knowledge discovery is important at Texas A&M, highlighting the school's role as a research-intensive university.

As another example, the mission statement of Glendale Community College in California reads:

> Glendale Community College serves a diverse population of students by providing the opportunities and support to achieve their educational and career goals. We are committed to student learning and success through transfer preparation, certificates, associate degrees, career development, technical training, continuing education, and basic skills instruction.

This statement illustrates Glendale Community College's emphasis on preparing students for careers and serving a broad range of students with specific academic and professional goals.

A third example is the mission statement of Endicott College in Massachusetts, which begins by stating:

> Shaped by a bold entrepreneurial spirit, Endicott College offers students a vibrant academic environment that remains true to its founding principle of integrating professional and liberal arts with experiential learning including internship opportunities across disciplines.

Endicott's mission mentions an emphasis on "experiential" learning, which is evident through the connection of professional experiences with academics and the availability of internships for students. Students who enroll at Endicott College should expect a practical, hands-on application of their learning throughout their coursework.

Of course, different students have different goals and reasons for pursuing undergraduate degrees. Sometimes those goals match the institution's mission fairly closely, but not always. What is your purpose in attending your college or university? How do your personal and professional goals fit within the school's goals and values?

Regardless of your purpose for attending college, the transition to college can be a challenging one. Vincent Tinto, a researcher interested in what helps students succeed as they make the transition to college, has identified and written extensively about three stages that students go through as they adapt to college: separation, transition, and incorporation.[*] At the separation stage, students might feel disconnected to prior communities and commitments, but successful students move through a transition stage and then find a way to connect themselves with new communities in college (incorporation). The separation stage can be very challenging, though, and knowing what resources you have available to you as you make the transition to college can be incredibly helpful.

Connect 1.1   **Identifying Your Goals within the Academic Community**

Find your school's mission statement (usually available in the "About" page of the school website). As you work through the following questions, think about how the mission of your school might align with your own interests and goals:

- What do you feel you are motivated to learn about? For example, if you had four hours with nothing to do except read and learn about one subject, what would you choose to read about? Or, if you could take only one class right now, but it could be any class you'd like, what would it be? Why?

- What goals do you hope to achieve by attending college?

- What connections do you see between your own goals and the mission of the university? How might the characteristics and mission of your college or university help you achieve your goals?

- What steps could you take to maximize your opportunity to explore your academic interests and achieve your goals?

---

[*]Tinto discusses these stages in "Stages of Student Departure: Reflections on the Longitudinal Character of Student Leaving," *Journal of Higher Education,* vol. 59, no. 4 (1988), pp. 438–55.

Writing within Academic Disciplines

As you enter the college community, you will discover different communities within it, each using writing to share knowledge and build our understanding of the world. When you take courses within these communities, you read and write within these specialized worlds. This book will give you tools and frameworks to meet these diverse and challenging assignments.

An important organizational feature of colleges and universities is the way they are divided into academic and professional disciplines. Depending on the school, this might take the form of departments, divisions, colleges, or other groupings. **Academic disciplines** are, broadly defined, areas of teaching, research, and inquiry that academics pursue. Sometimes these disciplines are listed in broad categories, such as psychology, English, biology, physics, and engineering. Within each academic discipline are more specialized communities of scholars.

At other times, disciplines are listed in more specialized categories that demonstrate the diversity of areas encompassed within higher education: for example, adolescent psychology, abnormal psychology, sociolinguistics, second language acquisition, molecular biology, physiology, astrophysics, quantum mechanics, civil engineering, mechanical engineering, computer science, Victorian poetry, and medieval literature.

While the specific divisions may differ according to the institution, most college and university faculties are grouped into departments or divisions of some sort, and those groupings usually correspond to similarities in how they approach the world from their disciplinary perspectives. Larger schools are typically further divided into colleges or schools-within-schools, which usually cluster together departments that are related to one another in some way. These groupings often, but not always, fall along common lines that divide departments into broader disciplinary areas of the humanities, social sciences, natural sciences, and applied fields. We use these broader categories when introducing you to different types of academic writing in Part Two.

For the purposes of this text, we're going to explore writing in different disciplinary areas that are grouped together according

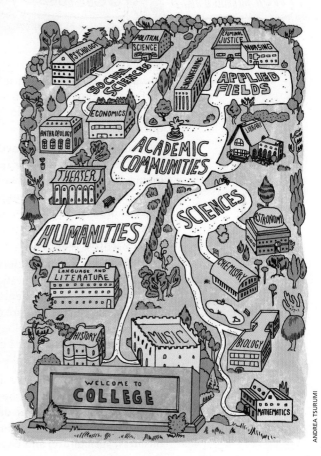

ANDREA TSURUMI

to (1) the kinds of questions that scholars ask in those disciplines and (2) the research strategies, or methods of inquiry, that they use to answer those questions. As mentioned earlier, we've divided various academic disciplines into four broad disciplinary categories: humanities, social sciences, natural sciences, and applied fields. As we talk about these four areas of study and the disciplines associated with them, both here and in Part Two of the book, you'll notice some similarities and differences within the categories:

- Scholars in the **humanities** usually ask questions about the human condition. To answer these questions, they often employ methods of inquiry that are based on analysis, interpretation, and speculation. Examples of academic disciplines that are generally considered part of the humanities are history, literature, philosophy, foreign languages, religious studies, and the fine arts. You'll find examples of the kinds of questions humanists ask—and how they write about them—in Chapter 7.

- Scholars in the **social sciences** usually ask questions about human behavior and society. To answer these questions, they often employ methods of inquiry that are based on theory building or empirical research. Examples of academic disciplines that are generally considered part of the social sciences are communication, psychology, sociology, political science, economics, and anthropology. You'll find examples of the kinds of questions social scientists ask—and how they write about them—in Chapter 8.

- Scholars in the **natural sciences** usually ask questions about the natural world. To answer these questions, they often employ methods of inquiry that are based on experimentation and quantifiable data. Examples of academic disciplines that are generally considered part of the natural sciences are chemistry, biology, physics, astronomy, and mathematics. You'll find examples of the kinds of questions natural scientists ask—and how they write about them—in Chapter 9.

- Scholars in **applied fields** might have their foundation in any one (or more) of the disciplinary categories, but their work is generally focused on practical application. Some disciplines that could fall under the category of applied fields are criminal justice, medicine, nursing, education, business, agriculture, and engineering. Each of these fields has elements that are closely aligned with the humanities, social sciences, and/or natural sciences, but each also focuses on application of that knowledge in specific contexts. You'll find examples of the kinds of questions scholars in applied fields ask—and how they write about them—in Chapter 10.

These categories are not perfectly distinct; they sometimes overlap with one another, and they are debatable. Sometimes you'll find that different institutions categorize certain classes as part of a particular disciplinary area through their General Education requirements, for example. Another institution might list a similar class as meeting a different requirement. You'll see examples of disciplinary overlap in the chapters in Part Two and in the student writing examples there. Regardless, the disciplinary categories of humanities, social sciences, natural sciences, and applied fields are useful for understanding some of the distinctions in the ways academics think and do research. One of the most useful things about understanding distinctions in how different disciplines approach subjects is understanding how they can work together to solve problems.

> ### Connect 1.2   Understanding Disciplinarity
>
> Look at your current course schedule. How might you classify the classes you're taking in terms of the four academic disciplines we've described: humanities; social sciences; natural sciences; applied fields? For each class, write for a few minutes about what characteristics of the class cause it to fit into the category you've chosen. Finally, compare your answers with a classmate's.

Entering Academic Conversations

As you think about the writing you will do in college, keep in mind that you are learning how to participate in the kinds of discussions that scholars and faculty members engage in about topics and issues of mutual interest. In other words, you're entering into academic conversations that have been going on for a while. As you are writing, you will need to think about who your audience is (other students? teachers? an audience outside of the academic setting?), who has already been participating in the conversations of interest to you (and perhaps who hasn't), and what expectations for your writing you'll need to follow in order to contribute to those conversations. (We'll have much more to say about the concept of audience in Chapter 3.)

As we explore the kinds of writing done in various disciplinary areas, you'll notice that different disciplines have different expectations for writing. In other words, faculty members in a particular discipline might expect a piece of writing to be structured in a particular way, or they might use specific kinds of language, or they might expect you to be familiar with certain research by others and refer to it in prescribed ways. Each of these expectations is an aspect of the writing conventions of a particular discipline. **Conventions** are the customs that scholars in a particular discipline follow in their writing.

Sometimes those conventions take the form of repeated patterns in structure or certain choices in language use, just to name a couple.

To prepare for writing in varied academic contexts, it might be helpful to think about why academics write. Most faculty members at institutions of higher education explain their responsibilities to the institution and their discipline in terms of three categories: their teaching, their research (which generates much of their writing), and their service (what they do outside of their research and teaching that contributes both to the school and to their discipline). Many academics' writing is related to communicating the results of their research, and it might be published or shared with academic audiences or more general audiences. In fact, a scholar might conduct a research project and then find that he or she needs to communicate the results of that project to a variety of audiences.

Imagine that a physiologist who studies diabetes has discovered a new therapy that could potentially benefit diabetic individuals. The researcher might want to publish the results of her study in an academic journal so that other scientists can read about the results, perhaps replicate the study (repeat it to confirm that the results are the same), and maybe expand on the research findings. She might also want to communicate the results of her research to doctors who work with diabetic patients but who don't necessarily read academic journals in physiology. They might read medical journals, though, so in this case the researcher would need to tailor her results to an audience that is primarily interested in the application of research results to patients. In addition, she might want to report the results of her research to the general public, in which case she might write a press release so that newspapers and magazines can develop news stories about her findings. Each of these writing situations involves reporting the same research results, but to different audiences and for different purposes. The physiologist would need to tailor her writing to meet the needs of each writing situation.

Connect 1.3 · Thinking about Academic Writing

Look for a published piece that has been written by one of the professors who you have for another class. Try to find something that you can access in full, either online or through your school's library. Some colleges and universities have lists of recent publications by faculty on their websites. Additionally, some faculty members list their publications on personal websites. You might also seek help from librarians at your institution if you aren't familiar with the library's resources. Then write your responses to the following questions:

- What does the professor write about?
- Where was the work published?
- Does your professor appear to be writing for other specialists, or does the audience appear to be nonspecialists?
- What surprised you most about your professor's published work?

Learning to Write in New Contexts

Many of your expectations for writing in college might be based on prior experiences, such as the writing you did in high school or in a work setting. Some students find that writing in college focuses less on personal experience and more on research than writing they've done in other contexts. Some students are surprised to find that writing instruction in college is not always paired with discussion of literature, as it often is in high school. While some colleges and universities use literature as a starting point for teaching writing, many other schools offer writing instruction that is focused on principles of **rhetoric**—the study of how language is used to communicate—apart from the study of literature. (Rhetoric will be discussed in detail in subsequent chapters throughout this book.) As you may have already experienced, many courses require you to write about different topics, in different forms, and for different audiences. Depending on your school, writing program, and instructor, the study of literature might be part of that approach, but you might also need to learn about the expectations of instructors in other disciplines.

Insider's View
Undergraduates Sam Stout, Gena Lambrecht, and Alexandria Woods on Academic Writing

Left to right: Sam, engineering; Gena, design; Alexandria, biology

QUESTION: How does the writing you did in high school compare to the writing you've done in college so far?

SAM: Well, in high school [teachers] mainly chose what we wrote about. And here in college they allow you to write about what you're going to be focusing on and choose something that's actually going to benefit you in the future instead of writing for an assignment grade.

GENA: Well, I thought I would be doing a lot more writing like in my AP English classes, which was analyzing literature and poems and plays and writing to a prompt that talked a lot about specific conventions for that type of literature.

ALEXANDRIA: I expected my college writing to be science-related—doing lab reports and research proposals—rather than what I did before college, in middle school and high school, which was just doing definition papers, analysis of books, and things like that.

Although the approaches toward teaching writing at various colleges and universities differ, we can talk about some common expectations for college-level writing. The Council of Writing Program Administrators (CWPA), a professional organization of hundreds of writing program directors from across the country, published a list of common outcomes for first-year writing courses that has been adapted for use by many schools. The first list of common outcomes was published in 2000, and it has been revised twice since then, most recently in 2014. The purpose of the list of outcomes is to provide common expectations for what college students should be able to accomplish in terms of their writing after finishing a first-year course, but the details of those expectations are often revised to fit a specific institution's context. For example, the CWPA's first outcome deals with "Rhetorical Knowledge" and emphasizes the importance of understanding how to shape your writing for different purposes and audiences. It states:

> By the end of first-year composition, students should
> - Learn and use key rhetorical concepts through analyzing and composing a variety of texts
> - Gain experience reading and composing in several genres to understand how genre conventions shape and are shaped by readers' and writers' practices and purposes
> - Develop facility in responding to a variety of situations and contexts calling for purposeful shifts in voice, tone, level of formality, design, medium, and/ or structure
> - Understand and use a variety of technologies to address a range of audiences
> - Match the capacities of different environments (e.g., print and electronic) to varying rhetorical situations
>
> http://wpacouncil.org/positions/outcomes.html

The statement introduces several specialized concepts and terms that we will describe in more detail throughout the book. You might also notice that the statement doesn't specify what kinds of writing students should do in their classes. It is left up to individual schools to determine what will be most helpful for their students.

Earlier in this chapter, we asked you to reflect on your goals for college. When you put your goals alongside the outcomes listed above, what potential connections do you see? As you compare your goals with the outcomes and the description of the writing course you are currently taking, what opportunities emerge? What might you be able to learn and practice in your writing course that will help you achieve your goals?

Connect 1.4   Understanding the Goals of Your Writing Course

Take a look at the goals, objectives, or outcomes listed for the writing course you are currently taking. You might look for a course description on the school's website or in a course catalog, or you might find goals or learning objectives listed in the course syllabus.

- What surprised you about the goals or objectives for your writing course?
- What is similar to or different from the writing courses you have taken before?

- What is similar to or different from the expectations you had for this course?
- How do the outcomes for the course align with your goals for writing and for college?
- What does the list of goals for your course tell you about what is valued at your institution?

Writing Project   Profile of a Writer

For this writing project, you will develop a profile of a writer in an academic field or profession of interest to you based on an interview you conduct. Under the guidance of your instructor, identify someone who is either a professor, graduate student, or upper-level student in your major (or a major that interests you) or a professional who works in a career that you could imagine for yourself. You might choose someone with whom you already have a connection, either through taking a class, having a mutual acquaintance, or enjoying a shared interest. Ask the person if you can interview him or her, either in person or through e-mail. Consider the descriptions of different disciplinary areas in this chapter, and write a profile of the writer that addresses questions about his or her writing, such as the following:

- What kinds of writing do people do in your field?
- What is the purpose of the writing you do in your field?
- What writing conventions are specific to and important to your research or work? How did you learn those conventions?
- What kinds of writing do you do most often in your work?
- What was your experience the first time you attempted to do those kinds of writing?
- What expectations do you have for students or new professionals who are learning to write in this field?
- What are the biggest writing challenges you've faced in your work?
- What advice would you give to students who are learning to write in your discipline to help them succeed?

Be sure to follow up your questions by asking for specific examples if you need more information to understand your interviewee's responses. In addition, you might ask to see an example of his or her writing to use as an illustration in your profile. Don't forget to thank the person for taking the time to respond to your questions.

A profile of a writer should do two things: (1) make a point about the person being interviewed (in this case, your point should focus on the person's writing) and (2) include details about the person's experiences that help develop the point.

Incorporate the person's responses into an essay that uses the interview to make a specific point about his or her development and experience as a writer.

···

Insider Example

Student Profile of a Business Professional

Rubbal Kumar, a sophomore at the University of Arizona, conducted an interview with Benu Badhan, a software engineer from India. Kumar is a computer science major, and he interviewed Ms. Badhan to learn more about the expectations for writing in his future profession. Through his interview with Ms. Badhan, Kumar learned that writing is very different for a software engineer than for a computer science major, but the writing he does as a computer science major will still prepare him well for his future career.

Rubbal Kumar's Draft of Interview Questions

1. Why did you choose this specific profession? What interested you in becoming a computer scientist?
2. What is your specific area of expertise in computer science, and why did you choose to specialize in that area?
3. What different types of writing are involved in computer science?
4. Is there any specific set of rules for writing in the IT field? If yes, then how is it different from the kinds of writing students are typically taught in school?
5. Did you face any difficulties in understanding the expectations for writing in computer science? How did you overcome those difficulties?

Rubbal Kumar's Final Essay

Profile of a Writer: Benu Badhan

Benu Badhan is a software engineer at Infosys, an information technology consulting company. She has been working in this field for about five years and her specialty includes software testing: manual testing and automation. She has completed her Bachelors in Technology in Computer Science from the Indian Institute of Technology, Mumbai, and completed her Masters from Delhi University, New Delhi. She worked for two different IT firms, Calsoft and Wipro, before joining Infosys.

In an in-person interview, she told me that writing expectations in an IT firm are totally different in comparison with college writing. She said, "In college, we had to write 4–5 page essays, but in the workplace there are totally different conventions." At work, software engineers are expected to write programming codes, and along with each programming

A key point of the profile, followed by examples from the interview

Quotation that emphasizes the differences between college and IT writing

code, they have to explain the function of each line using the comment feature. Comments are the description of the logic used to write the code. Commenting on the code is necessary because a programmer may inherit the features of existing code in his or her own code. Therefore, to transfer code successfully, comments are necessary. In this way, if someone else reads the code, the comments make understanding the logic far easier. She said that comments are the heart of the code because without comments another person cannot easily understand the programming code.

When I asked further about whether college had prepared her for writing comments clearly for her code, she replied that if there had been no college writing then she would have had difficulty. She also said that college writing prepares students to express things clearly and concisely, and this is one of the requirements in the IT field. She said that whether it is college writing or workplace writing, quality matters instead of quantity.

> A second key point, which builds from the first one

Apart from writing comments in programming code, another form of writing she engages in frequently is writing email. In order to communicate effectively with colleagues, she mentioned that it is important to have good email etiquette. She said that without good communication skills, a person cannot survive in an IT company. In addition to commenting on code and writing email, there are video conference calls and PowerPoint presentations which demand good communication skills. Sometimes she has to lead projects, so leadership qualities and clear communication with a team are also important. As an example, she described working on an idea proposal with her project group and drawing on skills she had learned through college writing. She is convinced that college writing prepares students for other writing assignments in their careers.

> A paragraph elaborating on the second key point with examples from the interview

I learned through my conversation with Ms. Badhan that workplace writing is different from college writing in computer science, but the academic writing we do in college prepares us well for what we will be asked to do in the workplace. The workplace is competitive, so it is important to have good writing skills, communication skills, and leadership qualities, and to be a good problem solver. Through my interview with Ms. Badhan, I learned that in order to be successful in writing in the workplace I must also perform well in my writing in college. While the writing conventions may change in the IT industry, the foundation built in college writing is essential.

> The central point of the profile

Discussion Questions

1. Read through Rubbal Kumar's interview questions of Badhan. What was his purpose in interviewing Badhan? What did he want to understand?

2. Was there anything that surprised you in the profile? If so, what was it?

3. If you were going to add a question to Rubbal's interview, what would it be? Why would you add that question?

tip sheet

An Introduction to Academic Writing

- **The institution you attend has a specific focus.** You may find it helpful to identify this focus and understand how it fits with your academic and career goals.

- **Colleges and universities are divided into disciplinary areas.** You might see these areas at your school as departments, divisions, and/or colleges. In this book, we talk about four broad disciplinary areas: humanities, social sciences, natural sciences, and applied fields.

- **Academic writing and professional writing follow unique conventions.** When academics and professionals write, they often follow conventions specific to their writing situations and to their disciplinary and career areas.

- **In college writing courses, we focus on principles of rhetoric, or how language is used to communicate.** This focus will give you skills to adapt to any writing situation.

Writing: Process and Reflection

This chapter has two main purposes: (1) to introduce and discuss the concept of a writing process and (2) to support the development of your reflective writing skills to help you better understand the writing processes that you use. The culminating project for this chapter is a literacy narrative, a genre of reflective writing that can help you develop agency in understanding who you are, see how and why you've come to view writing the way you do, and discover what direction your academic and professional career might take based on what you discover about yourself. This is particularly relevant if you are trying to decide what to major in, what career to choose, or whether the major or career you're considering is the right one for you. Reflective writing emerges as a powerful tool for understanding the values and experiences that have shaped you, as well as how those values and experiences may align with the academic major you are considering.

In Chapter 1, we discussed the Council of Writing Program Administrators' recommended goals for college writing classes. Listed below are their recommended goals related to college students' writing processes, highlighting skills you need to develop an effective writing process and to succeed in college. As you see, they value reflection in writing.

> By the end of first-year composition, students should
>
> - Develop a writing project through multiple drafts
> - Develop flexible strategies for reading, drafting, reviewing, collaborating, revising, rewriting, rereading, and editing
> - Learn to give and to act on productive feedback to works in progress

ANDREA TSURUMI

- Use composing processes and tools as a means to discover and reconsider ideas
- Reflect on the development of composing practices and how those practices influence their work

In this chapter, we will look at what is meant by these goals and offer opportunities for you to explore how they apply to the work you will be doing in college and beyond.

Developing Your Writing Process

When you think about major writing assignments you have written in the past, how would you describe the steps you took to complete them? You will have written a lot of things by the time you reach college, and when you're asked to write a new assignment for a new class, you may find it helpful to think about how you've written most successfully in the past. How many revisions do you usually work through on a major assignment? Do you like to receive feedback from peers, an instructor, a parent, or a tutor as you are drafting? What types of feedback are most helpful to you? If you have to write an assignment that requires multiple days of drafting, or even weeks, what are the steps you use to maintain focus and consistency?

The **writing process** consists of all the steps you use when writing. You might already be familiar with some of the commonly discussed steps of the writing process from other classes you've taken. Often, writing teachers talk about some variation of the following elements of the writing process, each of which offers an opportunity to discover and reconsider ideas:

- **Prewriting/Invention**   Prewriting/invention is the point at which you gather ideas for your writing. There are a number of useful brainstorming strategies that students find helpful in the processes of gathering their thoughts and arranging them for writing. A few of the most widely used strategies are freewriting, listing, and idea mapping:

  Freewriting, as the term implies, involves writing down your thoughts in a free-flow form, typically for a set amount of time. There's no judgment or evaluation of these ideas as they occur to you. You simply write down whatever comes to mind as you consider a topic or idea. Later, of course, you revisit what you've written to see if it contains ideas or information worth examining further.

  Listing is a way of quickly highlighting important information for yourself. You start with a main idea and then just list whatever comes to mind. These lists are typically done quickly the first time, but you can return to them and rework or refine them at any point in the writing process.

Idea mapping is a brainstorming technique that is a favorite among students because it allows you to represent your ideas in an easy-to-follow map. Idea mapping is sometimes referred to as *cluster mapping* because as you brainstorm, you use clusters of ideas and lines to keep track of the ideas and the relationships among them.

- **Research**   Sometimes research is considered a separate step in the writing process, and sometimes it is part of prewriting/invention. Of course, depending on the nature of your project, there might be a considerable amount of research or very little research involved. We explore some strategies for conducting research in more detail in Chapter 5.

- **Drafting**   At the drafting stage, you get ideas down on paper or screen. You might already realize that these stages don't happen in isolation in most cases; drafting might occur while you're doing prewriting/invention and research, and you might go back and forth between different stages as you work.

- **Peer Review**   Writers often benefit from seeking the feedback of others before considering a project complete. This is called **peer review**, which is only one stage in your writing process, so be sure to consider the point at which it will be the most beneficial to you.

- **Revising**   At the **revision** stage, a writer takes another look at his or her writing and makes content-level and organizational changes. This is different from the final step of editing/proofreading.

- **Editing/Proofreading**   Finally, the writer focuses on correcting grammatical, mechanical, stylistic, and referential problems in the text.

Insider's View
Mathematician Patrick Bahls on the Writing Process

"The more formally recognized genres of writing in my discipline would be research articles or expository articles or reviews of one another's work. Sometimes

you'll see technical reports, depending on what area you're working in. Statisticians will frequently write technical reports for folks for whom they're doing consulting or for government work.

"But I think the day-to-day writing, to me, is much richer and often goes overlooked. When you think about the finished product of a five- or six-page research article—I'll look back over the notes that I would've written to generate the work to end up with that article. And even if you only see five or six pages of polished writing, I look back over my notes and see a hundred or two hundred pages of just scribbles here and scribbles there."

Flexible Strategies

While the writing process list described above suggests that writers go through each of the steps in sequence in order to complete a writing project, the process is in fact much more fluid, as you likely know from your own experiences. Depending on the rhetorical context of a writing task, these processes might shift in importance and in the order in which you do them.

Imagine you get a last-minute writing assignment at work. You would progress through these stages rather quickly, and you might not have time for more than a cursory peer review. If you're writing a paper for a class, however, you might be able to do initial prewriting, research, and drafting well before the project's deadline. As we discuss different types of scholarly writing in this text, you might also consider how the writing process for each of these types of writing can vary. For instance, when conducting an experimental study, the research stage of the process will take a significant portion of the time allocated to the project.

If you are rigid, set in your ways, and unable to adapt to a variety of demands, you're going to have trouble. By contrast, if you are flexible and adaptable in your approach to collaborating, writing, and learning more broadly, you will be much more likely to succeed. Everybody brings a different set of experiences to a classroom, and your experiences have gotten you this far, so you certainly have some successful strategies already.

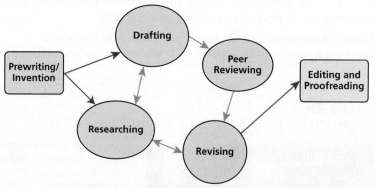

Writers move through multiple stages in the writing process, but the order and importance of stages vary according to the rhetorical context.

Multiple Drafts

By now, drafting is a skill you have probably developed quite well. The hard part about drafting is just doing it. We live busy lives and sometimes put off work until the last minute. For some writing assignments, you might be able to get away with last-minute writing. For more complicated projects, however, you may need to develop your assignment over the course of several weeks or months. A lot of this time may be spent analyzing an assignment sheet, reading examples of the kinds of assignments you're asked to write, brainstorming topics, highlighting or annotating sources you've found to support your points, writing an outline, and drafting. These steps are all part of a well-developed writing process that will be discussed throughout this chapter.

Writers often find it helps to avoid writer's block to think of the first draft as just a rough attempt to formulate ideas. But the work doesn't end with the first draft. Effective writers also take time for **revision** of their drafts, stepping away from the draft for a bit and then coming back to see the draft with fresh eyes (re-vision). At this stage, writers often make changes in the content and substance of their writing, filling in gaps or editing out areas where they are redundant. They might change part of the draft to fit the audience better, or they might reorganize parts of the draft so that it makes more sense to a reader. These kinds of revisions are different from the surface-level grammatical and mechanical changes writers make when editing. While this might seem like a lot to think about as you write, just keep in mind that becoming a better writer takes practice, but developing a writing project through multiple drafts can take your work to a higher level.

Don't be too hard on yourself. Sometimes the expectations for what you have to write can overwhelm you or just aren't interesting to you, and the motivation to stay on task and do a little bit of work each day on an assignment can be hard to come by. The keys are to stay focused, to understand the purpose of the assignment, and to remain as open and engaged as possible.

Connect 2.1 **Reflecting on Your Writing Process**

Describe the most complicated writing assignment you've written prior to this course. It could be for any class, not necessarily an English class.

- What was the class, the topic, and the purpose of the assignment?
- What writing processes did you use to maintain your focus when drafting the assignment? If you're able to name several specific steps you took to maintain your focus while remaining open to improving your drafts, chances are you've developed some good drafting skills.
- Did the assignment require you to be flexible as you worked through the stages of your draft? Were you open to making changes based on feedback? Did you try any new ways of generating ideas or organizing your material or connecting with readers?

Giving and Acting on Feedback

Many of the skills that demand flexibility in writing are demonstrated in peer review activities. **Peer review** is the process of reviewing a peer's writing while a project is in a drafting phase in order to provide feedback to improve the work, or of having your own work reviewed by a peer. When you think of peer review, perhaps you think of fixing grammar, punctuation, and spelling issues—content we would refer to as surface-level improvements. While that kind of feedback is important, equally important is the more variable and flexible feedback that shapes the direction or ideas in a peer's writing. These might be called deeper-level revisions.

Essential too, and often overlooked, is the understanding that giving feedback is itself a skill that is developed in the peer review process, and it is also one that requires flexibility. Often we tend to focus only on the end product of the paper that will be graded, but the skill of giving effective feedback to peers is one that requires excellent social skills, generosity, and intellect. Furthermore, the ability to give constructive feedback to peers is a highly sought-after skill relevant to a variety of careers beyond college. To give effective feedback on someone else's writing, you must be able to read the writing from different perspectives and write comments that will be helpful to the author—this requires flexibility in both your reading and writing.

Giving Productive Peer Review Feedback: A Sample Draft with Comments

Below, you will see a draft of student Jack Stegner's literacy narrative project for a first-year composition class that has been peer-reviewed by one of his classmates. The assignment was to tell a personal story to other students about how the writer changed or developed as a reader, writer, or speaker. Jack's reviewer focused on asking questions about deeper-level issues in his paper:

- **Ideas/Content**   Are the writer's ideas clear and fully developed? Does the writer fulfill the main objective of the assignment and tell a story about literacy development?

- **Organization**   Is the writing focused, directed, and easy to follow? Where does the essay go off track? Where does the writer need to develop the connection between points?

- **Paragraph Development**   Are the ideas in each paragraph clearly linked? Where could the writer provide more information to help the reader understand the point?

If you are doing peer review within the Achieve platform available with this text, then you'll find these kinds of deeper-level issues defined as "draft goals," with accompanying questions to help focus your reading and commenting.

We will discuss the literacy narrative in more detail later in this chapter as an example of reflective writing. As you read Jack's literacy narrative, pay attention to the comments left by his peer reviewer. Do you think these comments will be helpful to Jack as he thinks about how to revise his paper?

You'll notice that the peer reviewer doesn't comment about grammar, punctuation, and spelling matters, and she often phrases her feedback in the form of questions and points to things she would like to know more about. She helps Jack see his own writing through another perspective, which will help Jack develop flexibility in his own writing. This ability to give and receive effective feedback is a skill that can be developed with practice and guidance and is relevant to many careers beyond college.

Jack Stegner's Draft of a Literacy Narrative, with Peer Review Feedback

Orientation to high school was a big thing for me when I was fourteen. I was at one of the best high schools in the country getting ready to start my future life. I was excited yet nervous at the same. I came from a school where I had known kids my whole life and it was different seeing these new faces. I was afraid to talk to anyone since I felt like everyone knew each other. I got my school ID photo taken as I heard a man yelling from the crowd telling freshman to get in line. I looked over and saw this lean man with dark blonde hair and eyes as blue as the sky. As a tiny freshman I was scared to get even close to this man. That was before I realized he was one of the best teachers I would ever have.

> I like how you end the paragraph with a surprise. I'm not clear, though, on how this orientation day story ties to the idea of your literacy development.

The next day I walked into my fourth period classroom, and the tall lean man from yesterday was there standing in front of the class. I rolled my eyes to the back of my head saying, "Great, I have to deal with this guy the entire year." The first thing he did was assign us seats, which I wasn't used to, coming from a public school to a private school. He stood in front of the class and said his name was Mr. Alumbaugh and that he was going to be teaching us for the next school year. Then he asked us to write a paper that was due the next day discussing why we decided to go to De La Salle. I left class that day wanting to transfer out. I was already depressed as well not having many friends at the school. I came home crying to my mom saying how I didn't want to go back and how I wanted to go to the high school all my friends were going to which was Northgate. She told me at the end of the year if you still feel the same way we can transfer you out.

> Why did this make you want to transfer out? What issues were you having with writing? It would be good to know how you are feeling about your writing at this point.

A few months went by. I was still at De La Salle but still depressed from not having much of a social life. My friend Lauren wanted me to go out with her friend Natalie. We went on a few dates and we started to catch feelings for each other. Although I was her boyfriend and was friends with her friends I still didn't have many male friends. Then one day in English, Natalie was texting me during class when Mr. Alumbaugh saw. He then took my phone

> The story of this day is really vivid. The details about how you met Natalie seem to go off track, though.

and started texting Natalie as my whole class was laughing at me. I was so embarrassed being called out and having everyone laugh at me. After class however, my friend till this day as well, Chris came up to me and asked if I could join him and his group for lunch. I was finally invited to something and although I was embarrassed I was happy to be made an example of to get noticed.

Can you connect the story of your growing happiness at school with the story of your reaction to the assignment? I'm not clear how the ideas in this paragraph fit together.

In the Spring, I was conditioning for football and track, had to give my girlfriend attention, and had to juggle school and social life as well. I was starting to become closer with my classmates and actually making friends. I ended up forgetting about my friends at Northgate and even not wanting to go there. I was starting to become happy and realizing that people did care about me and that they did know me. In English, Mr. Alumbaugh assigned us homework to go up in front of the class and just talk about ourselves for two minutes. At first, I laughed, saying to myself "That's too easy of an assignment." When it actually came to writing about it though, I was puzzled and had no idea what to write about. I went to Mr. Alumbaugh's room one day after class ended and asked if he could help me with the assignment. He looked at me smiled and said, "Jack I can come up with a five minute speech about you and who you are. Just write how other people perceive you."

Was this helpful advice? Did you follow it?

The day of the presentation came and I was calm. It felt like I wrote a pretty good speech about myself, good enough to be confident about speaking it to the class. My name was called up and as I stood there the butterflies came out of nowhere, reminding me of the beginning of the year. I started speaking "Hello my name is . . ." I looked down at my paper when suddenly Mr. Alumbaugh yelled "Stop! Cut!" I was startled. Mr. Alumbaugh said that he could tell I was nervous but I didn't need to look down to see what my name was. The class laughed and I laughed about it, shaking off my nerves. He then said, "Go ahead and try again." I read my speech about myself and my goals in life, and I actually got the best grade in the class. Ever since that day in Mr. Alumbaugh's class, I have never been nervous to give a speech to an audience or to a class. He congratulated me personally and we had a great friendship after that year.

I'm interested to know more about what happened to make you so confident. It seems like the only thing your teacher did was tease you and yell at you. What did you learn from him that made you change?

You'll notice that the peer reviewer doesn't comment about grammar, punctuation, and spelling matters, and she often phrases her feedback in the form of questions and points to things she would like to know more about. She helps Jack see his own writing through another perspective, which will help Jack develop flexibility in his own writing. This ability to give and receive effective feedback is a skill that can be developed with practice and guidance and is relevant to many careers beyond college.

Responding to Peer Review Feedback

It can be difficult to read feedback from others on your writing, especially if you thought your draft was close to final and your peer reviewers raise big concerns. Responding to peer review feedback is a moment in the writing process that helps you develop flexibility. You are not required to do everything that a peer reviewer suggests, nor do you have to answer every question that is posed. If you have multiple peer reviewers, you might even find that they contradict one another. Your job is to take their feedback seriously, however, and weigh how to respond in a way that improves your project.

Professional writers usually welcome the chance to find out how readers react to their work before it is published, and they use the feedback to see their work through a reader's eyes. They ignore feedback that goes against what they are trying to accomplish, but they use it to focus on places where their readers aren't understanding them or where their readers offer good ideas. Often writers use feedback from peers or teachers to develop a **revision plan**, which maps out the kinds of big picture changes the writer would like to make and the necessary steps to make those changes. For example, after peer review, a writer might see the need for more evidence to support a particular point and make notes about further library research in the revision plan. Having such a plan makes the revision process more manageable and focused.

Connect 2.2   **Giving and Acting on Feedback**

- Reflect on your experiences as a peer reviewer. Did you have a clear sense of what to focus on in the draft you reviewed? Do you think you gave helpful feedback? What did you find most challenging about reviewing someone else's work? What was most rewarding?

- Reflect on your experiences receiving peer review feedback. Were you open to what your readers had to say? Was the feedback helpful to you in revising? If not, what advice would you give to your peer reviewers?

Reflection and Writing

Reflection—and reflective writing—is a powerful tool for understanding your strengths, your weaknesses, and your unique way of seeing the world. Reflection is the act of looking back over experiences in a questioning way in order to create insights. Reflective writing, which can take such forms as diaries, memoirs, blogs, and letters, is writing that processes one's personal experiences and organizes those experiences in a meaningful way. Just as you might use some form of reflective writing to understand and develop a relationship or skill, you can use reflective writing to develop as a writer.

Scholarship in writing studies suggests that the habits of mind most essential to transferring knowledge gained in one context (say this class) to another context (say a senior-level writing-intensive course in your major) are metacognition and flexibility/adaptability. Metacognition is the awareness of one's own thought processes. If your awareness of how you think and process knowledge is highly developed, you'll be able to take knowledge you acquire and more readily draw from that knowledge in another instance. This is where reflective writing is especially helpful because reflective writing improves metacognition.

Reflecting throughout the Writing Process

When you consider your literacy development over the span of your life, it is easy to see marked improvement. When you were a small child, for example, you first learned the alphabet, how to hold a pencil or crayon, and how to make the shapes of letters that would later become words and sentences. What's harder to see are the subtle changes that take place over a shorter span of time, such as a single semester of college. Perhaps you pick up only a few skills: knowledge about when to ask a peer to review your writing, how to insert a direct quotation into a paper, or how to create a graph from data you've collected. Each of these small skills accumulates with others over time to prepare you for the kinds of writing and research that will serve you in a career beyond college.

Reflecting on the progress you are making and the things you are learning can help your overall development as a writer in a couple of ways. First, it helps you feel a sense of accomplishment in what you have learned. Even small steps can accumulate over time to help your writing development in big ways. Second, reflecting on what we have learned can help us discover ways to apply what we have learned and build on it in the future.

As you approach your assignments, look for opportunities to reflect throughout the writing process. Consciously consider the choices you're making and what you're learning as a writer. What are the most challenging parts of the assignment? What do you need direction or help with? What do you like best about your paper? These are just some of the reflection questions that can support your growth as a writer.

Reflecting on Your Story as a Writer

In academic writing classes, the **literacy narrative** is one of the most commonly used reflective genres. A literacy narrative is an essay that reflects on how someone has developed literacy over time. It is a form of reflective writing that draws on the writer's memories and experiences, and as such it is non-fiction. In this context, the word *literacy* means more than the ability to read and write. It also means the ability to communicate and so accomplish things in a specific context or contexts. The purpose of the genre is to reflect on your identity as a literate person, as someone who has or needs to develop a skill. When done well, the literacy narrative makes meaning from experience and helps you to better understand yourself, why you feel the way you do about the skills you have gained, and how to chart a path forward in your life, drawing from the knowledge you have acquired.

A literacy narrative need not be confined to an academic setting. As we've begun to explore, literacy can mean much more than the ability to read and write, and the attitudes we bring to a classroom are informed by thousands of experiences that may have nothing to do with a classroom, teachers, or reading and writing directly. A literacy narrative might encompass the story of how you learned to speak and act as a softball player, YouTube celebrity, or employee at a movie theater. That kind of literacy narrative might explore the slang, codes of behavior, dress, or attitudes that others impressed upon you. Your instructor may have specific guidelines about the kinds of events she wants to see in your literacy narrative. The underlying theme, though, should be literacy (either narrowly or broadly defined), how you came to be literate, and what your feelings and attitudes about literacy are.

Characteristics of a Literacy Narrative

A literacy narrative almost always includes the following characteristics:

1. a main idea (or point) regarding your literacy development
2. scene writing (specific settings with a location and time)
3. use of sensory detail to describe the scenes (sight, sound, smell, touch, taste)
4. the "I" point of view

Effective narratives generally involve a struggle, obstacle, or challenge that you overcame. The struggle could be emotional (shame or anxiety, for example), or it could be physical or situational (perhaps you learned how to read with the help of a single mother who was working two jobs). All struggles appeal to emotions and as such can inspire readers to find persistence, passion, and perseverance, or to overcome challenges.

● **Main Idea**   Probably the most important aspect of a literacy narrative is the guiding principle or main idea of your narrative. This should be something you have a sense of before you get far into the drafting phase of your essay, but it may well develop or change as you write. For some students, it takes writing a full draft of a paper to really begin to see what the main idea is and what point they are trying to make.

The main idea of your literacy narrative should be tied to your identity, how you view literacy, and how your views developed through experiences good and bad. One activity that helps to brainstorm ideas is to list five words that describe your personality.

● **Scenes**   In a literacy narrative, a scene consists of a specific time and location. The bus stop on the morning of your first day of high school, the classroom where you took the SAT, an auditorium stage where you gave a speech, or your kitchen table where an adult helped you learn to spell your name when you were four years old. These are specific scenes. They take place at a specific location over a fairly short amount of time.

An additional word or two about scene length: If the scene you're envisioning takes place over more than a few hours, it likely ceases to be a scene.

Your entire freshman year of high school, for example, isn't a scene. However, one specific lunch period in the cafeteria during your freshman year when you and a friend decided to ditch school would be a scene. The tighter the timeline and location are in your mind, the more vivid the scene will be when you write it.

A literacy narrative written for a college class will usually be between four and ten pages. This affords you the space to describe approximately three scenes from your life that informed how you view reading, writing, language, and education. What would they be? Can you connect the scenes to the main idea you would like to convey about your identity as a student?

● **Sensory Details**   So you decide on a scene. Then what? Writers rely on their five senses—sight, sound, touch, smell, and taste—to describe scenes vividly. To use sensory detail, you absolutely must use your imagination and memory.

Using sensory detail is like painting. The key is to blend your sensory details to create an impression. Make use of as many senses as you can.

Rather than summarize huge chunks of time (your entire middle school experience, for example), decide on three specific scenes with short time spans and fixed locations that paint an impression of who you are, how your views of reading and writing were shaped in an instant of time, and then make use of all the sensory details you can to paint that scene.

● **"I" Point of View**   One of the most commonly asked questions in a first-year writing course is "Can I use the 'I' (first-person) point of view in my paper?" It seems that many college students arrive having been taught contradictory rules about using the "I" point of view for writing in a class. Let's try and clarify this rule for you once and for all.

Use or non-use of the "I" point of view in a paper for a class totally depends on the genre in which you are writing. When writing in the literacy narrative genre, you should make use of the "I" point of view. You are telling your story from your life, and the "I" point of view is the most appropriate point of view to use. In a scientific report, however, it might not always be helpful or appropriate to use the "I" point of view.

> **Connect 2.3**   **Drafting a Scene for a Literacy Narrative**
>
> • Brainstorm a list of at least three specific scenes you could choose from that best illustrate your literacy development.
> • Choose one and make notes about where the scene happened (location), how long the scene took place (ideally, between a few minutes and a few hours), who was in the scene, and how the scene helped shape your identity.

The purpose of the literacy narrative is for you to reflect on and tell the story of your literacy development. Effective narratives have a beginning, middle, and end, and a literacy narrative follows a series of connected scenes (perhaps three) that illustrate points regarding how you developed your skills, identity, and views of yourself and others as a literate person.

Your instructor may give you more direction about how to define literacy for the purpose of this assignment, but you could focus on the following lists of questions:

Academic Literacy

- What are your first memories of writing in school?
- How did you learn about the expectations for writing in school?
- Can you think of a time when you struggled to meet the requirements of a school writing assignment? What happened?

Technological Literacy

- What early memories do you have of using technology?
- How do you use technology now to communicate in your daily life? What technologies are most important to you for work, for school, and/or for personal commitments?

Workplace Literacy

- What writing and communication skills are expected in the occupation you aspire to when you graduate? How will you develop those skills?
- Can you think of a time when you encountered a task at work that you didn't know how to accomplish? What did you do? How did you address the challenge?

Social and/or Cultural Literacy

- Have you ever been in a social situation where you didn't know how to act? What did you do?
- What groups do you identify with, and what expectations and shared beliefs make that group cohesive?

In a narrative essay, explore the development of your own literacy. You might do this chronologically, at least as you start writing. Be specific in identifying how you define literacy and how you developed your abilities. In your narrative and analysis, provide examples from your experience, and show how they contribute to the development of that literacy. Ultimately, your narrative should be directed to a particular audience for a particular purpose, so think of a context in which you might tell this story. For example, a student who is studying to be a teacher might write about his early literacy experiences and how they led to an interest in teaching other children to read and write. Or an applicant for a job requiring specific technological ability might include a section in an application letter that discusses her development of expertise in technological areas relevant to the job. Be imaginative if you like, but make sure that your narrative provides specific examples and makes a point about your literacy development that you believe is important.

Insider Example
Student Literacy Narrative

The following literacy narrative was written by first-year college student Michaela Bieda regarding her self-awareness that her strengths and skills did not always align well with the expectations that schools, teachers, and peers had about what a "good student" should be. In her literacy narrative, Bieda reflects on the awakening she had through learning her strengths in an academic context and how a teacher contributed to her developing self-awareness of her individuality, her strengths, and her identity. Bieda makes use of all of the aspects of the literacy narrative we've introduced so far: a main idea, scenes, sensory details to describe those scenes, and the "I" point of view.

My Journey to Writing

As a young kid, I struggled a lot in school. I was that student who had a hard time being able to focus and maintain that focus. I was easily distracted, and my eyes and mind would wander rather than listen and watch my teacher. I even fell asleep in class at times either as a result of over-stimulation that I couldn't handle or maybe an underlying depression, knowing I just couldn't cope in a regular classroom or keep up with my fellow students who didn't seem to share my mindset. I remember many a teacher telling my parents, "Micki just doesn't apply herself. She's smart but she's lazy." I wasn't lazy, and I wasn't sure if I was smart or not. I just knew that I couldn't sit still at my desk and do what all the other kids were able to do. Nothing in school held my interest. The traditional way of presenting the three R's didn't hold my attention. I would much rather daydream, waiting to go home and work on my art projects, designing and coloring a world I created. The world of academia had already labeled me ADHD, where I thought of myself as creative. My parents were well aware of the skills I had as well as the ones I didn't have. They thought that by changing schools, I might not resent schoolwork and teachers so much. When I was in 4th grade, I went to another school, but since it was just another private Jewish day school, nothing much was different. "Mom,"

"I" point of view

Michaela sets up a problem that leads to the main point.

I complained almost from the first day at the new school, "I've got the same books and the same schedule. All that's happened is that I have to make new friends." The change of schools didn't result in an attitude change for me or a new understanding—and possible appreciation—by my new set of teachers. As they say, "Same old, same old."

A new scene

An important character is introduced.

In 5th grade, I remember sitting at circular tables, waiting for the teacher to come into the classroom. The school principal walked in and announced, "Class, this is Mrs. Crincolli. Please make her feel welcome." As usual, I wasn't really paying attention to the person entering the room, but I did perk up when she had us decorate nametags and stand them up on our desks. Finally! An art project! And it had a practical application! I was thrilled. It meant so much to me to be able to perform a task I knew I could excel at. I loved my nametag, and I have kept it all these years as a tangible marker of my first school success. From that point on, I started noticing how different I felt about going to school. I had never been so excited to see what Mrs. Crincolli was going to ask us to do next. For her part as a caring teacher, she noticed my lack of success on tests yet how good my writing and art projects were. She took the time to work with me to help me find ways to understand and remember the material for tests. I was a tricky learner because, with a mind that tried to absorb a billion things at once, prioritizing one thing to concentrate on took skills I didn't innately have but had to acquire. Mrs. Crincolli helped me to believe that I could learn that skill and then apply it. I can still hear her voice in my head, encouraging me:

Dialogue adds specific detail.

"Give it a whirl, Micki. You can do it."

By the time I hit 8th grade, I had fallen in love with writing, whether formal essays or free-form association. Mrs. Crincolli had also introduced me to the stories and poetry of Edgar Allan Poe. His dark Gothic elements spoke to me, and I tried writing stories and poems—not just emulating him but in my own voice as well. My favorite writing in school was free thought writing. Every day in class, we students had about 10 minutes to write in our journals. We could use the teacher's prompt or just go off on a personal tangent of feeling. Thanks to Mrs. Crincolli, from 5th grade on, I grasped that writing and literature could appeal to anyone needing a creative outlet. Mrs. Crincolli had been so clever in the types of assignments she gave and the books we were assigned to read in class. I always identified something in my life with what I had to write about or the characters and plots I had to follow. The lack of direction and purpose I'd felt before Mrs. Crincolli entered my school life was now replaced by the joy of expressing myself on paper . . . or a screen. I wanted to impress her and the other teachers I had in each successive grade. In each English class I had with Mrs. Crincolli, the way she presented curriculum was so different from the usual textbook approach. Everything she had us students do was interesting, encouraging, and provocative. She had us constantly thinking out of the box, which was something I never thought I could do before she became my mentor.

I became very close with Mrs. Crincolli, spending time after class to help her with her bulletin boards. Eventually during my high school years, I became her Teacher's Assistant. Throughout high school under her tutelage, I learned to appreciate English even more and felt my strength in those skills more than any other class. I remember on more than one occasion, counting pages of younger classes' writing journals. So many of those students just scribbled or wrote random words in order to get the required number of pages completed. I shook my head, sad that these youngsters hadn't yet caught on to the value of journal writing or the joy of exploring oneself through language.

When it came time to graduate from high school, I reflected on the many years I had developed a real relationship with words—using and understanding them—as well as the prize of having a friendship with Mrs. Crincolli. My school, like so many others, had the usual awards ceremony at graduation. Special to my school though was the tradition that each teacher spoke about one student who had made a real impact during high school. I was sitting far in the back of the assembly with my mom as the slide show of our senior class played. All the other students in my class and our teachers sat together, watching this heartwarming video under twinkly lights tangled in the trees. One by one, each teacher walked up to the front of the gathering. When it was Mrs. Crincolli's turn, my mom whispered to me, "I just know she'll talk about you." I wanted that to happen so badly—for her to know and share how much she meant to me and also how much I meant to her. My heart overflowed and so did my tears as she started to talk . . . about ME! She mentioned not only how I had been her student for so many years, but one of the first friends she had at the school—someone who put herself out for a teacher with the only expectation of learning as much as she could. I was so grateful that she understood just how I felt. She was the one, the pivotal one at the pivotal point in my life who made such a difference and such a contribution to me as a person as well as a writer. I don't have to wonder whether she knows how important she is to me or whether she has done her job as a teacher. We both know, and I cherish her and the confidence she gave me to celebrate a creative mind and channel it to positive and productive ends.

> Sensory detail

> The main point of the narrative: Mrs. Crincolli helped Michaela identify her own strengths.

Discussion Questions

1. What would you say Michaela Bieda learned about herself by writing her literacy narrative? What evidence suggests this?

2. What kind of major and career could you see someone with Michaela's strengths going into that would make her happy?

3. What relationships or events from your own life contributed the most to how you see yourself as a student? How did they contribute?

tip sheet	Writing: Process and Reflection

- **You should work to achieve specific goals** related to your writing process during your writing classes:
  - Develop a writing project through multiple drafts.
  - Develop flexible strategies for reading, drafting, reviewing, collaborating, revising, rewriting, rereading, and editing.
  - Learn to give and to act on productive feedback to works in progress.
  - Use composing processes and tools as a means to discover and reconsider ideas.
  - Reflect on the development of composing practices and how those practices influence your work.

- **Revision is an important stage in the writing process.** Feedback from peer reviewers can help writers see their drafts through readers' eyes.

- **Your purpose in using reflective writing is to process experiences** you've had in order to better understand how those experiences shape you and your writing. It is helpful to reflect on what you are learning about yourself as a writer throughout your writing life.

- **A literacy narrative is a reflective writing genre** used to process the experiences you've had that shape your views of reading, writing, and how you communicate with others.

Reading and Writing Rhetorically

You read and write in many different situations: at school, at home, with your friends, and maybe at work. You might, for instance, compose a private reflection about a personal goal in a journal, read a news article and post about it to your followers on social media, record science lab observations for your instructor in a logbook, or make plans with a friend through text messaging. You could probably name many other situations in which you read and write on a daily basis.

But have you ever considered how the experiences of reading and writing are different in these situations? You're performing the same act (reading or writing a text), but elements of the experiences might change from one situation to another:

- the way your text looks
- the medium or technology you use
- the tone that is most appropriate for your text
- the diction, or the particular words you use (or that you avoid)
- the grammar and mechanics you use

Understanding that a writer's choices depend on the specific demands of each writing situation is central to rhetoric, the study of how language is used to communicate. By learning to *write rhetorically* in different academic disciplines, you will gain a deeper awareness of the expectations that your readers bring to the communication and how these expectations inform your decisions about how to shape your own writing. By learning to *read rhetorically*, you will develop the ability to analyze unfamiliar and even difficult texts and become acquainted with the moves that writers make in different disciplines.

ANDREA TSURUMI

Understanding Rhetorical Context

Writing takes place in a **rhetorical context** of four key elements:

- who the **author** is and what background and experience he or she brings to the text
- who the intended **audience** is for the text
- what **topic** (or issue) the author is addressing
- what the author's **purpose** is for writing

Each of these elements has an impact on the way a text is written and interpreted. Consider for a moment how you might communicate about your last job in a text message to a friend in comparison with how you might write about it in an application letter for a new job. Even though the author is the same (you) and the topic is the same (your last job), the audience and your purpose for writing are vastly different. These differences would affect the choices you make as a writer—how you characterize your experience, what details you select to share, your word choice, the format of your communication, and even perhaps the medium through which you choose to deliver it. In turn, how the reader reacts to your writing (with an emoji? with a phone call for an interview?) also depends on the rhetorical situation.

Insider's View
Karen Keaton Jackson, Writing Studies Scholar, on Rhetorical Context

"Purpose and audience essentially shape every decision you will make as a writer. Once you have your topic, your purpose and audience help you decide how you're going to structure your sentences, how you're going to organize your essay, what word choices you will make, and what tone you will choose."

Sometimes writing situations call for more than one audience as well. You might address a **primary audience**, the explicitly addressed audience for the text, but you might also have a **secondary audience**, an implied audience who also might read your text or be interested in it. Imagine you were to write a job application letter as an assignment for a business writing class. Your primary audience would likely be your instructor, but a secondary audience could be a future prospective employer if you also were to write the letter as a template to use when beginning your job search.

In academic settings, these elements of rhetorical context shift as well, depending on the discipline within which you're writing. Consider another example that illustrates how a student's research topic might shift based on the needs of different academic audiences: Imagine a student has decided to research the last presidential election for a school assignment. If the research assignment were given in a history class, then the student might research and write about other political elections that provide a precedent for the outcome of the recent election and the events surrounding it. The student would be approaching the topic from a historical perspective, which would be appropriate for the context of the discipline and audience (a history professor). If the student were writing for an economics class, he or she might focus on the economic impact of elections and how campaign finance laws, voter identification laws, and voters' socioeconomic statuses affected the election. Even though the author, audience, topic, and purpose seem similar at first glance (they're all academic research assignments, right?), the student would focus on different questions and aspects of the topic when examining the election from different disciplinary perspectives and for different audiences. Other elements of the student's writing would likely shift, too, and we'll discuss those differences in Part Two of this book.

Connect 3.1   **Identifying Rhetorical Context**

Think about a specific situation in the past that required you to write something. It could be any kind of text; it doesn't have to be something academic. Then briefly describe the rhetorical context of that piece of writing. Consider the following questions:

- What was your background and role as the author?
- Who was the audience?
- What was the topic?
- What was your purpose for writing?

Understanding Genres

Writing typically takes place within communities of people who are interested in similar subjects and who use writing to accomplish shared goals. They might use similar vocabulary, formats for writing, and grammatical and stylistic rules—these are conventions or customary practices that have evolved within the community. Think, for example, of sports writers who report for newspapers or real estate attorneys who handle sales transactions. In a sense, these writers and their audiences speak the same "language." As you read and analyze the writing of academic writers, we'll ask you to notice and comment on the conventions that different disciplines use in various rhetorical contexts. When you write, you'll want to keep those conventions in mind, paying attention to the ways you should shape your own writing to meet the expectations of the academic community you are participating in. In Part Two, we'll give you the tools to identify conventions in different disciplines.

Academic writing communities—and writing communities at large—also often work in shared genres. **Genres** are approaches to writing situations that share some common features, or conventions, related to form and content. They may be described as categories of writing, such as driving directions, thank-you notes, and résumés, that writers rely on to deliver what their audience needs to know. Cookbook writers, for example, use the recipe genre to guide readers in making a dish. They know readers expect certain content—ingredients, measurements, oven temperatures, and preparation directions—and they typically follow the format of presenting the list of ingredients first and then providing step-by-step directions as a series of directives. Genres evolve, but they help writers by providing a framework so they don't have to start from scratch in every writing situation. In the illustration shown here, cookbook author Johanna Kindvall offers an innovation on the recipe genre by using images instead of words to show a recipe's steps.

Academic writing includes such genres as abstracts, mathematical proofs, research proposals, and lab reports, among many others. If you've ever produced one of these genres as a student, then you would have experience with some of the conventions that make them unique. Lab reports, for example, have a number of conventional features, including standardized headings (like "Methods"

one egg yolk

one oz 70% dark chocolate

one egg white

one tsp sugar

Chocolate Mousse (serves one)

JOHANNA KINDVALL

and "Results") that organize and control the flow of information, and they tend to rely on passive voice constructions to report the actions researchers took as part of their experiment. These are only a couple of the conventional features of lab reports. In the writing project for this chapter, you will be introduced to the academic genre of rhetorical analysis, as well as to the particular form that rhetorical analysis takes in the discipline of English. As we introduce additional academic genres throughout this book, our goal is not to have you identify a formula to follow for every type of academic writing, but rather to help you understand the expectations of a writing situation—and how much flexibility you have in meeting those expectations—so that you can make choices appropriate to the genre.

Insider's View
Moriah McCracken, Writing Studies Scholar, on Genre

"I think my favorite genre still remains what I call the 'handout genre.' Because I do a lot of conference presentation, this is a very particular kind of genre I produce that varies depending even on the conference I'm going to. . . . I also spend a lot of time writing professional development materials for our faculty. Just this week I was making handouts for them that could serve as quick references so they know where to go to find particular kinds of information. . . . I also spend a lot of time creating handouts for parents that try to translate the disciplinary pedagogical work that happens in my field for an audience who may not be familiar."

Connect 3.2   Thinking about Genre

Think back to the rhetorical situation you identified in Connect 3.1, "Identifying Rhetorical Context." What *genre* were you writing in, and how did you learn the expectations of that genre? Identify a few choices that you made because of the genre.

Writing Rhetorically

Writing is about choices. Although genres can provide a framework, writing is not a firm set of rules to follow. There are multiple choices available to you any time you take on a writing task, and the choices you make will help determine how effectively you communicate with your intended audience, about your topic, for your intended purpose. The first step in making writing choices for a project is analyzing the rhetorical context for which you are writing so that your choices will have the effect you intend. You'll think about the following four rhetorical elements:

- **What You, as the *Author*, Bring to the Writing Situation**   How do your background, experience, and position relative to the audience shape the way you write? Understanding what you bring to a writing situation can help you determine how best to represent yourself to your intended audience: Based on your knowledge and past experiences, do you present yourself as an expert or assume the position of someone new to a discussion or a topic? Do you choose to acknowledge explicitly the values and biases that inform your awareness of a topic or issue?

- **Who Your Intended *Audience* Is**   Should you address a specific audience? Has the audience already been determined for you (e.g., by your instructor)? What do you know about your audience? What does your audience value? Understanding your intended audience can help you make critical decisions about how best to shape an audience's experience of your text at every level of your writing: Are you writing for an audience for whom specialized language, or jargon, is appropriate? Do you structure or organize your writing according to the conventional expectations of the audience? Should you employ logical or emotional appeals (or both), based on your intended audience?

- **What Your *Topic* Is**   What are you writing about? Has the topic been determined for you, or do you have the freedom to focus your topic according to your interests? What is your relationship to the topic? What is your audience's relationship to it? Understanding your own awareness of a topic can help you determine, for instance, whether and when you should broaden or narrow your topic scope, the appropriateness of citing source material in your writing, as well as whether or not you should address your audience directly or indirectly.

- **What Your *Purpose* Is for Writing**   Why are you writing about this topic, at this time? For example, are you writing to inform? To persuade? To entertain? Understanding your purpose(s) and the expected outcomes for your writing is critical to achieving your aims and can help to establish your audience and topic. Such an understanding can also assist in shaping the overall tone of your writing, the method through which you communicate, as well as the level of formality in your writing, among other considerations.

In addition to analyzing the rhetorical context of any writing situation, you will also want to think about genre expectations. That is, you'll want to consider if your writing situation is suited to communicating in a specific genre. Should your letter to the local newspaper, for instance, follow the content and form conventions for the genre of a letter to the editor? Of course, you'll always want to keep in mind that some writing choices are more likely to be more effective than others based on the conventions expected for certain situations. Sometimes, too, you might choose to break with conventional or genre expectations in order to make a point or draw attention to what you are writing. Regardless, it's important to consider genre expectations as part of your analysis of any writing situation.

Connect 3.3   Thinking about Rhetorical Context

Think back to the rhetorical situation you identified in Connect 3.1, "Identifying Rhetorical Context." Consider that situation more analytically now, using the following questions to expand on your answers:

- As the *author*, how did your background, experience, and position relative to the audience shape the way you created your text?

- Were you addressing a specific *audience*? Was the audience already determined for you? What did you know about your audience? What did your audience value or desire?

- What was your text about? Was the *topic* determined for you, or did you have the freedom to focus your topic according to your interests? What was your relationship to the topic? What was your audience's relationship to it?

- What was your *purpose* for creating a text about that topic, at that time? For example, were you writing to inform? To persuade? To entertain?

Reading Rhetorically

One of the best ways to learn about choices that fit your rhetorical situation and genre is by reading. Not reading simply to absorb what a text says, but reading to analyze how the text says it, so that you can deepen your understanding of the moves that writers make. We want you to *read rhetorically*, paying close attention to the different elements of rhetorical context that help to shape the text and the ways a writer responded to that context. In this book, you will read rhetorically both academic and popular writing, by professional and student writers, and so build your repertoire of strategies for your own writing.

Questions for Rhetorical Reading

When you read a written text rhetorically, you'll study the text to see how it reflects the four elements of the rhetorical situation as well as the genre:

- **Author** The author's biography may be provided along with the text, or you could do a quick Google search if not. What background, experience, knowledge, and potential biases does the author bring to the text? Does the author use biographical details to establish credibility or connection with the reader?

- **Audience** Where was this text published, and who are the typical readers for this publication? Is the author writing to other scholars in the field, or does the publication have a general audience of people who are not experts? How much prior knowledge does the audience have, and can you see that reflected in how the author defines terms and provides background knowledge? Does the author seem to assume that the text's audience will agree with the findings or position, or does the author anticipate objections? Are there multiple audiences (primary and secondary)?

- **Topic** What is the author's topic? How does the author approach the topic, and what kind of attitude does the author assume toward the topic? In what ways does the topic itself contribute to the ways the text is shaped?

- **Purpose** What does the author hope to achieve? Is the author writing to inform, to entertain, or to persuade? Is the author's purpose stated explicitly, or is it implied?

- **Genre** Is the author writing in a recognizable genre? Why is the genre appropriate to the needs of the audience and the author's purpose? Does the author alter any of the conventional expectations for the genre? If so, what might be the author's reasoning for doing so?

Noticing rhetorical elements and analyzing an author's choice of genre when you read will help you become a careful and critical reader of all kinds of texts. When we use the term *critical*, we don't use it with any negative connotations. Instead, we use it in the way it works in the term *critical thinking*, meaning that you will begin to understand the relationships among author, audience, topic, and purpose by paying close attention to context.

Reading Visuals

The strategies for understanding rhetorical context and for reading rhetorically are applicable to both verbal and visual texts. In fact, any rhetorical event, or any occasion that requires the production of a text, establishes a writing

a different degree of freedom

Zipcar for Universities offers the convenience of car ownership without the hassles of having a car on campus.

The **author** is Zipcar.

The **topic** is getting away from campus.

The **audience** is college students.

The **purpose** is to persuade students to use Zipcar's product to get away from campus.

situation with a specific rhetorical context. Consider the places you might encounter visual advertisements, as one form of visual texts, over the course of a single day: in a magazine, on a website, in stores, on billboards, on television, and so on. Each encounter provides an opportunity to read the visual text rhetorically, or to consider how the four elements of author, audience, topic, and purpose work together to shape the text itself (in this case, an advertisement). The Facebook advertisement from Zipcar shown above, for example, creates a specific rhetorical context for an audience of college students. Notice how it employs both written text and images that are specifically targeted to its intended audience.

Connect 3.4   Reading Rhetorically

With the direction of your instructor, choose a verbal or visual text to read and analyze. As you read the text, consider the elements of rhetorical context. Make notes about who the author is, who the intended audience is, what the topic is, and what the author's purpose is for writing or for creating the text. Later in the chapter, we'll ask you to provide evidence for your points and analyze how these elements work together to influence the way the text is written.

Analyzing the Rhetorical Context: A Sample Annotated Text

When you read rhetorically, you analyze a text through a particular lens. When you write in the genre of **rhetorical analysis**, you present the findings of your rhetorical reading to an audience. We'll provide several opportunities for you to conduct rhetorical analyses in this book, since it is one of the ways you will begin to discover the features of writing across different academic contexts.

In a rhetorical analysis paper, the writer uses a rhetorical framework to understand how the context of the text helps to create meaning. One framework you might use involves walking through the different elements of rhetorical context to examine a piece of writing in detail:

- **Author**   What does the author bring to the writing situation?
- **Audience**   Who is the author addressing, and what do they know or think about this topic?
- **Topic**   What is the author writing about, and why did he or she choose it?
- **Purpose**   Why is the author writing about this topic, at this time?

These four components of the rhetorical context function together dynamically. You might analyze the author's background and experience and how he or she develops credibility in the text. Or you could make assertions about the author's primary and secondary audiences based on the author's choices regarding style and language. Although you should focus on one or more of the elements of rhetorical context, you will want to keep in mind that all four of the rhetorical context components function together to shape how someone writes or speaks.

The following text offers an example of what to look for when reading rhetorically. It also serves as the text for the "Insider Example: Student Rhetorical Analysis" at the end of the chapter. The genre is a government letter, one that George H. W. Bush, the forty-first president of the United States (and father of the forty-third president, George W. Bush), sent to Iraqi president Saddam Hussein on January 5, 1991, shortly before the United States, in cooperation with over thirty other countries, launched an assault to expel Iraqi forces from Kuwait. The letter was published by global news organizations a week later. Bush's letter is the kind of document you might analyze in a history or political science class; you'll also encounter contemporary versions of letters and speeches from world leaders in your everyday reading as a citizen. The U.S. military action that Bush warns of came in response to Iraq's invasion and annexation of Kuwait in 1990, and it became a part of the history that is now referred to as the First Gulf War. While the events that precipitated this letter occurred several decades ago, it is a helpful artifact for understanding the complicated power dynamics at play in the U.S. involvement in ongoing events in the Middle East.

Letter to Saddam Hussein

GEORGE H. W. BUSH

Mr. President,

We stand today at the brink of war between Iraq and the world. This is a war that began with your invasion of Kuwait; this is a war that can be ended only by Iraq's full and unconditional compliance with UN Security Council resolution 678.

I am writing to you now, directly, because what is at stake demands that no opportunity be lost to avoid what would be a certain calamity for the people of Iraq. I am writing, as well, because it is said by some that you do not understand just how isolated Iraq is and what Iraq faces as a result.

I am not in a position to judge whether this impression is correct; what I can do, though, is try in this letter to reinforce what Secretary of State James A. Baker told your foreign minister and eliminate any uncertainty or ambiguity that might exist in your mind about where we stand and what we are prepared to do.

The international community is united in its call for Iraq to leave all of Kuwait without condition and without further delay. This is not simply the policy of the United States; it is the position of the world community as expressed in no less than twelve Security Council resolutions.

We prefer a peaceful outcome. However, anything less than full compliance with UN Security Council resolution 678 and its predecessors is unacceptable. There can be no reward for aggression.

Nor will there be any negotiation. Principles cannot be compromised. However, by its full compliance, Iraq will gain the opportunity to rejoin the international community. More immediately, the Iraqi military establishment will escape destruction. But unless you withdraw from Kuwait completely and without condition, you will lose more than Kuwait. What is at issue here is not the future of Kuwait—it will be free, its government restored—but rather the future of Iraq. This choice is yours to make.

The United States will not be separated from its coalition partners. Twelve Security Council resolutions, twenty-eight countries providing military units to enforce them, more than one hundred governments complying with sanctions—all highlight the fact that it is not Iraq against the United States, but Iraq against the world. That most Arab and Muslim countries are arrayed against you as well should reinforce what I am saying. Iraq cannot and will not be able to hold on to Kuwait or exact a price for leaving. You may be tempted to find solace in the diversity of opinion that is American democracy.

The **primary audience** for President Bush's letter is Iraqi President Saddam Hussein. The formal opening salutation is one conventional feature of the **genre** of a letter.

U.S. President George H. W. Bush establishes the **topic** of his letter: an impending war with Iraq. The timeliness and urgency of the situation provide context for and contribute to the need for Bush's letter to Hussein.

The **purpose** of President Bush's letter is "to warn" the Iraqi president of the consequences for Iraq and its people should he choose not to comply fully with the UN Security Council resolution. Bush also underscores Iraq's "isolation" in its actions and the unity of the "world community's" opposition to those actions.

The **author** of this letter is President Bush, but he makes clear that he represents the will of the American people as well as that of the "international community."

President Bush includes multiple references to "coalition partners," and these partners, whose support for U.S. military action is crucial, are an important **secondary audience** for the president's letter. Another audience is clearly the people of the United States.

You should resist any such temptation. Diversity ought not to be confused with division. Nor should you underestimate, as others have before you, America's will.

Iraq is already feeling the effects of the sanctions mandated by the United Nations. Should war come, it will be a far greater tragedy for you and your country. Let me state, too, that the United States will not tolerate the use of chemical or biological weapons or the destruction of Kuwait's oil fields and installations. Further, you will be held directly responsible for terrorist actions against any member of the coalition. The American people would demand the strongest possible response. You and your country will pay a terrible price if you order unconscionable acts of this sort.

I write this letter not to threaten, but to inform. I do so with no sense of satisfaction, for the people of the United States have no quarrel with the people of Iraq. Mr. President, UN Security Council resolution 678 establishes the period before January 15 of this year as a "pause of good will" so that this crisis may end without further violence. Whether this pause is used as intended, or merely becomes a prelude to further violence, is in your hands, and yours alone.

I hope you weigh your choice carefully and choose wisely, for much will depend upon it.

Connect 3.5   Thinking about "Letter to Saddam Hussein"

Twitter had not yet been created when George H. W. Bush wrote this letter to Hussein. Imagine, however, that Bush had tried to communicate his message in a single tweet. Write what you think that tweet would be (280 characters maximum). Other than length, what are the most striking differences between the two communications, in your opinion?

Writing Project   Rhetorical Analysis

In this paper, you will analyze the rhetorical situation of a text (written or visual) of your choosing. You might want to choose something already published so that you know that the author(s) has finished making revisions and has had time to think through important rhetorical choices. Alternatively, you might choose something unpublished that was produced for an academic, personal, work, or other context. Start by reading the text carefully and rhetorically. Use the elements of rhetorical context—author, audience, topic, and purpose—to analyze and understand the choices the author has made in the text.

In addition to describing the rhetorical features of the article, you will also explore why you believe the author made certain choices. For example, if you're analyzing a blog entry on a political website, you might discuss who the author is and review the author's background. Then you could speculate about the writing choices the author has made and how the author's background might have influenced those choices.

Consider what conclusion you can draw about the text, and highlight that as an assertion you can make in the introduction to your analysis. The body of your paper should be organized around the rhetorical features you are analyzing, demonstrating how you came to your conclusion about the text.

In your conclusion, reflect on what you have found. Are there other issues still to be addressed? What other rhetorical strategies could be explored to analyze the work further? Are there surprises in the choices the author makes that you should mention?

Keep in mind that your essential aim is to analyze, not to evaluate. Additionally, you'll want to keep in mind your own rhetorical situation as a writer. Consider how you'll represent yourself as the author, your purpose for writing, your topic, as well as the needs of your audience.

....

Insider Example
Student Rhetorical Analysis

The following is a student rhetorical analysis of the letter written from George H. W. Bush to Saddam Hussein. As you read this analysis, consider how the student, Sofia Lopez, uses audience, topic, and purpose to construct meaning from Bush's letter. Additionally, pay attention to how Sofia uses evidence from the letter to support her assertions. These moves will become more important when we discuss using evidence to support claims in Chapter 4.

The Multiple Audiences of George H. W. Bush's
Letter to Saddam Hussein

President George H. W. Bush's 1991 letter to Saddam Hussein, then the president of Iraq, is anything but a simple piece of political rhetoric. The topic of the letter is direct and confrontational. On the surface, Bush directly calls upon Hussein to withdraw from Kuwait, and he lays out the potential impact should Hussein choose not to withdraw. But when analyzed according to the rhetorical choices Bush makes in the letter, a complex rhetorical situation emerges. Bush writes to a dual audience in his letter and establishes credibility by developing a complex author position. By the conclusion of the letter, Bush accomplishes multiple purposes by creating a complex rhetorical situation.

The introduction outlines the writer's approach to analyzing Bush's letter. She announces her intent to focus on audience and purpose and show that the rhetorical situation is complex.

While Bush's direct and primary audience is Saddam Hussein, Bush also calls upon a much larger secondary audience in the first sentence of the letter by identifying "the world" as the second party involved in the imminent war that the letter is written to prevent. Bush continues to write

In this paragraph, the writer outlines potential audiences for Bush's letter in more detail.

the letter directly to Hussein, using second person to address him and describe the choices before him. Bush also continues, however, to engage his secondary audience throughout the letter by referring to resolutions from the UN Security Council in five separate paragraphs (1, 4, 5, 7, and 9). The letter can even be interpreted to have tertiary audiences of the Iraqi and the American people because the letter serves to justify military action should Hussein not comply with the conditions of the letter.

In this paragraph, the writer explores the ways Bush is able to align himself with multiple audiences. The writer points to specific references to the international community and other Arab and Muslim countries to support this idea about audience.

— Because Bush is addressing multiple audiences, he establishes a complex author position as well. He is the primary author of the letter, and he uses first person to refer to himself, arguably to emphasize the direct, personal confrontation in the letter. He constructs a more complex author position, however, by speaking for other groups in his letter and, in a sense, writing "for" them. In paragraph 4, he speaks for the international community when he writes, "The international community is united in its call for Iraq to leave all of Kuwait. . . ." He draws on the international community again in paragraph 6 and refers to his coalition partners in paragraph 7, aligning his position with the larger community. Additionally, in paragraph 7, he builds his credibility as an author by emphasizing that he is aligned with other Arab and Muslim countries in their opposition to Hussein's actions. Writing for and aligning himself with such a diverse group of political partners helps him address the multiple audiences of his letter to accomplish his purposes.

The writer concludes her analysis by summarizing her ideas about the stated and implied audiences for this letter and how the letter works within a complex rhetorical situation.

— While the primary and literal purpose of the letter is to call upon Iraq to withdraw from Kuwait and to outline the consequences of noncompliance, Bush accomplishes additional purposes directly related to his additional audiences and the complex author position he has established. The primary purpose of his letter, naturally, is addressed to his primary audience, Saddam Hussein. The construction of the letter, however, including the repeated mention of UN Security Council resolutions, the invocation of support from other Arab and Muslim countries, and the reference to other coalition partners and the international community, serves to call upon the world (and specifically the United Nations) to support military action should Hussein not comply with the conditions of the letter. The construction of a letter with a complex audience and author allows Bush to address multiple purposes that support future action.

Discussion Questions

1. What does Sofia Lopez identify as Bush's purpose? How does she support that interpretation of Bush's purpose?

2. Whom does Sofia see as Bush's audience? How does she support that reading of the letter?

3. What might you add to the analysis from a rhetorical perspective?

tip sheet — Reading and Writing Rhetorically

- **It is important to consider rhetorical context as you read and write.** Think about how the following four elements have shaped or might shape a text:
  - Who the *author* is, and what background and experience he or she brings to the text
  - Who the intended *audience* is
  - What issue or *topic* the author is addressing
  - What the author's *purpose* is for writing

- **Genres are approaches to writing situations that share some common features, or conventional expectations.** As you read and write texts, consider the form of writing you're asked to read or produce: Is it a recognizable genre? What kinds of conventional expectations are associated with the genre? How should you shape your text in response to those expectations?

- **Writing rhetorically means crafting your own text based on an understanding of the four elements of your rhetorical context.** Specifically, you consider how your understanding of the rhetorical context should affect the choices you make as a writer, or how your understanding should ultimately shape your text.

- **Reading rhetorically means reading with an eye toward how the four elements of author, audience, topic, and purpose work together** to influence the way an author shapes a text, verbal or visual or otherwise.

- **A rhetorical analysis is a formal piece of writing that examines the different elements of the rhetorical context of a text.** It also often considers how these elements work together to explain the shape of a text targeted for analysis.

CHAPTER

4

Developing Arguments

Many writing situations, both academic and non-academic, require us as writers to persuade audiences on a particular topic—that is, to develop an argument. When we refer to arguments, we don't mean heated, emotional sparring matches. Rather, we use **argument** to refer to the process of making a logical case for a particular position, interpretation, or conclusion. Of course we all experience and participate in these kinds of arguments around us every day as we decide where to eat dinner with friends, what classes to take, or which movie to download or concert to see. We are immersed in these kinds of popular arguments constantly through advertisements, marketing campaigns, social media posts, and texting with friends, and so we are adept at critically thinking about arguments and persuasion in those contexts.

In academic settings, arguments are frequently more developed and nuanced because the authors are arguing for a particular interpretation or conclusion or action based on the results of research. To make such an argument effectively, academics must develop clear, persuasive texts through which to present their research. These arguments are built on **claims**—arguable assertions—that are supported with evidence from research. The unifying element of any academic argument is its primary or central claim, and although most sustained arguments make a series of claims, there is usually one central claim that makes an argument a coherent whole. Our goal in this chapter is to introduce you to some of the basic principles of argumentation and to help you write clear central claims and develop successful arguments, especially in your academic writing.

ANDREA TSURUMI

Understanding Proofs and Appeals

Aristotle, a rhetorician in ancient Greece, developed a method of analyzing arguments that can be useful to us in our own reading and writing today. He explained that arguments are based on a set of proofs that are used as evidence to support a claim. He identified two kinds of proofs: inartistic and artistic. Inartistic proofs are based on factual evidence, such as statistics, raw data, or contracts. Artistic proofs, by contrast, are created by the writer or speaker to support an argument. Many arguments contain a combination of inartistic and artistic proofs, depending on what facts are available for support. Aristotle divided the complex category of artistic proofs into three kinds of **rhetorical appeals** that speakers and writers can rely on to develop artistic proofs in support of an argument:

- Appeals to **ethos** are based on credibility or character. An example might be a brand of motor oil that is endorsed by a celebrity NASCAR driver. Another example could be a proposal for grant money to conduct a research study that discusses the grant writer's experience in successfully completing similar research studies in the past. In both examples, the speaker's or writer's experiences (as a NASCAR driver or as an established researcher) are persuasive elements in the argument.

- Appeals to **logos** are based on elements of logic and reason. An example might be an argument for change in an attendance policy that reveals a correlation between attendance and grades. The argument relies on logic and reason because it presents a relationship between attendance and grades and draws a connection to the policy, emphasizing how a change in the policy might affect grades.

- Appeals to **pathos** are based on emotions. Emotion can be a powerful motivator to convince an audience to hear an argument. An example might include telling the story of a program that helps homeless teenagers complete high school by finding shelter, food, and social support that enables them to improve their living conditions. Perhaps the program is in need of financial assistance in order to continue helping homeless teens. A story that features one or two specific teens who have come through the program and successfully completed high school would be an example of an appeal to emotion.

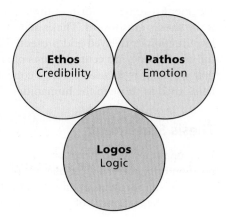

These types of appeals are present in arguments in both academic and non-academic settings. Many arguments, and often the most effective ones, include elements of more than one kind of appeal, using several strategies to persuade an audience. Based on the example above about a program that helps homeless teens, imagine that there is a campaign to solicit financial donations from the public to support the program. Now consider how much more persuasive that campaign would be if other appeals were used in addition to an emotional appeal. The campaign might develop an argument that includes raw data and statistics (an inartistic proof), the advice of civic leaders or sociological experts (ethos), the demonstration of a positive cause-and-effect relationship of the program's benefits in teens' lives (logos), along with a story of one teen, describing how she became homeless and how the program helped to get her back on her feet (pathos). Understanding the structure of arguments, and knowing the potential ways you can develop your own arguments to persuade an audience, will help you to write more effectively and persuasively.

Connect 4.1   Thinking about Rhetorical Appeals

Choose a text to read that makes a claim. Consider something that interests you—perhaps an advertisement, or even your college's or university's website recruiting page for prospective students. Write about the kinds of rhetorical appeals you notice. Do you see evidence of ethos? Logos? Pathos? Is the argument drawing on statistics or raw data, an inartistic proof?

Making Claims

The unifying element of any academic argument is its primary or central claim. In American academic settings, the central claim is often (but not always) presented near the beginning of a piece so that it can tie the elements of the argument together. A form of the central claim that you're likely familiar with is the **thesis statement**. Thesis statements, whether revealed in an argument's introduction or delayed and presented later in an argument (perhaps even in the conclusion), are central claims of arguments. They are typical of writing that is primarily focused on civic concerns, as well as writing in some academic fields such as those in the humanities.

Thesis Statements

Imagine for a moment that you've been asked to write an argument taking a position on a current topic like cell phone usage, and you must decide whether or not to support legislation to limit cell phone use while driving. In this instance, the statement of your position is your claim. It might read something like this: "We should support legislation to limit the use of cell phones while driving," or "We should not support legislation to limit the use of cell phones while driving." Although there are many types of claims, the statement "We should pass legislation to limit the use of cell phones" is a claim of proposal or policy, indicating that the writer will propose some action or solution to a problem. We could also explore claims of definition ("Cheerleading is a sport") or claims of value ("Supporting a charity is a good thing to do"), just to name a few.

Literary analysis, a genre commonly taught in high school English classes, usually presents a thesis statement as part of the introduction. You may be familiar with a thesis statement that reads something like this: "Suzanne Collins's *Hunger Games* is a dystopian novel that critiques totalitarian regimes and empowers young women who are far too often marginalized and oppressed." This thesis statement makes a claim in support of a specific interpretation of the story. Regardless of the specific type of claim offered, the argument that follows it provides evidence to demonstrate why an audience should find the claim persuasive.

Thesis versus Hypothesis

In an academic setting, thesis statements like those typical of arguments in the humanities are not the only kind of unifying claim you might encounter. In fact, arguments in the natural and social sciences are often organized around a statement of hypothesis, which is different from a thesis statement. Unlike a thesis statement, which serves to convey a final position or conclusion on a topic or issue that a researcher has arrived at based on study, a **hypothesis** is a proposed explanation or conclusion that is usually either confirmed or denied on the basis of rigorous examination or experimentation later in a paper. This means that hypothesis statements are, in a sense, still under consideration by a writer or researcher. A hypothesis is a proposed answer to a research question. Thesis statements, in contrast, represent a writer's or researcher's conclusion(s) after much consideration of the issue or topic.

Consider the following examples of a hypothesis and a thesis about the same topic:

Hypothesis	Thesis
Decreased levels of sleep will lead to decreased levels of academic performance for college freshmen.	College freshmen should get at least seven hours of sleep per night because insufficient sleep has been linked to emotional instability and poor academic performance.

The hypothesis example above includes several elements that distinguish it from the thesis statement. First, the hypothesis is written as a prediction, which indicates that the researcher will conduct a study to test the claim. Additionally, it is written in the future tense, indicating that an experiment or study will take place to prove or disprove the hypothesis. The thesis statement, however, makes a claim that indicates it is already supported by evidence gathered by the researcher. A reader would expect to find persuasive evidence from sources later in that essay.

We highlight this distinction in types of claims to underscore that there is no single formula for constructing a good argument in all academic contexts. Instead, expectations for strong arguments are bound up with the expectations of particular writing communities. If you write a lab report with the kind of thesis statement that usually appears in a literary analysis, your work would likely convey the sense that you're a novice to the community of writers and researchers who expect a hypothesis statement instead of a thesis statement. One of the goals of this text is to help you develop awareness of how the expectations for good argumentation change from one academic context to the next.

Developing Reasons

When writing an academic argument that requires a thesis statement, you can choose how detailed to make that thesis statement. When we introduced thesis statements as a type of claim, we asked you to consider two possible statements on the topic of cell phone use while driving: "We should/should not support legislation to limit the use of cell phones while driving." You can also refer to these two possible forms as *simple thesis statements* because they reveal a writer's central position on a topic but do not include any reasoning as support for that position. When reasons are included as logical support, then you can think about the thesis statement as a *complex thesis statement*.

Consider the following simple thesis statement and supporting reasons:

Simple Thesis   We should support legislation to limit the use of cell phones while driving.

Reasons   They are an unnecessary distraction.
They increase the incidence of accidents and deaths.

When you combine the simple statement of position or belief with the reasons that support it, then you have a more complex, and fuller, thesis statement:

Complex Thesis   We should support legislation to limit the use of cell phones because they are an unnecessary distraction for drivers and because they increase needless accidents and deaths on our roadways.

Although constructing complex thesis statements allows you to combine your statement of position, or your central claim, with the reasons you'll use to defend that position, you may frequently encounter arguments that do not provide the reasons as part of the thesis. That is, some writers, depending on their rhetorical context, prefer to present a simple thesis and then reveal the reasons for their position throughout their argument. Others choose to write a thesis that both establishes their position and provides the reasoning for it early on. An advantage of providing a complex thesis statement is that it offers a road map to the reader for the argument that you will develop.

You also want to be careful not to limit your positions to being only for or against something, especially if you can think of alternative positions that might be reasonable for someone to argue. Often, there are multiple sides to an issue, and we miss the complexity of the issue if we acknowledge only two sides. For example, in light of the usefulness of cell phones for navigation and for emergency situations, you may choose to present a thesis that identifies the complexity of the issue and takes a more nuanced position: *Although cell phones can sometimes be helpful to drivers in a number of ways, including navigating travel routes and in emergency situations, we should support legislation to limit the use of cell phones because they are generally an unnecessary distraction for drivers and because they increase needless accidents and deaths on our roadways.* By acknowledging the complexity of an issue or topic on which they're taking a position as part of the thesis statement, writers can appear more credible and trustworthy.

Connect 4.2   Constructing Thesis Statements

Generate a list of six to eight current social issues that require you to take a position. Consider especially issues that are important to your local community. Choose one or two to focus on for the other parts of this activity.

Next, explore multiple positions. Consider competing positions you can take for each of the issues you identified. Write out a simple thesis statement for those positions. Then list as many reasons as you can think of to support each of those positions. It might be helpful to connect your simple thesis statement to your reasons using the word *because*. This activity can help you to strengthen your argument by anticipating rebuttals or counterarguments. We'll take these issues up in more detail later in the chapter.

Finally, combine your simple thesis with your reasoning to construct a complex thesis for each potential position. Write out your thesis statements.

Supporting Reasons with Evidence

Reasons that support a claim are not particularly powerful unless there is evidence to back them up. Evidence that supports an argument can take the form of any of the rhetorical appeals. Let's look again at the complex thesis from the previous section: "We should support legislation to limit the use of cell phones because they are an unnecessary distraction for drivers and because they increase needless accidents and deaths on our roadways." In order to generate the reasons, the writer relied on what he already knew about the dangers of cell phone use. Perhaps the writer had recently read a newspaper article that cited statistics concerning the number of people injured or killed in accidents as a direct result of drivers using their phones instead of paying attention to the roadways. Or perhaps the writer had read an academic study that examined attention rates and variables affecting them in people using cell phones. Maybe the writer even had some personal knowledge or experience to draw upon as evidence for his position. Strong, persuasive arguments typically spend a great deal of time unpacking the logic that enables a writer to generate reasons in support of a particular claim, and that evidence can take many forms.

● **Personal Experience**   You may have direct experience with a particular issue or topic that allows you to speak in support of a position on that topic. Your personal experience can be a rich resource for evidence. Additionally, you may know others who can provide evidence based on their experiences with an issue. Stories of personal experience often appeal to either ethos (drawing on the credibility of the writer's personal experience) or pathos (drawing on read- ers' emotions for impact). Sometimes these stories appeal to both ethos and pathos at the same time. Imagine the power of telling the story of someone you know who has been needlessly injured in an accident because another driver was distracted by talking on the phone.

● **Expert Testimony**   Establishing an individual as an expert on a topic and using that person's words or ideas in support of your own position can be an effective way of bolstering your own ethos while supporting your central claim. However, the use of expert testimony can be tricky, as you need to carefully establish what makes the person you're relying on for evidence an actual expert on the topic or issue at hand. You must also consider your audience—whom would your audience consider to be an expert? How would you determine the expert's reputation within that community?

The use of expert testimony is quite common in academic argumentation. Researchers often summarize, paraphrase, or cite experts in their own disci- pline, as well as from others, to support their reasoning. If you've ever taken a class in which your instructor asked you to use reputable sources to support your argument, then you've probably relied on expert testimony to support a claim or reason already. As evidence for our complex thesis, imagine the effectiveness of citing experts who work for the National Transportation and Safety Board about their experiences investigating accidents that resulted from inattentive driving due to cell phone use.

● **Statistical Data**   Statistics frequently serve as support in both popular and academic argumentation. Readers tend to like numbers, partly because they seem so absolute and scientific. However, it is important, as with all evidence, to evaluate statistical data for bias. Consider where statistics come from and how they are produced, if you plan to use them in support of an argument. Additionally, and perhaps most important, consider how those statistics were interpreted in the context of the original research reported. What were the study's conclusions? Imagine the effectiveness of citing recently produced statistics (rates of accidents) on the highways in your state from materials provided by your state's Department of Transportation.

● **Research Findings** Writers also often present the findings, or conclusions, of a research study as support for their reasons and claims. These findings may sometimes appear as qualitative, rather than just statistical, results or outcomes.

When selecting the types and amounts of evidence to use in support of your reasons, be sure to study your rhetorical context and pay particular attention to the expectations of your intended audience. Some audiences, especially academic ones, are less likely to be convinced if you only provide evidence that draws on their emotions. Other audiences may be completely turned off by an argument that relies only on statistical data for support. Above all, select support that your audience will find credible, reliable, and relevant to your argument.

Insider's View
Criminologist Michelle Richter on Quantitative and Qualitative Research

"There are a few ways to really look at research. One is more of a quantitative approach. I know one individual in our field who publishes twenty, thirty, many papers a year. Because he's proficient in statistics, he can take the same data set, and run it three, four different times with different research questions in mind. I think it's great. I think it's expedient. But there are limitations. If I told you three out of four women may experience a completed sexual assault or an attempted sexual assault in the course of their lifetimes, does that mean every woman? Does that mean specific women, specific geographic areas, critical age periods? With a lot of the quantitative data, we often have a need for context.

"The other way is the more qualitative. And that's an area that I absolutely love. For me, it's interview based. Sometimes it's very hard to quantify, to put in numerical form. But you do get that background, like why someone decided to drive drunk, or why someone decided to start using drugs at the age of ten. I think that's a really good supplement for the numbers.

"Research that combines the qualitative and quantitative is fantastic. The problem is that it can be expensive; it's time consuming; and there are hurdles with IRB [Institutional Review Board] because you are sometimes asking people directly about things that might be personal or traumatic for them."

Choose any one of the complex thesis statements you constructed in Connect 4.2, "Constructing Thesis Statements." Then identify two potential target audiences for your arguments. Freewrite for five to ten minutes in response to the following questions about these audiences' likely expectations for evidence:

- What does each audience already know about your topic? That is, what aspects of it can you assume they already have knowledge about?

- What does each audience need to know? What information do you need to make sure to include?

- What does each audience value in relation to your topic? What kinds of information will motivate them, interest them, or persuade them? How do you know?

- What sources of information about your topic might your audiences find reliable, and what sources would they question? Why?

Understanding Assumptions

Any time you stake a claim and provide a reason, or provide evidence to support a reason, you are assuming something about your audience's beliefs and values, and it is important to examine your own assumptions very carefully as you construct arguments. Though assumptions are often unstated, they function to link together the ideas of two claims.

Let's consider a version of the claim and reason we've been looking at throughout this chapter to examine the role of assumptions: "We should support legislation to limit the use of cell phones while driving because they increase needless accidents and deaths on our roadways." In this instance, the claim and the reason appear logically connected, but let's identify the implied assumptions that the reader must accept in order to be persuaded by the argument:

Claim	We should support legislation to limit the use of cell phones while driving.
Reason	They increase needless accidents and deaths on our highways.
Implied Assumptions	We should do whatever we can to limit accidents and deaths.
	Legislation can reduce accidents and deaths.

Many audiences would agree with these implied assumptions. As a result, it would likely be unnecessary to make the assumptions explicit or provide support for them. However, you can probably imagine an instance when a given audience would argue that legislating people's behavior does not affect how people actually behave. To such an audience, passing laws to regulate the use of cell phones while driving might seem ineffective. As a result, the audience might actually challenge the assumption(s) upon which your argument rests, and you may need to provide evidence to support the implied assumption that "legislation can reduce accidents and deaths."

A writer who is concerned that an audience may attack his argument by pointing to problematic assumptions might choose to explicitly state the assumption and provide support for it. In this instance, the writer might consider whether precedents exist (e.g., the effect of implementing seat belt laws, or statistical data from other states that have passed cell phone use laws) that could support the assumption that "legislation can reduce accidents and deaths."

Connect 4.4   Considering Assumptions and Audience

In Connect 4.3, you considered the most appropriate kinds of evidence for supporting thesis statements for differing audiences. This time, we ask you to identify the assumptions in your arguments and to consider whether or not those assumptions would require backing or additional support for varying audiences.

Begin by identifying the assumption(s) for one of your thesis statements. Then consider whether or not those assumptions need backing as the intended audience for your argument changes to the following:

- a friend or relative
- a state legislator
- an opinion column editor
- a professional academic in a field related to your topic

Anticipating Counterarguments

Initially, it may strike you as odd to think of counterarguments as a strategy to consider when constructing an argument. However, anticipating **counterarguments**—the objections of those who might disagree with you—may actually strengthen your argument by forcing you to consider competing chains of reasoning and evidence. In fact, many writers actually choose to present counterarguments, or rebuttals of their own arguments, as part of the design of their arguments.

Why would anyone do this? Consider for a moment that your argument is like a debate. If you are able to adopt your opponent's position and then explain why that position is wrong, or why her reasoning is flawed, or in what ways her evidence is insufficient to support her own claim, then you support your own position. This is what it means to offer a **rebuttal** to potential counterarguments. Of course, when you provide rebuttals, you must have appropriate evidence to justify dismissing part or all of the counterargument. By anticipating and responding to counterarguments, you also strengthen your own ethos as a writer on the topic. Engaging counterarguments demonstrates that you have considered multiple positions and are knowledgeable about your subject.

You can also address possible counterarguments by actually conceding to an opposing position on a particular point or in a limited instance. Now, you're probably wondering: Why would anyone do this? Doesn't this mean losing your argument? Not necessarily. Often, such a concession reveals that you're developing a more complex argument and moving past the pro/con positions that can limit productive debate.

Imagine that you're debating an opponent on a highly controversial issue like free college tuition. You're arguing that tuition should be free, and your opponent makes the point that free tuition could have the effect of lowering the quality of education an institution is able to offer. You might choose to concede this possibility, but counter it by explaining how varying tuition costs among different kinds of universities contribute to socioeconomic stratification. Though you acknowledge the validity of your opponent's concerns, you are able to make a case that the social damage caused by the current system makes that risk acceptable. That is, you could qualify your position by acknowledging your opponent's concerns and explaining why you feel that your argument is still valid. In this case, your opponent's points are used to adjust or to qualify your own position, but this doesn't negate your argument. Your position may appear even stronger precisely because you've acknowledged the opponent's points and refined the scope of your argument as a result.

Insider's View
Astronomer Mike Brotherton on Counterarguments

"In science, we're really worried about which side is right, and you discuss both sides only to the extent of figuring out which one's right. It's not one opinion versus another. It's one set of ideas supported by a certain set of observations against another set of ideas supported, or not supported, by the same set of observations, and trying to figure out which one is a better explanation for how things work."

Analyzing an Argument: A Sample Annotated Text

One way to understand the process of developing a persuasive argument is to study how others structure theirs. We have annotated the opinion piece below to point out some of the key features of argument that you've just learned about. The author is an inequality researcher at the Institute for Policy Studies, and his essay was published on several news sites in October 2019. In the Writing Project at the end of the chapter, we invite you to find your own text to analyze and annotate, while taking the next step of putting your observations in essay form.

Student Athletes Are Workers; They Should Get Paid

BRIAN WAKAMO

> The author's position is clear based on the article's title.

California has fired the first shot in the fight against the unfair pay practices of the NCAA. The state's new Fair Pay to Play Act, just signed by Gov. Gavin Newsom, allows for college athletes to profit off their own name and likeness.

In other words, if you're a college athlete in California, come January 2023, you can make money off things like the sale of jerseys with your name on them, as well as endorsements and autographs.

The NCAA, which currently bans student athletes from receiving any compensation at all, is angry about the law. And every state should adopt it.

The bill, which passed with overwhelming support and enjoyed the backing of superstars like LeBron James, is a major step toward leveling the playing field (pardon the pun) with the NCAA, which rakes in more than a billion dollars in revenue from college sports.

The bulk of that money comes from television and marketing rights—which means that AT&T Halftime Show during March Madness, which shows all those player highlights, is bringing in the big bucks for the NCAA.

Coaches also hit the jackpot in this system: College football or basketball coaches were the highest paid public employees in 39 states as of 2016. Meanwhile, stories of their players struggling to eat while working near-full work weeks are all too common.

NCAA rules dictate that these "student-athletes" are allowed to put only 20 hours a week toward their athletic careers. Yet the NCAA also put out a survey reporting that many of them work at least 30 hours a week, and often more than 40 hours, on their sport.

So, for all intents and purposes, these players are workers, breaking their backs for their bosses and employers to get rich.

Former football star Tim Tebow, who supports the NCAA's ban on paying players while raking in cash for itself, said that the push to pay student athletes comes out of a "selfish culture, where it's all about us."

But when these athletes are significantly more likely to suffer chronic injuries long-term than non-college athletes—the CDC says there are around 201,000 injuries in college sports a year—who really is being selfish? The people risking their bodies, or the ones making money off that damage?

Only a small percentage of these young people risking life and limb even have a chance of making a professional career out of it.

According to the NCAA's own breakdown, only 1.6 percent of football players go on to be drafted into major professional leagues. And for basketball players, it's even lower, with just 1.2 percent of men and 0.9 percent of women going pro.

So what good is this system? The NCAA and its defenders say it provides kids with an education, and that's what the whole system is about: they're students first, athletes second. They trot out stats that more than 80 percent of student-athletes end up getting a degree.

But with athletes working full workweeks to train—never mind actually competing—do their schools really care about their education? It's no wonder that story after story comes out about cheating scandals related to players trying to stay academically eligible.

The NCAA even acknowledges it doesn't have a responsibility to ensure education quality.

Margin notes:

The author makes his thesis explicit here: Every state should adopt California's law that "allows for college athletes to profit off their own name and likeness."

The author makes an appeal to pathos.

The author provides a chain of evidence to support a reason for supporting the new law: "Players are workers, breaking their backs for their bosses and employers to get rich."

The author presents a counterargument in favor of the current system.

The author responds to the counterargument by citing a statistic from the Centers for Disease Control and Prevention (CDC).

The author presents another counterargument that favors the current system.

In short, the NCAA runs a system where athletes destroy their bodies, often don't get a quality education, and struggle to make ends meet, with little chance of going pro—all while the coaches and the NCAA executives make money hand over fist off their labor.

The author sums up his reasons for supporting the California law.

It's a completely exploitative system, where these kids can't even start a side business or win a car in a promotional contest without being punished.

So yes, college athletes should absolutely be paid. The California bill is a starting point, and an important one at that. Let's expand it and allow every student athlete to get paid, in every state and at every college.

The author reiterates his call to support the California law and calls for its expansion.

Connect 4.6   **Thinking about "Student Athletes Are Workers"**

What was the most persuasive point in this essay from your point of view? What was the least persuasive point?

Writing Project   **Rhetorical Analysis of an Argument**

For this project, we ask you to consider the ways in which rhetorical context and appeals work together to create an argument. To begin, choose an argument that you can analyze based on its rhetorical context and the appeals it uses to persuade the intended audience. Then, drawing on the principles of rhetorical analysis from Chapter 3 and the discussion of developing arguments in this chapter, compose an analysis examining the argument's use of appeals in light of the rhetorical situation the argument constructs. These questions will be central to your analysis:

- **Rhetorical Context**   How do the elements of the rhetorical context—author, audience, topic, and purpose—affect the way the argument is structured?

- **Rhetorical Appeals**   Does the argument use the appeals of ethos, logos, and/or pathos, and why?

Keep in mind that a rhetorical analysis makes an argument, so your analysis should have a central claim that you develop based on what you observed through the frameworks of rhetorical context and rhetorical appeals. Make your claim clear, and then support it with reasons and evidence from the argument.

Insider Example
Student Analysis of an Argument

Muhammad Ahamed, a student in a first-year writing class, wrote the following analysis of an argument as a course assignment. He used elements of rhetorical analysis and argument analysis to understand the persuasive effects of the argument he chose.

Rhetorical Appeals in "Letter from Birmingham Jail"

Martin Luther King Jr.'s "Letter from Birmingham Jail" is an important document in the history of the American Civil Rights Movement. The letter, which King began writing after being arrested and jailed in Birmingham, Alabama, in April 1963 for "parading without a permit," is directed at a primary audience of eight white clergymen who argued that the Birmingham protests calling for an end to racial segregation and discrimination were "unwise and untimely" and that they should not occur illegally or in the streets. Instead, the clergymen argued, the issues needed to be debated and resolved in the courts. King offers a forceful response to the white clergymen's position in his letter, and he employs the rhetorical appeals of ethos, pathos, and logos to support the goals, methods, and timing of the Birmingham protests for racial justice.

King uses a number of strategies to bolster his ethos as a writer and powerful voice for racial equality. One of these strategies is the respectful manner in which he addresses his audience of "dear fellow clergymen" throughout the letter. Early on in the letter, King refers to the clergymen as "my friends" and acknowledges that they are "men of good will" whose criticisms appear "sincerely set forth." He maintains a respectful tone throughout the body of the letter, in which he lays out the arguments against the protests put forth by the clergymen and offers his response. The respectful tone of the letter extends through the letter's concluding sections. There, he asks his audience to forgive him if anything in the letter "overstates the truth or indicates an unreasonable impatience," and he concludes the letter by expressing a sincere wish to meet the clergymen, "not as an integrationist or a civil-rights leader but as a fellow clergyman and a Christian brother." King's tone and respectful engagement with his audience support his ethos and would likely further his aim of moving the religious leaders closer to his position.

King further bolsters his own ethos by making specific reference to well-known authorities and established thinkers throughout his letter. On more than one occasion, for example, he provides support for his positions by referencing Socrates: "Just as Socrates felt it was necessary to create a tension in the mind so that individuals could rise from the bondage of myths and half truths to the unfettered realm of creative analysis and objective appraisal, so must we see the need for nonviolent gadflies." King also references T. S. Eliot to support his argument for nonviolent protest

The author establishes the focus of his analysis: King's letter.

The author explains the rhetorical context for King's letter.

The author presents his thesis.

In this paragraph, the author explores one way the letter supports King's ethos: his respectful tone.

In this paragraph, the author explores how King uses references to others' words and ideas to support his own ethos.

as a means to address racial discrimination and to encourage his audience to examine its support of police action, even when that action is relatively nonviolent in nature: "The last temptation is the greatest treason: To do the right deed for the wrong reason." King cites numerous other authoritative sources as well, including Thomas Jefferson and Abraham Lincoln, and these references strengthen his response to the criticism that the actions of the protestors are extreme by situating their actions within the wider history of political and social upheaval in the United States. The history of the United States, after all, is filled with instances of progress that resulted from protests. King's references reveal him as one steeped in knowledge of the past, and they provide support for his authority to defend the actions of the protestors.

> The author provides multiple examples to support his argument.

Perhaps the most powerful way that King bolsters his ethos with his intended audience of fellow clergymen is by demonstrating his knowledge and understanding of the Bible and of the history of Christianity itself. King establishes his own authority as a minister when he reveals his familial connections to the church: "Yes, I love the church. How could I do otherwise? I am in the rather unique position of being the son, the grandson, and the great grandson of preachers." Throughout the body of his letter, King relies on his knowledge of the Bible to provide support for the cause of the protestors. To respond to the clergymen's criticism that the protestors are outside agitators, for instance, King relies on the Bible to support the protestors' actions: "I am in Birmingham because injustice is here. . . . Just as the Apostle Paul left his village of Tarsus and carried the gospel of Jesus Christ . . . to the far corners of the world, so am I compelled to carry the gospel of freedom beyond my own home town." To respond to the clergymen's characterization of the protestors as "extreme," King once again provides biblical precedent for the actions of the protestors. In this instance, he compares the actions of the protestors to Jesus Christ himself: "Though I was initially disappointed at being categorized as an extremist . . . I gradually gained a measure of satisfaction from the label. Was not Jesus an extremist for love[?] . . . Perhaps the South, the nation, and the world are in dire need of creative extremists." Repeatedly, King provides rationales for the positions and actions of the protestors that are rooted in biblical precedents.

> In this paragraph, the author explains how King's strategic references to the Bible and the history of Christianity further support his ethos.

King ends his letter by expressing his worry that the church, which he describes as the "arch defender of the status quo," may lose power to affect people's lives if it chooses not to engage in positive social action and engagement: "But the judgment of God is upon the church as never before. . . . Every day I meet young people whose disappointment with the church has turned into outright disgust." By highlighting his deep familiarity with the Scriptures and choosing biblical precedents as support for the protestors' actions, and by acknowledging his deep concern for the future of the church in the letter's conclusion, King reinforces his ethos and strengthens the power of his arguments to move his primary audience of ministers.

The author concludes this section by highlighting the likely effects of King's strategies on his audience.

King's letter also employs the use of pathos, or emotional appeals, to move his audience. One of the clergymen's criticisms levied against the protestors concerned the timing of the protests. The clergymen felt that the protestors should exhibit more patience as the issues of racial desegregation and justice were litigated in the courts. King responds to this criticism with a powerful emotional appeal comprised of a series of scenes of human suffering that have resulted from racism: "But when you have seen vicious mobs lynch your mothers and fathers at will and drown your brothers and sisters at whim; when you have seen hate filled policemen curse, kick and even kill your black brothers and sisters . . . then you will understand why we find it difficult to wait." King also strategically employs an emotional appeal to criticize the inaction of the church by positing the beauty and majesty of the Southern land against the effects of racial prejudice: "On sweltering summer days and crisp autumn mornings I have looked at the South's beautiful churches with their lofty spires pointing heavenward. . . . Over and over I have found myself asking, 'What kind of people worship here? Who is their God?' . . . In deep disappointment I have wept over the laxity of the church." King's balanced use of emotional appeals would be powerfully affecting for any audience, but this is especially true for his primary audience of ministers who are deeply invested in the life and future of the church.

Throughout this paragraph, the author explores King's use of pathos by providing and commenting on specific examples.

At the heart of King's letter are a series of logical arguments, or appeals to logos, that are driven by the structure of the letter as a series of rebuttals to his audience's objections to the Birmingham protests. One of the clergymen's criticisms was directly related to the illegal nature of the protests. In his response to this criticism, King makes a cogent argument to distinguish just and unjust laws, which he defines as "out of harmony with the moral law." If there are unjust laws, then, his argument is that "one has a moral responsibility to disobey unjust laws," and he relies on St. Thomas Aquinas as an authoritative source to support his contention that an unjust law is really no law at all. King essentially dismantles one of the clergymen's

In this section, the author explores a specific strategy of logical appeals that King employs to support his argument.

objections to the protests by presenting a logical case for reinterpretation of the situation. He also addresses the clergymen's objection to the protests on the grounds that they precipitate violence by appealing to their logic. He explicitly wonders about their reasoning: "But is this a logical assertion?" Instead, King maintains, to stand against the actions of the protestors because they may precipitate violence would be similar to "condemning a robbed man because his possession of money precipitated the evil act of robbery." On multiple occasions, King unravels the logic of the clergymen's position against the protests and offers a clearer, more informed reasoning to favor the timing and methods of the protests.

One of the more soaring logical appeals King makes comes when he considers a future America in which racial discrimination and injustice are vanquished. He argues passionately about the inevitability of the outcome of the protests in Birmingham and beyond, based on the history of the United States themselves, because, as he puts it, the "goal of America is freedom." Since the history of the United States is one of progress toward more freedom, and he can trace that history with specific evidence, then the outcome is clear: "We will win our freedom because the sacred heritage of our nation and eternal will of God are embodied in our echoing demands."

King's "Letter from Birmingham Jail" responds to a specific rhetorical situation. Primarily, it is designed to rebut the concerns of a group of clergymen who resisted the timing and methods of the Birmingham protest for racial justice. To support this purpose, King utilizes the rhetorical appeals of ethos, pathos, and logos. He effectively establishes and bolsters his own ethos as a minister and civil rights activist. He further details a number of scenes that compel his audience to connect emotionally to the experiences of the protestors and to develop sympathy for their cause, and he develops a number of logical counterarguments that have the effect of undermining the clergymen's objections to the protests. Beyond the specific strategies King employs to move his primary audience, however, his text remains a powerful example of persuasion that remains applicable today.

The author's concluding paragraph provides a brief overview of King's letter and acknowledges its rhetorical strength.

Work Cited

King, Martin L., Jr. "Letter from Birmingham Jail." *The Martin Luther King, Jr. Research and Education Institute*, https://swap.stanford .edu/20141218230016/http://mlk-kpp01.stanford.edu/kingweb/popular _requests/frequentdocs/birmingham.pdf. Accessed 1 Sept. 2020.

Discussion Questions

1. Where does Muhammad Ahamed state his thesis? Why do you think he phrases his thesis in the way that he does?

2. How does Muhammad use logos in his own argument? Why do you think he relies on logos to support his thesis?

3. Which claim(s) do you find most convincing for Muhammad's rhetorical situation? Why?

tip sheet   Developing Arguments

- **Presenting an argument is different from merely stating an opinion.** Presenting and supporting an argument mean establishing a claim that is backed by reasons and evidence.

- **The unifying element of any academic argument is its primary or central claim.** A unifying claim may take the form of a thesis, a hypothesis, or a more general statement of purpose. There are numerous kinds of claims, including claims of value, definition, and policy.

- **Reasons are generated from and supported by evidence.** Evidence may take the form of inartistic proofs (including statistics and raw data) or artistic proofs, including the rhetorical appeals of ethos (appeal to credibility), logos (appeal to reason and logic), and pathos (appeal to emotion).

- **Claims presented as part of a chain of reasoning are linked by (often) unstated assumptions.** Assumptions should be analyzed carefully for their appropriateness (acceptability, believability) in a particular rhetorical context.

- **Considering and/or incorporating counterarguments is an excellent way to strengthen your own arguments.** You may rebut counterarguments, or you may concede (or partially concede) to them and qualify your own arguments in response.

- **Analyzing others' arguments is a good way to develop your skills at arguing,** particularly in an academic context.

Academic Research

Most of us undertake some kind of research as part of our everyday lives. Imagine for a moment that you have a leaky kitchen faucet you'd like to fix. Unless you're already quite skilled at plumbing work, you may need to consult sources to help you develop a plan to fix the faucet. In this instance, you might consult YouTube videos that demonstrate how a leaking faucet can be fixed, or you might collect information from websites that offer advice about addressing plumbing issues. Or imagine you're in charge of planning a beach vacation with friends. To do so, you may need to consult travel websites to determine the likely costs of the vacation, read reviews of hotels where you're considering staying to help inform the rooms you book, and study maps to determine the best ways to get from one place to another while you vacation. In both of these scenarios, you would be engaging in research. That is, you would be gathering information by examining your own experiences or consulting sources to help you answer questions or accomplish tasks.

Research in the academic context is similar to the kinds of research we conduct in our everyday lives. Students and scholars draw on their own experiences and consult sources to help them answer questions or accomplish tasks. A historian, for example, might study personal journals and newspapers from a particular time to help him understand the social impact of a major historical event. The historian might also consult the work of other scholars who have studied and can provide some insight into the same historical event. Or, before undertaking a series of laboratory experiments to try to answer a question, a biologist may consult the work of other scholars who have already studied the same biological phenomenon. The work of these scholars may inform the biologist's questions as well as the design of her own laboratory experiments. Regardless of their particular research methods, which we'll discuss in more detail in later chapters, these scholars would be engaged in a process of creating knowledge that can be shared with others.

ANDREA TSURUMI

Academic writing, then, is largely focused on sharing the insights that students and scholars gain from their research. The historian might communicate his findings in a new book. The biologist might present the results of her research in a poster presentation at an academic conference or as an article for a peer-reviewed academic journal. Once published, either in the form of a book, a poster presentation, a journal article, or otherwise, the research of these scholars may also become source material for other scholars' research. In this way, these scholars' research would contribute to an ongoing process of creating new knowledge that is the core objective of academic inquiry.

Throughout this chapter, we'll introduce you to some of the basic building blocks of academic research. You'll have the opportunity to consider a research question, to evaluate sources appropriate to that research question, as well as to produce your own researched argument as a starting point for your further participation in academic conversations.

Developing a Research Question

Research projects have all kinds of starting points. Sometimes we start them because a course instructor or an employer asks us to. At other times, we embark on research projects because we want to learn about something on our own. In all these cases, though, the research we undertake typically responds to a question or to a set of questions that we need to answer. These are called **research questions**.

Good research questions are context specific. In other words, a research question that's appropriate for one rhetorical situation may not be appropriate for another. Just as there are various public contexts you encounter on a daily basis for which you may be asked to write an argument, there are also multiple academic contexts in which you may be asked to engage in research. A research question that is appropriate for a literature course in an academic context, for instance, would be quite different from the kind of research question you'd likely ask in a chemistry class. For any research assignment, you want to make sure that you analyze carefully your rhetorical context before undertaking the project. Regardless of your rhetorical context, whether public or academic, there are some general criteria you should consider whenever you're asked to begin a research project or develop a research question.

● **Personal Investment** Does your question concern a topic or issue you care about? Writers tend to do their best work when writing about issues in which they have a personal investment. Even if you're conducting research in a course with a topic that has been assigned, you should always consider how you might approach the topic from an angle that matters to you or that brings in your unique point of view. Your personal investment and level of interest in the topic of your research can greatly impact the kinds of questions you ask of that topic, but they may also influence your level of commitment to, and the quality of, your research.

● **Scope** Is your question too broad or too narrow? If a research question is too broad, then it may not be feasible to respond to it adequately in the scope of your research assignment. If it's too narrow, though, it might not be researchable; in other words, you might not be able to find enough sources to support a solid position on the issue. Consider if there's a way you can broaden or narrow your question to an aspect of an issue or topic that is of the most importance to you. When constructing an academic research question, also keep in mind that your question probably should not be answerable with a simple "yes" or "no" response. Good academic research questions typically require more complex and nuanced answers.

● **Researchable Subject** Is the topic of your research question researchable? Can your question be answered using either primary or secondary research? You'll want to keep in mind that some research questions (as with certain topics and issues) are more appropriate for academic research than others. If a project or assignment you're working on calls for research, and particularly secondary research, then you'll want to formulate a research question that allows you to engage academic source materials to help build your response. This means scholars or other researchers have already contributed to the discussion about your topic in such a way that their contributions might be useful to support your own argument.

● **Feasibility** Is the scope of the research question manageable, given the amount of time you have to research the issue and the amount of space in which you will make your argument? Most research projects, and especially those you undertake for a class, are bound by deadlines; there's usually a due date for turning over your project to your peers or your instructor for review. It's important to keep in mind the amount of time you have available to collect sources and study them, as well as to draft and revise your project. The scope of your research question can affect the type and number of resources you'll need to study to construct a full answer, so it's important to consider any time limitations you may have for completing your project. Additionally, some writing projects have word or page number limitations, and you'll want to make sure you can fully develop a response to your research question within the bounds of those limitations.

● **Contribution** Will your response to your question contribute to the ongoing conversation about the issue? A focused research question sometimes comes from reading previously published materials on a topic or issue. If you are able to review what others have already written on a topic before conducting a study or making an argument of your own on that topic, then you will know what still needs to be understood, explained, or debated. In this way, you may identify a gap in what is already known or understood about a topic in order to build a research question that, when answered, could help fill that gap. This is how researchers continue to contribute to ongoing conversations.

Although we can consider the formulation of a research question the first step in any research project, you should note that research, especially in an academic context, is a highly recursive process. In fact, it's quite common for scholars to formulate an initial research question and begin researching only to find that they need to change their initial research question on the basis of actual research. A good research question, then, is one that has been arrived at after much consideration. Sometimes it is developed only after some initial researching has already taken place. Ultimately, though, a good research question provides focus for a research project by explicitly revealing the general topic or issue that is the subject of inquiry. It may also provide, usually implicitly, clues about the kind of research that will be required to answer the question.

Connect 5.1   **Writing a Research Question**

As you begin your research project, identify a research question that will guide your research and keep you on track. Start by brainstorming a list of possible research questions for ten minutes, and then use the criteria identified above to narrow down your list to a research question that might work for you. If your answer to any of the questions is a definitive "No," then the research question might not be a good choice, or you might need to revise it to make it work for your research project.

Choosing Your Sources

You can gather several different types of sources to respond to a research question. Some of your sources may serve the purpose of simply helping you understand or define your inquiry topic. Other sources may be useful for helping you support or refute another's claims as part of your own argument. Regardless of how your sources are ultimately used as part of your researched argument, you should begin by searching for sources that provide specific evidence to address aspects of your research question. Additionally, you'll always want to keep your target audience in mind as you select your sources, taking into account the kinds of evidence that would likely be most convincing to your audience, whether you are targeting a public or academic audience. Depending on your specific research aims, you must also decide whether you will need to collect primary and/or secondary sources to support your aims.

Primary Sources

Primary sources provide first-hand, or direct, evidence that is useful for supporting an argument. Most research questions require engagement with some kind of primary sources, but the particular forms those sources take in an academic context vary from discipline to discipline.

In a number of academic disciplines, including law, literature, and the arts, for example, primary sources themselves are often the objects of inquiry. If you're making a claim about how to interpret a work of art and you've studied the piece carefully for images and symbols that you discuss in your argument as evidence, for instance, then the work of art is your primary source. Researchers who study the past, like those in the fields of history, may rely on primary sources like newspapers, personal journals, or photographs to provide first-hand evidence to support their conclusions about a particular historical moment.

Scholars in other academic disciplines, including many fields in the social and natural sciences, often rely on data they've gathered from conducting experiments as evidence for their arguments. Imagine a research team that has designed and conducted a survey of people's experiences with a particular social phenomenon, like culture shock. In this case, the results the researchers gathered from their survey are a primary source from which they can provide evidence to answer a research question or support their arguments about the experience of culture shock.

We will delve more deeply into the specifics of research methods in the disciplines in Part Two, but it's important to note that primary sources can take a number of forms. Gathering appropriate primary sources to respond to a particular research question may take a researcher from an archive or museum to a laboratory or library, and it may involve employing any of a number of primary data-collection methods, like interviews, surveys, and experiments to gather first-hand evidence.

Secondary Sources

Based on the scope of your argument and the expectations of your audience, you may also need to engage **secondary sources**, or sources that offer commentary on or description or analysis of primary sources. For example, let's say that your literature professor wants you to offer an interpretation of a poem. You study the poem carefully as your primary source and arrive at a conclusion or claim about the work. But imagine that the assignment also requires you to use scholarly opinions to support your own position or interpretation. As a result, you spend time in the library or searching online databases to locate articles or books by scholars who provide their own interpretations or perspectives on the poem. The articles or books you rely on to support your interpretation are secondary sources because the interpretations were developed by others, commenting on the poem. Likewise, if you cite as part of your own argument the results of a study published by others in an academic journal article, then that article serves as a secondary source of information to you. Some commonly used secondary sources include scholarly books, journal articles, review essays, textbooks, and encyclopedias.

Many of the researched arguments you will produce in college will require you to use both primary and secondary sources as support for your arguments. Even if the main evidence used to support an academic research project comes from primary sources, though, secondary sources can provide you with an overview of what other scholars have already argued with regard to a particular issue or topic. Keep in mind that academic writing and research essentially comprise a series of extended conversations about different issues, and secondary sources may help you understand what part of the conversation has already happened before you start researching a topic on your own, or before you consider entering an established conversation on a topic or issue. Besides revealing what others have already said about a topic, secondary sources may also be useful for providing support for particular claims you might make as part of a broader argument. Scholars often cite the findings and results of other scholars' research to support their own positions.

Connect 5.2 Using Primary and Secondary Sources

Read closely each of the general research questions provided below and consider how each might be researched using both primary and secondary sources. What would those sources be, and how might they offer support to help a researcher respond to the research question?

- What are the effects of food insecurity among students at my college or university?
- What is the meaning of Robert Frost's poem "Stopping by Woods on a Snowy Evening"?
- What are the effects of continuous blacklight exposure on the growth of sunflowers?

Searching for Sources

In Part Two, we discuss collecting and using primary evidence to support claims in specific disciplinary areas or genres in more detail. In the following sections, though, we provide support for collecting secondary sources, which build a foundation for research and writing in academic contexts.

There are many ways to search for sources. Most students today think immediately of the Internet when they consider ways to begin locating secondary sources. No doubt, the Internet can be a highly valuable resource for identifying and collecting potential sources for research projects, both public and academic. When using the Internet to locate sources, however, you should keep in mind that there's a difference between conducting general searches for resources on topics and conducting the kind of narrow and specific searches that will be most useful for academic arguments. How you conduct research on the Internet, including the various online tools you use to search the Internet's vast resources, will impact the volume and appropriateness of the sources you locate for your particular research aims.

For some students, too, the image of a physical library comes immediately to mind when they think of locating sources. No doubt, physical libraries are an excellent resource. In addition to housing any number of possible resources, many libraries also offer workshops on how to locate and use sources effectively, so you should make sure you're knowledgeable about any online or in-person resources offered by your community or college libraries to support your research. For most students engaged in academic research, their institution's library also provides access to more specialized tools to assist in the location of appropriate secondary sources for research projects. In the following sections, we provide a brief introduction to some of the strategies and resources you might use as you undertake your own research projects.

Search Terms and Search Engines

When you search for secondary sources to support the development of a research study or to support a claim in an argument, it's important to consider your **search terms,** the key words and phrases you'll use while you're searching. Let's say, for example, that you're interested in understanding the effects of using cell phones while driving, a topic we explored in Chapter 4. In such a case, you might begin your research with a question that reads something like this:

What are the effects of using cell phones while driving?

The first step in your research process would likely be to find out what others have already written about this issue. To start, then, you might temporarily rephrase your research question to this:

What have others written or argued about the effects of using cell phones while driving?

To respond, you'll need to identify the key terms of your question that will focus your search for secondary sources about the subject. You might highlight some of the key terms in the question:

> What have others written or argued about the effects of using **cell phones** while **driving**?

Let's say you wanted to start by seeing what you could gather from a general search engine such as Google before visiting your library website. If you started by typing "cell phones and driving" into the search bar, your search would return more than 28 million results, from public service ads to news articles to statistics from insurance companies, to name a few. As a result, you may choose to narrow your search to something that emerges as a specific issue, like "reaction time." Doing so reduces the number of hits to 2 million, which is still far too many results to review. The academic sources that might best inform your work will be buried in this overwhelming list of results.

Instead, you might choose to search Google Scholar (scholar.google.com) to understand the ongoing conversation among scholars about your topic. Conducting a search for "cell phones and driving accidents and reaction time" in Google Scholar returns more than 32,000 results:

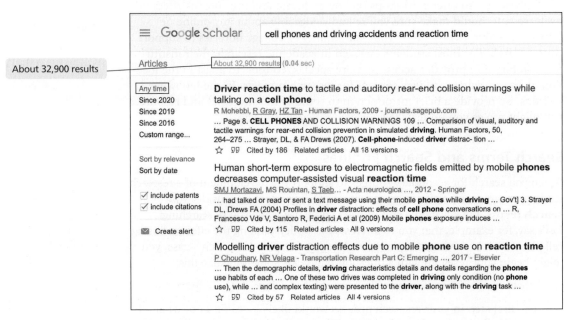

About 32,900 results

If you take a close look at the left-hand side of the screen, however, you'll notice that you can limit your search in several additional ways. By limiting the search to sources published since 2020, you can reduce your results significantly:

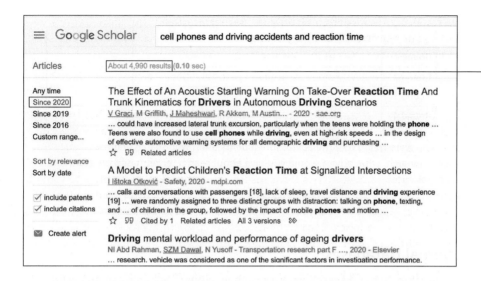

About 4,990 results

You can continue refining your search until you end up with a more manageable number of hits to comb through. Although the number is still large, thousands of results are more manageable than millions. Of course, you would likely need to continue narrowing your results. As you conduct this narrowing process for your topic of inquiry, you are simultaneously focusing in on the conversation you originally wanted to understand: what scholars have written about your topic. Consider the criteria that would be most meaningful for your project as you refine your search by revising your search terms. Also note that Google Scholar is not the only search engine to work with academic sources; you might also try Microsoft Academic.

Connect 5.3   Generating Search Terms

Think of a controversial social issue that interests you. We chose driving while using a cell phone, but you should choose something you would potentially be interested in learning more about. Then follow these instructions:

- What search terms would you enter into Google Scholar or another specialized search engine? List your search terms in the box for Round 1 below, and then try doing a search using your preferred web search engine. How many hits did you get? Write the number in the box for Round 1.

- Now consider how you might refine or narrow your search terms based on the resources you were able to locate in Round 1. Write your new search terms in the box for Round 2. Try the search again and record the number of hits.

- Follow the instructions again for Rounds 3 and 4. →

	Search Terms	Number of Hits
Round 1		
Round 2		
Round 3		
Round 4		

If you were going to write advice for students using web search engines for research, what advice would you give about search terms, based on this experience?

Journal Databases

While more general search engines such as Google Scholar can be useful starting points, experienced academic researchers generally rely on more specialized databases to find the kinds of sources that will support their research most effectively. When you are conducting academic research on a topic of current scholarly inquiry, we recommend that you use these databases to find peer-reviewed journal articles. You may wonder why we don't recommend first scouring your library's catalog for books. The answer is that academic books, which are often an excellent source of information, generally take much longer to make their way through the publishing process before they appear in libraries. Publishing the results of research in academic journal articles, however, is a faster method for academics to share their work with their scholarly communities. Academic journals, therefore, are a valuable resource precisely because they offer insight into the most current research being conducted in a field.

In addition to timeliness, academic journal articles offer credibility. Unlike many general interest publications, academic journals publish research only after it has undergone rigorous scrutiny through a peer-review process by other scholars in the relevant academic field. Work that has gone through the academic peer-review process has been sent out, with the authors' identifying information removed, and reviewed by other scholars who determine whether it makes a sufficiently significant contribution to the field to be published. Work published in a peer-reviewed academic journal has been approved not only by the journal's editor but also by other scholars in the field.

One way of searching for journal articles through your school's library is to explore the academic databases by subject or discipline. These databases usually break down the major fields of study into the many subfields that make up smaller disciplinary communities. Individual schools, colleges, and universities choose which databases they subscribe to. In the following image from North Carolina State University's library website, you can see that the social sciences are divided into various subfields: anthropology, communication & media, criminology, and so on.

Select databases by subject (see all)

		Not sure where to start? Search General/Multi-Subject databases.
Agriculture	Anthropology	
Design	Communication & Media	
Education	Criminology	
Engineering	Economics	
Humanities	Family & Consumer Sciences	
Life Sciences	History	
Management	History of Science & Technology	
Mathematics	Information Science & Technology	
Natural Resources	Law	
Physical Sciences	Linguistics	
	Operations Research	
Social Sciences	Political Science	
	Psychology	
Textiles	Public Administration	

Let's say you need to find information on post-traumatic stress disorder (PTSD) among veterans of the Iraq War that began in March 2003. You spend some time considering the subfields of the social sciences where you're most likely to find research on PTSD: history, sociology, political science, and psychology, for instance. If you choose to focus on the psychological aspects of PTSD, then you would likely select "Social Sciences" and then "Psychology." When you select "Psychology" from the list of available disciplines, typically you'll see a screen that identifies major research databases in psychology, along with some related databases. Choosing the database at the top of the page, "PsycINFO," gains you access to one of the most comprehensive databases in that field of study.

Psychology

Databases

PsycINFO

PsycINFO, from the American Psychological Association (APA), contains more than 2 million citations and summaries of scholarly journal articles, book chapters, books, and dissertations, all in psychology and related disciplines, dating as far back as the 1800s. The database also includes information about the psychological aspects of related fields such as medicine, psychiatry, nursing, sociology, education, pharmacology, physiology, linguistics, anthropology, business, law and others. Journal coverage, which spans 1887 to present, includes international material selected from nearly 2,000 periodicals in more than 25 languages.

Selecting "PsycINFO" grants access to the PsycINFO database via a search engine—in this case, EBSCOhost. You can now input search terms such as "PTSD and Iraq War veterans" to see your results. Notice that the search engine allows you to refine your search in a number of ways, similar to the criteria that you can use in Google Scholar: you can limit the years of publication for research articles, you can limit the search to sources that are available full-text online, you can limit the search to peer-reviewed journal articles, and more. If you limit your search for "PTSD and Iraq War veterans" to peer-reviewed journal articles available in full-text form online, then the results look something like this:

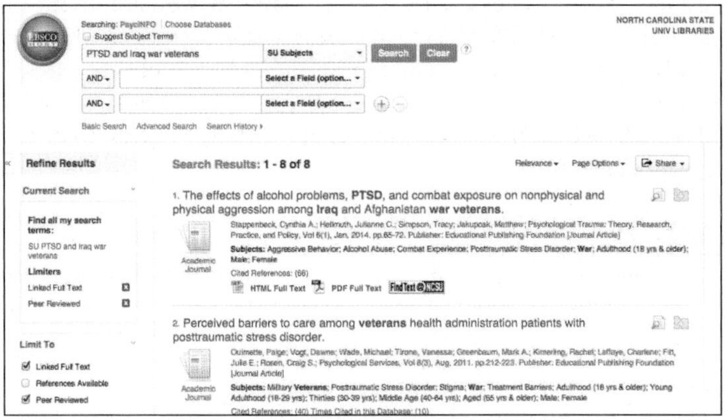

You can now access the texts of journal articles that you find interesting or that might be most relevant to your research purposes. Depending on the number and content of the results, you may choose to revise your search terms and run the search again.

Connect 5.4 Generating Sources from an Academic Database

For this activity, use the same controversial social issue you relied on to complete Connect 5.3. This time, however, try conducting your search using a more specialized academic database that is appropriate to your topic, such as PSYCINFO or Sociological Abstracts. Input each of the four sets of search terms from Connect 5.3 into the database and record the number of hits yielded. As you conduct your search, using each of the search terms, take a few minutes to peruse the kinds of results that are generated by each search.

	Search Terms	Number of Hits
Round 1		
Round 2		
Round 3		
Round 4		

In what ways are the results of your academic database search similar to those you found from a web search engine? In what ways are the results different? What factors, besides using different terms, could account for any difference in the results?

Evaluating Sources:
Scholarly versus Popular Works

If you use a search engine that limits your results to scholarly journals, you can assume that your sources are reliable. If, however, you are doing a broader search, you'll need to be able to evaluate your sources more carefully. To review, **scholarly sources** are produced for an audience of other scholars, and **popular sources** are produced for a general audience. Scholarly sources have undergone a peer-review process prior to publication, while popular sources typically have been vetted only by an editor.

Examples of Scholarly Sources	Examples of Popular Sources
Academic Journals Most journal articles are produced for an audience of other scholars, and the vast majority are peer-reviewed before they are published in academic journals.	*Magazines* Like newspaper articles, magazine articles are typically reviewed by editors and are intended for a general reading audience, not an academic one.
Books Published by Academic Presses Academic presses publish books that also go through the peer-review process. You can sometimes identify academic presses by their names (e.g., a university press), but sometimes you need to dig deeper to find out whether a press generally publishes scholarly or popular sources. Looking at the press's website can often help answer that question.	*Newspapers* Most newspaper articles are reviewed by editors for accuracy and reliability. However, they typically provide information that would be of interest only to a general audience. They are not specifically intended for an academic audience. A newspaper might report the results of a study published in an academic journal, but it will generally not publish original academic research.

Although it may seem easy to classify sources into one of these two categories, there are sources that fall outside these publication types. In those cases, there are other elements of the source that you can explore to see if the source has the qualities of a scholarly work. Imagine that you locate a study published on the Internet that you think would be a really good source for your research. It looks just like an article that might appear in a journal, and it has a bibliography that includes other academic sources. However, as part of your analysis of the source, you discover that the article, published only on a website, has never been published by a journal. Is this a scholarly work? It might be. Could this still be a useful scholarly work for your purposes? Perhaps. Still, as a writer and researcher, you would need to know that the article you're using as part of your own research has never been peer-reviewed or published by a journal or an academic press. This means that the validity of the work has never been assessed by other experts in the field. If you use the source in your own work, you would probably want to indicate that it has never been peer-reviewed or published in an academic journal as part of your discussion of that source.

Answering the following questions about your sources can help you evaluate their credibility and reliability:

1. Who are the authors?
2. Who is the intended audience?
3. Where is the work published?
4. Does the work rely on other reputable sources for information?
5. Does the work seem biased?

As a writer, you must ultimately make the decisions about what is or is not an appropriate source, based on your goals and an analysis of your audience. Answering the questions above can help you assess the appropriateness of sources.

Connect 5.5   Evaluating Sources

For this exercise, look at an essay that you wrote for a class in the past. Choose one of the sources listed in the essay's bibliography and find it again. Then consider these questions:

- Who are the authors? Do they possess any particular credentials that make them experts on the topic? With what institutions or organizations are the authors associated?

- Who is the intended audience—the general public or a group of scholars? How do you know? →

- Where is the work published? Do works published there undergo a peer-review process?
- Does the work rely on other reputable sources for information? What are those sources, and how do you know they are reputable?
- Does the work seem biased? How do you know this? Is the work funded or supported by individuals or parties who might have a vested interest in the results?

Summarizing, Paraphrasing, and Quoting from Sources

Once you've located and studied the sources you want to use in a research paper, then you're ready to begin considering ways to integrate that material into your own work. There are a number of ways to integrate the words and ideas of others into your research, and you've likely already had experience summarizing, paraphrasing, and quoting from sources as part of an academic writing assignment. For many students, though, the specifics of how to summarize, paraphrase, and quote accurately are often unclear, so we'll walk through these processes in some detail.

Summarizing

Summarizing a text is a way of condensing the work to its main ideas. A summary therefore requires you to choose the most important elements of a text and to answer these questions: *What* is this work really trying to say, and *how* does it say it? Composing a summary of a source can be valuable for a number of reasons. Writing a summary can help you carefully analyze the content of a text and understand it better, but a summary can also help you identify and keep track of the sources you want to use in the various parts of your research. You may sometimes be able to summarize a source in only a sentence or two. We suggest a simple method for analyzing a source and composing a summary:

1. Read the source carefully, noting the *rhetorical context*. Who composed the source? For whom is the source intended? Where was it published? What issue or topic is the author addressing? What is the author's purpose for writing? Identify the source and provide answers to these questions at the beginning of your summary, as appropriate.

2. Identify the *main points*. Pay close attention to topic sentences at the beginnings of paragraphs, as they often highlight central ideas in the overall structure of an argument. Organize your summary around the main ideas you identify.

3. Identify *examples*. You will want to be able to summarize the ways the writer illustrates, exemplifies, or argues the main points. Though you will likely not discuss all of the examples or forms of evidence you identify in detail as part of your summary, you will want to comment on one or two, or offer some indication of how the writer supports his or her main points.

The following excerpt is taken from the text of Warren E. Milteer Jr.'s "The Strategies of Forbidden Love: Family across Racial Boundaries in Nineteenth-Century North Carolina":

> In an era in which women in general had limited opportunities for work and faced significant wage discrimination, free women of mixed ancestry had to consider the financial security and social standing of potential mates. For a poor woman looking to move up financially, a relationship with a well-established white man who was willing to build a long-term relationship was a promising opportunity. A white man could not directly pass on the benefits of whiteness to a woman of color and her children as he could for a white woman and her children. White enforcement of racial boundaries limited free people of color's access to certain exclusively white networks, therefore limiting a white man's ability to extend his social connections. However, a white man could convey property obtained through connections to these networks and, as long as he lived, he could pass on some of the intangible benefits of being part of middle- and upper-class white social circles.

A summary of this part of Milteer's text might read something like this:

> In "The Strategies of Forbidden Love: Family across Racial Boundaries in Nineteenth-Century North Carolina," Warren E. Milteer Jr. acknowledges that free women of mixed ancestry could improve their social and economic lot by developing relationships with well-to-do white men. He develops this point by identifying parameters that could both potentially support and undermine the advantages of such relationships (615).

You'll notice that this summary eliminates discussion of the specific details about such relationships that Milteer provides. Though Milteer's ideas are clearly condensed and the writer of this summary has carefully selected the specific ideas to be summarized in order to further his or her own aims, the core of Milteer's argument is accurately represented.

Paraphrasing

Sometimes a writer doesn't want to summarize a source because condensing its ideas risks losing part of its importance. In such a case, the writer has to choose whether to paraphrase or quote directly from the source. **Paraphrasing** means translating the author's words and sentence structure into your own for the purpose of making the ideas clear for your audience. A paraphrase may be the same length or even longer than the part of a text being paraphrased, so the purpose of a paraphrase is not really to condense a passage, as is the case for a summary.

Often, writers prefer to paraphrase sources rather than to quote from them, especially if the exact language from the source isn't important, but the ideas are. Depending on your audience, you might want to rephrase highly technical language from a scientific source, for example, and put it in your own words. Or you might want to emphasize a point the author makes in a way that isn't as clear in the original language. Many social scientists and most scientists routinely paraphrase sources as part of the presentation of their own research because the results they're reporting from secondary sources are more important than the exact language used to explain the results. Quotations should be reserved for instances when the exact language of the original source is important to the point being made. Remember that paraphrasing requires you to restate the passage in your own words and in your own sentence structure. Even if you are putting the source's ideas in your own words, you must acknowledge where the information came from by providing an appropriate citation.

To illustrate both inappropriate and appropriate paraphrasing of a passage, let's look at this paragraph taken from William Thierfelder's article "Twain's *Huckleberry Finn*," published in *The Explicator*, a journal of literary criticism:

> An often-noted biblical allusion in *Huckleberry Finn* is that comparing Huck to the prophet Moses. Like Moses, whom Huck learns about from the Widow Douglas, Huck sets out, an orphan on his raft, down the river. In the biblical story, it is Moses's mother who puts him in his little "raft," hoping he will be found. In the novel, Huck/Moses takes charge of his own travels.

The following paraphrase of the first two sentences of Thierfelder's passage is *inappropriate* because it relies on the language of the original text and employs the author's sentence structure even though some of the language has been changed and the paraphrase includes documentation:

> William Thierfelder suggests that Huckleberry is often compared to the prophet Moses. Huck, an orphan like Moses, travels down a river on a raft (194).

By contrast, an *appropriate* paraphrase that uses new language and sentence structure might look like this:

> William Thierfelder notes that numerous readers have linked the character of Huckleberry Finn and the biblical figure of Moses. They are

both orphans who take a water journey, Thierfelder argues. However, Moses's journey begins because of the actions of his mother, while Huck's journey is undertaken by himself (194).

Quoting

Depending on your rhetorical context, you may find that **quoting** the exact words of a source as part of your argument is the most effective strategy. The use of quotations is much more common in some academic fields than in others. Writers in the humanities, for example, often quote texts directly because the precise language of the original is important to the argument. You'll find, for instance, that literary scholars often quote a short story or poem (a primary source) for evidence. You may also find that a secondary source contains powerful or interesting language that would lose its impact if you paraphrased it. In such circumstances, it is entirely appropriate to quote the text. Keep in mind that your reader should always be able to understand why the quotation is important to your argument. We recommend three methods for integrating quotations into your writing. (The examples below follow American Psychological Association style conventions; see "Understanding Documentation Systems" on pages 86–89 for more information about documentation styles.)

1. **Attributive Tags**   Introduce the quotation with a tag (with words like *notes*, *argues*, *suggests*, *posits*, *maintains*, etc.) that attributes the language and ideas to its author. Notice that different tags suggest different relationships between the author and the idea being cited. For example:

   De Niet, Tiemens, Lendemeijer, Lendemei, and Hutschemaekers (2009) argued, "Music-assisted relaxation is an effective aid for improving sleep quality in patients with various conditions" (p. 1362).

2. **Grammatical Integration**   You may also fully integrate a quotation into the grammar of your own sentences. For example:

   Their review of the research revealed "scientific support for the effectiveness of the systematic use of music-assisted relaxation to promote sleep quality" in patients (De Niet et al., 2009, p. 1362).

3. **Introduction with Full Sentence and Punctuation**   You can also introduce a quotation with a full sentence and create a transitional link to the quotation with punctuation, such as a colon. For example:

   The study reached a final conclusion about music-assisted relaxation: "It is a safe and cheap intervention which may be used to treat sleep problems in various populations" (De Niet et al., 2009, p. 1362).

Summarizing, Paraphrasing, and Quoting from Sources

Choose a source you have found on a topic of interest to you, and find a short passage that provides information that might be useful in your own research. Then complete the following steps:

1. Summarize the passage. It might help to look at the larger context in which the passage appears.

2. Paraphrase the passage, using your own words and sentence structure.

3. Quote the passage, using the following three ways to integrate the passage into your own text: (a) attributive tags, (b) grammatical integration, and (c) introduction with full sentence and punctuation.

Avoiding Plagiarism

Any language and ideas used in your own writing that belong to others must be fully acknowledged and carefully documented, with both in-text citations and full bibliographic documentation. Failure to include either of these when source materials are employed could lead to a charge of **plagiarism**, perhaps the most serious of academic integrity offenses. The procedures for documenting cited sources vary from one rhetorical and disciplinary context to another, so you'll always want to clarify the expectations for documentation with your instructor when responding to an assigned writing task. Regardless, you should always acknowledge your sources when you summarize, paraphrase, or quote, and be sure to include the full information for your sources in the bibliography of your project.

Insider's View
Karen Keaton Jackson, Writing Studies Scholar, on Plagiarism

"Many students come in who are already familiar with using direct quotations. But when it comes to paraphrasing and summarizing, that's when I see a lot of accidental plagiarism. So it's really important for students to understand that if you don't do the research yourself, or if you weren't there in the field or doing the survey, then it's not your own idea and you have to give credit."

Understanding Documentation Systems

Documentation systems are often discipline-specific, and their conventions reflect the needs and values of researchers and readers in those particular disciplines. For these reasons, you should carefully analyze any writing situation to determine which documentation style to follow. You'll find papers that model specific documentation systems in the disciplinary chapters in Part Two. You'll also find more detail on these systems in the Appendix. The three most commonly used documentation systems come from the Modern Language Association (MLA), the American Psychological Association (APA), and the Council of Science Editors (CSE).

Modern Language Association (MLA)

MLA documentation procedures are generally followed by researchers in the humanities. One of the most important elements of the in-text citation requirements for the MLA documentation system is the inclusion of page numbers in a parenthetical reference. Though page numbers are used in other documentation systems for some in-text citations (as in the APA system when quoting a passage directly), page numbers in MLA are especially important because they serve as a means for readers to assess your use of sources, both primary and secondary, and are used whether you are quoting, paraphrasing, or summarizing a passage. Page numbers enable readers to quickly identify cited passages and evaluate the evidence: readers may verify that you've accurately represented a source's intent when citing the author's words, or that you've fully examined all the elements at play in your analysis of a photograph or poem. Of course, this kind of examination is important in all disciplines, but it is especially the case in the humanities, where evidence typically takes the form of words and images.

Unlike some other documentation systems, the MLA system does not require dates for in-text citations, because scholars in this field often find that past discoveries or arguments are just as useful today as when they were first observed or published. Interpretations don't really expire; their usefulness remains valid across exceptionally long periods of time.

Learn more about the style guides published by the Modern Language Association, including the *MLA Handbook*, along with more information about the MLA itself, at www.mla.org.

American Psychological Association (APA)

APA documentation procedures are followed by researchers in many areas of the social sciences and related fields. Although you will encounter page numbers in the in-text citations for direct quotations in APA documents, you're much less likely to find direct quotations overall. Generally, researchers in the social sciences are less interested in the specific language or words used to report research findings than they are in the results or conclusions. Therefore, social science researchers are more likely to paraphrase information than to quote information.

Additionally, in-text documentation in the APA system requires the date of publication for research. This is a striking distinction from the MLA system. Social science research that was conducted fifty years ago may not be as useful as research conducted two years ago, so it's important to cite the date of the source in the text of the argument. Imagine how different the results would be for a study of the effects of violence in video games on youth twenty years ago versus a study conducted last year. Findings from twenty years ago probably have very little bearing on the contemporary social context and would not reflect the same video game content as today's games. As a result, the APA system requires the date of research publication as part of the in-text citation. The date enables readers to quickly evaluate the currency, and therefore the appropriateness, of the research being referenced.

Learn more about the *Publication Manual of the American Psychological Association* and the APA itself at its website: www.apa.org.

Council of Science Editors (CSE)

As the name suggests, the CSE documentation system is most prevalent among disciplines of the natural sciences, although many of the applied fields in the sciences, like engineering and medicine, rely on their own documentation systems. As in the other systems described here, CSE requires writers to document all materials derived from sources. Unlike MLA or APA, however, CSE allows multiple methods for in-text citations, corresponding to alternative forms of the reference page that appears at the end of research reports.

For more detailed information on CSE documentation, consult the latest edition of *Scientific Style and Format: The CSE Manual for Authors, Editors, and Publishers*. You can learn more about the Council of Science Editors at its website: www.councilscienceeditors.org.

Annotated Bibliographies

The **annotated bibliography** is a common genre in several academic disciplines because it provides a way to compile and take notes on—that is, annotate—resources that are potentially useful in a research project. Annotated bibliographies are essentially lists of citations, formatted in a consistent documentation style, that include concise summaries of source material. Some annotated bibliographies include additional commentary about the sources—perhaps a description of their rhetorical context or an evaluation of their usefulness for a particular research project or an explanation of how the sources complement one another within the bibliography (possibly by providing multiple perspectives). Although less common, some annotated bibliographies that are completed as part of a class project may include a brief introduction that identifies a student's research question and/or provides a brief overview of the research or reflection on the annotated sources.

You will want to be careful to follow closely any specific instructions you receive for the construction of your own projects. Annotated bibliographies are usually organized alphabetically, but longer bibliographies can be organized topically or in sections with subheadings. Each source entry gives the citation first and then a paragraph or two of summary, as in this example using MLA style:

> Carter, Michael. "Ways of Knowing, Doing, and Writing in the
> Disciplines." *College Composition and Communication,* vol. 58, no. 3,
> 2007, pp. 385–418.

> In this article, Carter outlines a process for helping faculty across
> different academic disciplines to understand the conventions of writing
> in their disciplines by encouraging them to think of disciplines as "ways
> of doing." He provides examples from his own interactions with faculty
> members in several disciplines, and he draws on data collected from

these interactions to describe four "metagenres" that reflect ways of doing that are shared across multiple disciplines: problem-solving, empirical inquiry, research from sources, and performance. Finally, he concludes that the metagenres revealed by examining shared ways of doing can help to identify "metadisciplines."

For an example of an annotated bibliography in APA style, see the Insider Example on page 90.

Writing Project   ## Annotated Bibliography

For this assignment, you should write an annotated bibliography that explores sources you've located to help you respond to a specific research question. Your purposes in writing the annotated bibliography are threefold: (1) to organize and keep track of the sources you've found on your own topic, (2) to better understand the relationships among different sources that address your topic, and (3) to demonstrate knowledge of the existing research about it.

To meet these purposes, choose sources that will help answer your research question, and think about a specific audience who might be interested in the research you're presenting. Your annotated bibliography should include the following elements:

- An introduction that clearly states your research question and describes the scope of your annotated bibliography: What led you to your research question? What makes your question important or meaningful? Why does your question need to be answered?

- Three to five scholarly sources (though you may include more, depending on the scope of the sources and the number of perspectives you want to represent), organized alphabetically, from any academic field you believe will help you construct an answer to your research question. If you choose a different organization (e.g., topical), provide a rationale for how you have organized your annotated bibliography in the introduction.

- An annotation for each source that includes the following:
  - A citation in a consistent documentation style. See the Appendix for citation information, but also note that the landing page of online articles often provides the citation elements in various style options.
  - A summary of the source that gives a concise description of the researchers' methods and central findings, focused on what is most important for responding to your research question
  - Relevant information about the authors or sponsors of the source to indicate credibility, bias, perspective, and the like
  - An indication of what this source brings to your annotated bibliography that is unique and/or how it connects to the other sources

Insider Example

Student Annotated Bibliography

The following annotated bibliography by Regan Mitchem, a student in a first-year writing course, is organized according to her instructor's directions, which asked students to provide only their research questions at the beginning of their projects as introductory material. Students were asked to include three to five annotated entries as part of their bibliographies. This annotated bibliography utilizes APA documentation style. It has been annotated to highlight consistent moves the student writer makes across the bibliographic entries. For a complete example of APA paper formatting, including a title page and running head, see the Insider Example on pages 191–98 in Chapter 8.

Benefits of Technology Integration in the Classroom

Research Question: What are the benefits of technology integration in the classroom?

Baylor, B. L., & Ritchie, D. (2002). What factors facilitate teacher skill, teacher morale, and perceived student learning in technology-using classrooms? *Computers & Education, 39*(4), 395–414. https://doi.org/10.1016/S0360-1315(02)00075-1

Baylor and Ritchie (2002), in the article "What Factors Facilitate Teacher Skill, Teacher Morale, and Perceived Student Learning in Technology-Using Classrooms?" explain that a teacher's openness to change and technology-supporting leadership can significantly influence acceptance of technology use, higher-level thinking, teacher technological abilities, and teacher morale. Baylor and Ritchie (2002) support their claims through a quantitative comparison of 94 classrooms from 12 schools across the United States with varying characteristics related to technology. They conclude that "although [they] found that administrators contribute to the positive interactions of technology in a school, of greater importance were teacher attributes" (Baylor & Ritchie, 2002, p. 412). The authors' purpose is to determine how technology can best be supported and utilized in the classroom setting for the benefit of students, teachers, and administrators. The authors write in a formal tone for an audience of administrators and policymakers seeking guidance on the use of technology in schools.

Dolch, C., & Zawacki-Richter, O. (2018). Are students getting used to learning technology? Changing media usage patterns of traditional and non-traditional students in higher education. *Research in Learning Technology, 26,* 2038–2055. http://dx.doi.org.prox.lib.ncsu.edu/10.25304/rlt.v26.2038

This student's project assignment asks that students present their research question as the introduction to their projects.

The student identifies the researchers' methods.

The student notes a finding that may be of particular interest to her research project.

All bibliographic entries should appear in a consistent documentation style. In this case, it's APA.

In their longitudinal study, "Are Students Getting Used to Learning Technology?" which surveyed over 1,000 students enrolled in German institutions of higher education, Dolch and Zawacki-Richter (2018) sought to examine the media use behavior of traditional and non-traditional students. They found that increasing numbers of students enrolling in fully online and technologically blended courses as well as the demand for more digital learning opportunities increasing among non-traditional students. Notably, they indicated "a clearly significant change is the direction towards the use of mobile devices" (Dolch & Zawacki-Richter, 2018, p. 2049). Their study indicates various implications of their findings for higher education settings. The researchers' purpose is to identify trends in student engagement with online media so that institutions of higher education might respond appropriately in their instructional design. They write for an audience of researchers and other educational professionals.

> The student indicates an overview of the researchers' purpose.

Erstad, O. (2003). Electracy as empowerment: Student activities in learning environments using technology. *Young, 11*(1), 11–28. https://doi-org. prox.lib.ncsu.edu/10.1177/1103308803011001073

In his article "Electracy as Empowerment: Student Activities in Learning Environments Using Technology," Erstad (2003) suggests that a balance in traditional teaching and use of technology could open opportunities for independent learning, add a new dimension to communication, and create a more student-centered system for teachers as they facilitate the learning process. Erstad (2003) supports his claims, based on case studies of three schools, to show that the "use of technology gives students tools for empowerment and some possibilities of moving students towards student-centered learning environments" (p. 25). The author's purpose is to encourage the integration of technological opportunities into learning environments so that students are more engaged in their subject material and can better understand their own learning abilities. Erstad (2003) writes in a persuasive tone to address an audience of teachers or education professionals.

> The student offers a general summary of the source.

> The student identifies potential audiences for the researchers' study.

A Supported Argument on a Controversial Issue

For this writing assignment, you will apply your knowledge from Chapter 4 about developing an argument and from this chapter on finding and documenting appropriate sources. The sources you find will be evidence for the argument you develop. We ask you to make a claim about a controversial issue that is of importance to you and support that claim with evidence to persuade a particular audience of your position. As you write, you might follow the steps below to develop your argument:

- Begin by identifying an issue that you care about and likely have some experience with. We all write best about things that matter to us. For many students, choosing an issue that is specific to their experience or local context makes a narrower, more manageable topic to write about. For example, examining recycling options for students on your college campus would be more manageable than tackling the issue of global waste and recycling.

- Once you have identified an issue, start reading about it to discover what people are saying and what positions they are taking. Use the suggestions in this chapter to find scholarly sources about your issue so that you can "listen in on" the conversations already taking place about your issue. You might find that you want to narrow your topic further based on what you find.

- As you read, begin tracking the sources you find. These sources can serve as evidence later for multiple perspectives on the issue; they will be useful both in supporting your claim and in understanding counterarguments.

- Identify a clear claim you would like to support, an audience you would like to persuade, and a purpose for writing to that audience. Whom should you talk to about your issue, and what can they do about it?

As you work to develop your argument, consider the various elements of an argument you read about in Chapter 4.

- Identify a clear central claim and determine if it should have a simple or complex thesis statement.

- Develop clear reasons for that claim, drawn from your knowledge of the issue and the sources you have found.

- Choose evidence from your sources to support each reason that will be persuasive to your audience, and consider the potential appeals of ethos, logos, and pathos.

- Identify any assumptions that need to be explained to or supported for your audience.

- Develop responses to any counterarguments you should include in your argument.

Insider Example

Student Argument on a Controversial Issue

The following sample student argument, produced in a first-year writing class, illustrates many of the principles discussed in Chapters 4 and 5. As you read, identify the thesis, reasons, and sources used as support for the argument. Notice also that the student writer, Jack Gomperts, followed CSE documentation conventions throughout his paper, in response to his instructor's direction to choose a documentation style appropriate to the subject of his argument. For a complete example of CSE paper formatting, including a title page and running head, see the Insider Example on pages 241–46 in Chapter 9.

Evaluating Hydration Levels in High School Athletes

Every day, high school athletes across the country put themselves at risk of heat-related injury, and even death, by failing to hydrate properly. Many athletes arrive at practice dehydrated and abandon proper hydration throughout activity. This habit not only puts athletes at an increased risk of injury, but also decreases their performance (Gibson-Moore 2014). Numerous researchers have explored exactly when and how much fluid an athlete needs to maintain proper hydration. Some experimenters focus on which fluids, such as water, sports drinks, milk, juice, or various other drink options, produce the best hydration. The most important factor in making sure athletes maintain hydration, however, is not telling them how to obtain hydration, but rather testing their hydration status. Often, athletes forget or ignore hydration when coaches simply tell them to stay well hydrated. If athletes know that they will undergo testing for hydration every day, they will be more likely to take action to achieve the proper hydration status. Scientists possess dozens of methods for testing hydration in athletes, and urine specific gravity and body mass measurements are the most practical for everyday use. Urine specific gravity requires only one drop of urine from an athlete, and body mass measurements require athletes to step on a scale. In addition, athletes must sign a contract with their school before participating in any athletic event associated with the school. Schools use these contracts to ensure that they are not liable for any injury experienced by an athlete. However, most schools do not include any information about hydration in their contracts, thus exposing athletes to severe risk. Altogether, schools should alter their athletic contracts to include hydration testing for athletes with urine specific gravity and body mass measurements.

> Argument begins by establishing a problem that exists

> Establishes the need for further exploration and action with regard to hydration in athletes

> Establishes a two-part central claim or position of the argument: schools should alter contracts to include hydration testing and they should use urine specific gravity and body mass measurements as the means to test hydration.

Consider the kinds of evidence the writer relies on in this paragraph, including evidence from personal experience. Are they effective? What function does this paragraph serve in the overall structure of the student's argument?

Every year, 10,000 high school athletes in the United States suffer from dehydration (Centers for Disease Control and Prevention 2010). This staggering number only includes injuries that health professionals have diagnosed and does not account for the numerous athletes who suffer from dehydration without realizing it. Personally, I have never witnessed an athlete who was diagnosed with a heat-related illness, but I have seen several athletes suffer injuries that trace back to dehydration. I played on several sports teams throughout my high school career and witnessed a common theme; coaches often tell athletes to stay hydrated, but fail to explain the importance of hydration. At many football games, several of my teammates suffered from cramps caused by dehydration. During my senior year of high school, an athlete collapsed at three of my cross-country meets because of overheating.

How does this paragraph support part of the writer's central position about testing athletes' levels of hydration? What reason is supported here?

The athletes who neglected proper hydration at my school did not do so without consequences. Many of them experienced concussions; at least ten to twelve athletes from various sports at my school received concussions every year. According to Dr. Meehan, "Every time you get [a concussion], there's some effect on the brain that doesn't go away, concussions have a cumulative effect" (Costa 2015). Concussions negatively impact student-athletes for their entire lives, whereas most sports-related injuries do not have detrimental long-term effects. Scientists believe a strong correlation exists between hydration statuses and concussion risks. They have begun to study cerebrospinal fluid, which surrounds the brain and reduces the impact of heavy blows. With less fluid, athletes have a smaller cushion for their brain; scientists believe even a two percent decrease in hydration severely decreases the amount of cerebrospinal fluid (DripDrop 2016).

This paragraph functions to support the writer's reasoning for his central position. What is the reason he presents to support his central claim or thesis?

In addition to concussions, dehydration can also lead to a variety of heat-related illnesses, such as heat cramps, heat exhaustion, heat stroke, or even death. Heat cramps cause involuntary muscle contractions and can be treated by stretching and rehydration. Heat exhaustion causes redness of skin, profuse sweating, nausea, and vomiting, and is treated as a medical emergency by immediate rehydration and applying ice to the core. Heat stroke is the complete inability to thermo-regulate and causes clammy skin, cessation of sweating, dizziness, nausea, and possible unconsciousness. In order to treat a person experiencing these symptoms, medical professionals immediately cool them in an ice bath or transport them to a trauma center (Gallucci 2014). Despite the consequences, many athletes and coaches overlook the problem of dehydration. According to the National Center for Catastrophic Sports Injury Research (2009), 40 high school football players have died from heat stroke since 1995. In addition, they report that dozens of athletes are hospitalized every year for heat-related illnesses, which directly correlates to hydration status. When as many as two thirds of young athletes arrive at practice dehydrated (Southwest Athletic Trainers' Association 2013), it is evident that high school athletic policies must be improved.

The writer incorporates evidence from statistics.

Once schools recognize the problem of dehydration, there are many possible solutions. Of the various methods, a combination of urine specific gravity and body mass measurements would be the most convenient and effective for daily use. Since urine specific gravity is easy to use and accurate, schools should utilize its capabilities. This system analyzes a drop of urine on the stage of a refractometer to evaluate the level of hydration in the athlete. If the device shows a value between 1.001 and 1.012, the athlete is likely over-hydrated. A value between 1.013 and 1.029 shows proper hydration, and values above 1.030 show dehydration (Armstrong 2005). The device needed to take these measurements can cost anywhere from $60 to $400 (Lopez 2006)—a small price for teams to pay to ensure the safety of their athletes. According to Armstrong (2005), urine specific gravity is the best method to test hydration in an everyday setting because of its reliability, accuracy, and ease of use. Scientists possess several additional methods for testing hydration. These methods, however, are not practical for athletes on a daily basis, although they produce a higher level of accuracy than urine specific gravity. For instance, urine specific gravity loses accuracy as athletes' muscle mass increases. Hamouti et al. (2010) found that urine specific gravity devices falsely classify athletes with high muscle mass as dehydrated far more often than athletes with low muscle mass.

Provides reasoning to support this particular method of hydration testing

Due to the slightly inaccurate measurements produced by urine specific gravity, coaches should use body mass measurements in addition to urine specific gravity to test hydration. Body mass measurements are even more efficient and less expensive to record than urine specific gravity measurements. In order for coaches to use body mass measurements to determine hydration, they must simply weigh their athletes before and after every practice. If the athletes' mass decreases by more than two percent, they are dehydrated (Armstrong 2005). In addition, if their body mass decreases by more than two percent from the beginning of practice one day to the beginning of practice the next day, they are likely dehydrated.

Provides further reasoning to support the methods of testing hydration levels in athletes

Body mass measurements provide a good estimate of hydration status. Recognizing that the body mass of high school athletes constantly changes due to growth, eating habits, and several other factors, coaches should use body mass measurements in addition to urine specific gravity. They should use urine specific gravity once on the athletes at the beginning of the season, and two to three times randomly throughout the season. This system will provide the coaches with more accurate results than body mass measurements, while not requiring athletes to place a drop of urine on a device every day. This process will ensure the safety of athletes on a daily basis and drastically decrease their risk for illness or death.

Despite the many benefits of hydration testing, some people might disagree with this proposal. Some might argue that regulating hydration status invades the privacy of an athlete and assumes unnecessary control of an athlete's life. I propose that students should decide how much fluid they need, how often they need it, and which drinks best produce hydration. Lopez (2006), Maughan (2010), and Johannsen (2015) all argue for different amounts and types of fluid for proper hydration. These decisions should be left to the athlete since each athlete differs in how much fluid they need for hydration. The schools should only take responsibility for making sure that their athletes are well hydrated. Schools and athletic organizations have put dozens of rules in place to ensure the safety of athletes, like the types of hits allowed in football. If schools have the authority to make rules that protect football players, schools have the power to implement rules and regulations that concern hydration. If implementing hydration regulations can save just one life, schools should do so as quickly as possible. A life is worth more than the few hundred dollars spent on urine specific gravity devices and portable scales. A life is worth more than the slight hassle of taking a few minutes before and after practice to measure athletes' body mass. These rules, however, could have potentially saved the 40 lives that have been lost since 1995 because of heat-related illnesses (National Center for Catastrophic Sports Injury Research 2009). Hydration testing might have prevented several thousand athletes from experiencing heat-related illness every year, or saved dozens of athletes from hospitalization. The slight intrusion on athletes' privacy is well worth saving dozens of lives.

In addition to the intrusion on athletes, some people might argue that coaches already carry immense responsibility, and adding these tests would place a heavier burden on the coaches. However, the coaches' job is to teach the athletes how to improve their play and to keep them safe from injury. The hydration requirements I propose align directly with a coach's responsibility. Although it could be considered a burden to require coaches to measure athletes' hydration status, this burden takes no more than 20 minutes a day to complete. Additionally, these regulations exist in accordance with the coach's job, which is to protect his or her athletes, and enhance the athletes' performance however possible. These tests will help coaches do their job more fully and provide better care for their athletes.

Altogether, hydration should be tested in athletes with a combination of urine specific gravity and body mass measurements because these tests will ensure that athletes are practicing and performing under safe conditions. Dehydration poses a problem in high schools all across America because many teens do not understand the importance of proper hydration. Therefore, they arrive at practice dehydrated, which leads to thousands of injuries a year. I propose that to solve this problem, schools should include a policy in their athletic contract regarding hydration. This policy should require athletes to be subject to three to four urine specific gravity tests throughout the season and two daily body mass measurements. Even though people might argue that these tests intrude on athletes' privacy and place a burden on coaches, the tests are capable of saving dozens of lives. I believe that this insignificant burden is well worth the sacrifice. I further propose that each athlete should be held responsible for determining how he or she can best achieve hydration. While researchers continue to find the best ways for athletes to maintain hydration, schools must take responsibility by implementing regulations to reduce the dangers associated with dehydration in athletics.

> Can you identify other potential counterarguments that might undermine the writer's position here?

> Do any of the writer's proposals, presented in the conclusion to the argument, surprise you as a reader? Why or why not?

References

> In CSE paper format, the References would start a new page.

> Notice the mix of sources the writer relies upon, both popular and academic, as well as any primary and secondary forms of research.

Armstrong LE. 2005. Hydration assessment techniques [Internet]. Nutr Res. [accessed 2016 Dec 9]; 63(6):S40–S54. Available from: https://www.ncbi .nlm.nih.gov/pubmed/16028571

Centers for Disease Control and Prevention. 2010. Heat illness among high school athletes—United States, 2005–2009 [Internet]. Morb Mortal Wkly Rep. [accessed 2016 Dec 9]; 59(32):1009–1053. Available from: https://www.cdc.gov/mmwr/preview/mmwrhtml/mm5932a1.htm

Coe S, Williams R. 2011. Hydration and health [Internet]. Nutr Bull. [accessed 2016 Dec 9]; 36(2):259–266. Available from: http://onlinelibrary.wiley .com/doi/10.1111/j.1467-3010.2011.01899.x/abstract

Notice the kinds of sources the author uses as support. If he were to conduct additional research for support, what kind of additional sources would you recommend he look to in order to strengthen his argument?

Costa S. 2015. Just how dangerous are sports concussions, anyway?: Concussions cause the brain to dangerously move back and forth inside the skull [Internet]. Huffington Post. [accessed 2016 Dec 9]. Available from: http://www.huffingtonpost.com/entry /the-truth-about-concussions_us_564a0043e4b045bf3deff7fc

DripDrop Hydration. 2016. Does dehydration increase an athlete's risk for concussion? [Internet]. [accessed 2016 Dec 9]. Available from: http://dripdrop.com/dehydration-increase-athletes-risk-concussion/

Gallucci J. 2014. Soccer injury prevention and treatment: A guide to optimal performance for players, parents and coaches. New York (NY): Demos Medical Publishing. p. 157–159.

Gibson-Moore H. 2014. Hydration and health [Internet]. Nutr Bull. [accessed 2016 Dec 9]; 39(1):4–8. Available from: http://onlinelibrary.wiley.com /doi/10.1111/nbu.12039/full

Hamouti N, Del Coso J, Avila A, Mora-Rodriquez R. 2010. Effects of athletes' muscle mass on urinary markers of hydration status [Internet]. Euro J Appl Physiol. [accessed 2016 Dec 9]; 109(2):213–219. Available from: https://www.ncbi.nlm.nih.gov/pubmed/20058021

Johannsen NM, Earnest CP. 2015. Fluid balance and hydration for human performance. In: Greenwood M, Cooke MB, Ziegenfuss T, Kalman DS, Antonio J, editors. Nutritional supplements in sports and exercise. Cham, Switzerland: Springer International Publishing. p. 105–119.

Lopez RM, Casa DJ. 2006. Hydration for athletes: What coaches can do to keep their athletes healthy and performing their best [Internet]. Coaches' Quarterly. [accessed 2016 Dec 9]. Available from: https://www .wiaawi.org/Portals/0/PDF/Sports/Wrestling/hydration4athletes.pdf

Maughan RJ, Shirreffs SM. 2010. Dehydration and rehydration in competitive sport [Internet]. Scand J Med Sci. [accessed 2016 Dec 9]; 20(3):40–47. Available from: http://onlinelibrary.wiley.com/doi/10.1111/j.1600 -0838.2010.01207.x/abstract

National Center for Catastrophic Sports Injury Research (US) [NCCSIR]. 2009. Annual survey of football injury research: 1931–2008 [Internet]. [accessed 2016 Dec 9]. p. 2–29. Available from: http://nccsir.unc.edu /files/2014/05/FootballAnnual.pdf

Southwest Athletic Trainers' Association. 2013. Statistics on youth sports safety [Internet]. [accessed 2016 Dec 9]. Available from: http://www .swata.org/statistics/

Discussion Questions

1. Whom do you think Jack Gomperts is targeting as his audience in this assignment? Why do you think that is his audience?

2. What kinds of sources does Jack rely on in his argument? How does he integrate them into his argument, and why do you think he has made those choices?

3. Are you convinced by the writer's argument? Why or why not? What would make this argument more persuasive and effective?

tip sheet   Academic Research

- **Research typically begins with a research question, which establishes the purpose and scope of a project.** As you develop research questions, keep in mind the following evaluative criteria: personal investment, debatable subject, researchable issue, feasibility, and contribution.

- **A researcher who has established a clear research focus, or who has generated a claim, must decide on the kinds of sources needed to support the research focus:** primary, secondary, or both.

- **While both scholarly and popular sources may be appropriate sources of evidence in differing contexts, be sure to understand what distinguishes these types of sources** so that you can choose evidence types purposefully.

- **Primary sources are the results of data that researchers might collect on their own.** These results could include data from surveys, interviews, or questionnaires. **Secondary sources include research collected by and/or commented on by others.** These might include information taken from newspaper articles, magazines, scholarly journal articles, and scholarly books, to name a few.

ANDREA TSURUMI

Inside Academic Writing

In Part Two you'll look at how writing works in each of the major
academic areas. You'll learn how the conventions and genres
of different disciplines represent a discipline's shared values.
Throughout these chapters, you'll be practicing skills of rhetorical
analysis that you can transfer to your future courses and careers.

6

Reading and Writing in Academic Disciplines

ANDREA TSURUMI

Now that you have an understanding of the fundamentals of rhetoric, argument, and working with sources, you are ready to analyze and practice writing in various academic disciplines. Keep in mind, though, that we do *not* expect you to master the writing of these communities by taking just one class or by reading one book. Instead, we introduce you to the concepts associated with **disciplinary discourse**, or the writing and speaking that is specific to different disciplines. Using these concepts, you can analyze future writing situations and make choices appropriate to the rhetorical contexts. It's worth noting that such rhetorical awareness may help you enter other **discourse communities**, or groups that share common values and similar communication practices, outside of your college classes as well, both socially and professionally.

As you study writing in the four broad disciplinary areas of humanities, social sciences, natural sciences, and applied fields in the chapters that follow, you'll focus on three defining elements: (1) research expectations, (2) conventions (expectations) of writing, and (3) genres (types) of writing. You'll learn that the conventions and genres of different disciplines are not just patterns to follow; rather, they represent the discipline's shared values. In other words, because scholars in the same discipline might have similar ways of thinking about an issue and what they can contribute to our understanding of it, they follow common ways of researching and sharing their results with others. We'll take a closer look at how values are reflected in such details as what to cover at the start of a paper or how to credit the work of others.

The information we offer you on different academic disciplinary conventions and genres in this book is not necessarily something to memorize, but rather something to view through the frame of *rhetorical analysis*. Ultimately, we want you to be able to look at an academic text and be able to do the following:

- understand the overall rhetorical context of the piece of writing: the author, the audience, the topic, and the purpose for writing
- identify and understand the disciplinary area—humanities, social sciences, natural sciences, applied fields—and make connections to what you know about that discipline
- identify the genre and study the conventions of writing for that genre, including the elements of structure, language, and reference (explained below)

The ability to look at writing through this framework will help you determine and follow the expectations for writing in different courses throughout your college career. It will also help you read the assignments in your other classes because you will understand some of the reasons that texts are written in the way that they are.

Using Rhetorical Context to Analyze Academic Writing

In Chapter 3, we introduced the concept of rhetorical context for analyzing different kinds of writing. Now we want to focus your attention on analyzing the rhetorical contexts of writing in different disciplines. Scholars write for different rhetorical contexts all the time, and they adapt their writing to the audience, topic, and purpose of the occasion. In this chapter, we'll look at two pieces of writing from astronomer Mike Brotherton, a member of the science faculty at the University of Wyoming. Each represents a type of writing that he does on a regular basis. Brotherton writes scholarly articles in his field to report on his research to an audience of other academics—his peers. He also sometimes writes press releases about his research, and these are intended to help journalists report news to the general public.

Analyzing Academic Writing: A Sample Annotated Text

Let's take a look at a press release that Brotherton composed in 2008 to announce his research team's findings on the evolution of galaxies and the black holes at their centers. As you read the press release, which we've annotated, keep in mind the elements of rhetorical context that are useful in analyzing all kinds of writing: author, audience, topic, and purpose. Specifically, consider the following questions:

- How might the fact that Brotherton is both the *author* of the press release and the lead researcher influence the way he wrote the press release? What might have been different if someone else had written the press release after talking to him about his research?

- Who do you think is the *audience* for this piece? Keep in mind that press releases are usually written to the media to encourage them to follow and report on a story. Science journalists often have the background to understand complex scientific topics and translate them for the public, but not all publications have science journalists on staff. What choices do you think Brotherton made that were specific to his audience for the press release?

- How does the *topic* of the press release affect the choices Brotherton made? Would you have made different choices to approach the topic for a general audience? What would they be?

- What is the *purpose* for writing the press release? How might that influence Brotherton's choices as a writer? Do you think he has met that purpose? Why or why not?

Excerpt from Hubble Space Telescope Spies Galaxy/Black Hole Evolution in Action

MIKE BROTHERTON

JUNE 2, 2008 — A set of 29 Hubble Space Telescope (HST) images of an exotic type of active galaxy known as a "post-starburst quasar" show that interactions and mergers drive both galaxy evolution and the growth of super-massive black holes at their centers. Mike Brotherton, Associate Professor at the University of Wyoming, is presenting his team's findings today at the American Astronomical Society meeting in St. Louis, Missouri. Other team members include Sabrina Cales, Rajib Ganguly, and Zhaohui Shang of the University of Wyoming, Gabriella Canalizo of the University of California at Riverside, Aleks Diamond-Stanic of the University of Arizona, and Dan Vanden Berk of the Penn State University. The result is of special interest because the images provide support for a leading theory of the evolution of massive galaxies, but also show that the situation is more complicated than previously thought.

Over the last decade, astronomers have discovered that essentially every galaxy harbors a super-massive black hole at its center, ranging from 10,000 times the mass of the sun to upwards of 1,000,000,000 times solar, and that there exists a close relationship between the mass of the black hole and properties of its host. When the black holes are fueled and grow, the galaxy becomes active, with the most luminous manifestation being a quasar, which can outshine the galaxy and make it difficult to observe.

Margin annotations:

Identifies the **topic** of the research study and its relevant findings

Identifies members of the research team, who are all **authors** of the study upon which the press release is based

Fulfills the **purpose** of a press release by stating the importance of the research project; appears in the first paragraph to make it prominent for the audience

Provides relevant background information about the topic for the **audience**

In order to explain the relationships between galaxies and their central black holes, theorists have proposed detailed models in which both grow together as the result of galaxy mergers. This hierarchical picture suggests that large galaxies are built up over time through the assembly of smaller galaxies with corresponding bursts of star formation, and that this process also fuels the growth of the black holes, which eventually ignite to shine as quasars. Supernova explosions and their dusty debris shroud the infant starburst until the activated quasar blows out the obscuration.

Brotherton and his team turned the sharp-eyed Hubble Space Telescope and its Advanced Camera for Surveys to observe a subset of these post-starburst quasars that had the strongest and most luminous stellar content. Looking at these systems 3.5 billion light-years away, Hubble, operating without the distortions of an atmosphere, can resolve sub-kiloparsec scales necessary to see nuclear structure and host galaxy morphology.

> Provides a brief overview of the study's methods

"The images started coming in, and we were blown away," said Brotherton. "We see not only merger remnants as in the prototype of the class, but also post-starburst quasars with interacting companion galaxies, double nuclei, starbursting rings, and all sorts of messy structures."

Astronomers have determined that our own Milky Way galaxy and the great spiral galaxy of Andromeda will collide three billion years from now. This event will create massive bursts of star formation and most likely fuel nuclear activity a few hundred million years later. Hubble has imaged post-starburst quasars three and a half billion light-years away, corresponding to three and a half billion years ago, and three and a half billion years from now our own galaxy is probably going to be one of these systems.

This work is supported by grants from NASA, through the Space Telescope Science Institute and the Long-Term Space Astrophysics program, and the National Science Foundation.

> Acknowledges funding support for the research project, giving credit to funding agencies that might also be **audiences** for the journalists' news articles

Insider's View
Astronomer Mike Brotherton on Writing for a General Audience

"It isn't always the case that scientists write their own press releases. Often, there are writers on staff at various institutions who specialize in writing press releases and who work with scientists. I've written press releases solo (e.g., the contribution included here) and in collaboration with staff journalists at the University of Texas, Lawrence Livermore National Laboratory, and the University of Wyoming. Press releases should be able to be run as news stories themselves and contain enough content to be →

adapted or cut to length. The audience for a press release is very general, and you can't assume that they have any background in your field. You have to tell them why your result is important, clearly and briefly, and little else.

"While I don't think my effort here is bad, it is far from perfect and suffers one flaw. Reporters picking up press releases want to know what single result they should focus upon. They want to keep things simple. I tried to include several points in the release, rather than focusing on a single result. Some reporters became distracted about the notion that the Milky Way and Andromeda would someday merge and might become a post-starburst galaxy, which was not a result of my research project. Even though it gave the work some relevance, in hindsight I should have omitted it to keep the focus on the results of my research."

Connect 6.1   **Reflecting on Rhetorical Context**

In his Insider's View, astronomer Mike Brotherton explains some of the specifics of writing a press release and what he sees as the strengths and weaknesses of his own press release. Review the press release with Brotherton's comments in mind, and explain whether you agree with his assessment of it. What advice might you give him for revising the press release?

Recognizing Academic Genres

As you know, different writing situations call for different types of writing, as the example of the press release illustrates. These different types of writing—from short items such as tweets, bumper stickers, and recipes to longer and more complex compositions such as PhD dissertations, annual reports, and novels—are called *genres*. We mentioned genres in Part One, but we want to dive a little deeper here to talk about the kinds of genres you'll encounter in academic contexts and how to analyze them.

Scholars write in many different genres depending on their disciplinary areas, the kinds of work they do, and the situation in which they're writing. You have probably written in several different academic genres in your education already. You might have written a literary analysis in an English class, a lab report in a science class, and a bibliography for a research paper; for this writing course, you may have already written a personal narrative, a rhetorical analysis, a supported argument, or an annotated bibliography. Each of these genres has a distinct purpose and set of expectations that you must be familiar with in order to communicate effectively with your intended audience. In the following chapters, you'll find information about writing in genres that you are likely to encounter as you advance in your studies—such as literary/artistic interpretations, reviews of academic literature, theory responses, observation logbooks, research proposals, lab reports, and memos. The goal is not to make you an expert in every academic genre, but rather to give you the opportunity to practice genre analysis using writing from the disciplines. The skills you will develop through this practice can be applied any time you are faced with a new genre.

Genres are not always bound by discipline, however. Some genres recur across disciplines because writers' purposes can be quite similar even in different fields. For example, you will find the genre of the literature review used by scholars across the curriculum when their purpose is to report on what others have written about a topic. Likewise, when reporting on their own research, many academics follow the IMRaD (Introduction, Methods, Results, and Discussion) format, or a variation of it, to record and publish results, regardless of their discipline. There might be some subtle differences from one discipline or one situation to another, but common elements are evident. Literature reviews and IMRaD-style reports are two examples of common genres of academic writing.

As you read Chapters 7 through 10 on humanities, the social sciences, the natural sciences, and applied fields, pay attention to which genres are repeated and how the conventions of those genres shift or remain constant from one disciplinary context to another.

Connect 6.2   **Reflecting on Academic Genres**

What do you already know about academic genres? What academic genres have you already worked with in high school and college? How did you learn the expectations of those genres?

Using Structure, Language, and Reference (SLR) to Analyze Genre Conventions

Earlier, we introduced two questions that are central to analyzing an academic text:

1. What is the rhetorical context?
2. What conventions are present in the text?

Understanding the rhetorical context is the first step toward understanding how a particular genre works. Knowing the audience and purpose for writing helps us to identify the situations in which different genres occur. To understand fully how a genre works, you must also understand the conventions that are present in the text and whether they follow the expectations for conventions in that genre.

Defining SLR

To understand the conventions that are present in the text, though, we need an additional framework for analysis. The categories of **structure, language, and reference (SLR)**[*] offer more specific help in analyzing the conventions of genres at a deeper level. Although discourse conventions vary from discipline to discipline, once you understand how to analyze writing through these categories, you can determine what conventions and choices are appropriate for nearly any writing situation.

● **Structure, or Format and Organization**   Written texts are often organized according to specific disciplinary conventions. For example, scholars in the social sciences and natural sciences usually organize experimental study reports with an introduction first, followed by a description of their research methods, then their data/results, then the analysis of that data, and finally a discussion and conclusion (IMRaD format, discussed in more detail in Chapters 8 and 9). By contrast, scholars in the humanities tend to write and value essays that are driven by a clear thesis (or main claim: what you are trying to prove) near the beginning of the essay that indicates the direction the argument will take. Scholars in the humanities do not tend, as much, to use headings to divide a text.

● **Language, or Style and Word Choice**   The language used in academic writing follows disciplinary conventions. Consider the use of qualifiers (words such as *might, could, likely*), which are often used in the natural and social sciences to indicate that, while the researchers feel confident in their interpretation of their results, there may be circumstances in which the results would be different. This might be the case, for example, in a study that has a small group of participants (Example: *The positive correlation between the variables likely indicates a strong relationship between the motivation of a student and his or her achievement of learning objectives*). When qualifiers are used in the humanities, however, they often demonstrate uncertainty and weaken an argument (Example: *Hamlet's soliloquies in Acts 2 and 4 might provide an interesting comparison because they frame the turning point of the play in Act 3*).

● **Reference, or Citation and Documentation**   The conventions of how scholars refer to one another's work can also shift by discipline. You might already know, for example, that many scholars in the humanities use the documentation style of the Modern Language Association (MLA), while those in the social sciences generally use the style guide published by the American Psychological Association (APA). More citation styles are listed and discussed in the Appendix. Conventions for how often scholars quote, paraphrase, and

---

[*]The SLR concept originated in the following essay: Patricia Linton, Robert Madigan, and Susan Johnson, "Introducing Students to Disciplinary Genres: The Role of the General Composition Course," *Language and Learning across the Disciplines,* vol. 1, no. 2 (1994), pp. 63–78.

summarize one another's work can also vary. We explain the rationale for these differences when discussing documentation in Chapters 7 and 8.

Analyzing Genre Conventions: A Sample Annotated Text

In the next example of Mike Brotherton's work, we'll look at the abstract and introduction to a scholarly journal article that he wrote with several co-authors. If we start with an understanding of the rhetorical context—that Brotherton and his co-authors are writing with the *purpose* of sharing research results and the *audience* of fellow astronomers—then we can move to understanding the conventions that are present in this type of writing. Considering the *structure, language,* and *reference conventions* used in the piece provides insight into the way such writing is structured within the sciences—and specifically in the field of astronomy.

As you read the excerpt from Brotherton's co-authored article, notice the structure, language, and reference conventions that we have pointed out in the annotations. The article contains a lot of specific scientific language, and for the purpose of your analysis right now it's not important to understand the concepts as much as it is to recognize some of the elements that make this writing unique from other writing you may have encountered in English classes in the past. Consider the following questions:

- Even though the entire article is not included, what conclusions can you draw about its **structure**? What comes first in the article, and how is it organized in the beginning?

- How would you describe the **language** that Brotherton and his co-authors choose to use in the article? What does it tell you about the audience for the article?

- What **reference** conventions does the article follow? Does the documentation style used for the parenthetical references look familiar? How often are other scholars cited, and what is the context for citing their work? What purpose do those references serve in the article?

Excerpt from A Spectacular Poststarburst Quasar

M. S. BROTHERTON, WIL VAN BREUGEL, S. A. STANFORD, R. J. SMITH, B. J. BOYLE, LANCE MILLER, T. SHANKS, S. M. CROOM, AND ALEXEI V. FILIPPENKO

ABSTRACT

We report the discovery of a spectacular "poststarburst quasar" UN J10252−0040 ($B = 19$; $z = 0.634$). The optical spectrum is a chimera, displaying the broad Mg II $\lambda 2800$ emission line and strong blue continuum characteristic of quasars, but is dominated in the red by a large Balmer jump and prominent high-order Balmer

> The language is highly specific and technical.

absorption lines indicative of a substantial young stellar population at similar redshift. Stellar synthesis population models show that the stellar component is consistent with a 400 Myr old instantaneous starburst with a mass of $\leq 10^{11}$ $M_\odot$. A deep, K_s-band image taken in ~0".5 seeing shows a point source surrounded by asymmetric extended fuzz. Approximately 70% of the light is unresolved, the majority of which is expected to be emitted by the starburst. While starbursts and galaxy interactions have been previously associated with quasars, no quasar ever before has been seen with such an extremely luminous young stellar population.

1. INTRODUCTION

Is there a connection between starbursts and quasar activity? There is circumstantial evidence to suggest so. The quasar 3C 48 is surrounded by nebulosity that shows the high-order Balmer absorption lines characteristic of A-type stars (Boroson & Oke 1984; Stockton & Ridgeway 1991). PG 1700 + 518 shows a nearby starburst ring (Hines et al. 1999) with the spectrum of a 10^8 yr old starburst (Stockton, Canalizo, & Close 1998). Near-IR and CO mapping reveals a massive (~10^{10} $M_\odot$) circumnuclear starburst ring in I Zw 1 (Schinnerer, Eckart, & Tacconi 1998). The binary quasar member FIRST J164311.3 + 315618B shows a starburst host galaxy spectrum (Brotherton et al. 1999).

In addition to these individual objects, *samples* of active galactic nuclei (AGNs) show evidence of starbursts. Images of quasars taken with the Hubble Space Telescope show "chains of emission nebulae" and "near-nuclear emission knots" (e.g., Bahcall et al. 1997). Seyfert 2 and radio galaxies have significant populations of ~100 Myr old stars (e.g., Schmitt, Storchi-Bergmann, & Cid Fernandes 1999). Half of the ultraluminous infrared galaxies (ULIRGs) contain simultaneously an AGN and recent (10–100 Myr) starburst activity in a 1–2 kpc circumnuclear ring (Genzel et al. 1998).

The advent of *IRAS* provided evidence for an evolutionary link between starbursts and AGNs. The ULIRGs ($L_{IR} > 10^{12}$ $L_\odot$) are strongly interacting merger systems with copious molecular gas $[(0.5 - 2) \times 10^{10}$ $M_\odot]$ and dust heated by both starburst and AGN power sources. The ULIRG space density is sufficient to form the quasar parent population. These facts led Sanders et al. (1988) to hypothesize that ULIRGs represent the initial dust-enshrouded stage of a quasar. Supporting this hypothesis is the similarity in the evolution of the quasar luminosity density and the star formation rate (e.g., Boyle & Terlevich 1998; Percival & Miller 1999). Another clue is that supermassive black holes appear ubiquitously in local massive galaxies, which may be out-of-fuel quasars (e.g., Magorrian et al. 1998). AGN activity may therefore reflect a fundamental stage of galaxy evolution.

We report here the discovery of a poststarburst quasar. The extreme properties of this system may help shed light on the elusive AGN-starburst connection. We adopt $H_0 = 75$ km s^{-1} Mpc^{-1} and $q_0 = 0$.

"The audience for a scientific journal should be experts in your field but also beginning graduate students. Articles should be specific, succinct, and correct. For better or worse, in scientific articles it is necessary to use a lot of qualifications, adverbs, and modifying phrases, to say exactly what you mean even though the result is not as strong or effective. Accuracy trumps strong writing here, although there is plenty of room for good writing. Every piece of writing, fiction or non-fiction, should tell an interesting story. The format for a scientific article is rather standard.

"There is also an abstract that gives a summary of all the parts of the paper. In many instances, the entire paper is not read but skimmed, so being able to find things quickly and easily makes the paper more useful. Audiences for scientific papers are often measured only in the dozens, if that. While popular papers can be read and used by thousands, most papers have a small audience and contribute to advancement in some niche or other, which may or may not turn out to be important.

"Some people cite heavily, and some people don't cite as heavily. Again, you need to keep in mind your audience and what's appropriate. In writing a telescope proposal, for instance, which is not quite the same as a scientific article but has the same conventions, some reviewers want you to cite a lot of things just to prove that you know the field. This is especially true for beginning students writing proposals."

Connect 6.3   Gathering Ideas for Analysis

In his Insider's View, Mike Brotherton provides some guidelines for thinking about the conventions of a scientific article through the lenses of structure, language, and reference. Which of his points might help you approach reading a scientific article in your courses?

Writing Project   Genre Analysis

The purpose of a genre analysis is to practice analyzing the rhetorical context and conventions of academic writing so that you have a method of approaching new genres that you encounter in your courses. You will be better able to complete this analysis after reading the following chapters, which provide more detail on academic writing in each of the main discipline areas.

For this project, you might analyze a single piece of academic writing or you might do a comparative analysis of two pieces of writing. For the comparative analysis, you could look at two articles on the same topic, either from different disciplines or from a popular and a scholarly source.

Whether you choose to analyze a single piece of academic writing or do a comparative analysis, start with these questions:

- What is the rhetorical context? Consider the author, audience, topic, and purpose of the article.
- What conventions are present in the text? Consider the structure, language, and reference conventions of the article.

ANALYZING A SINGLE TEXT

Find a full-length academic article in a discipline of your choice, or work with an article assigned by your instructor. Analyze the genre features of the article, considering the choices the writer or writers made. Why did they write the article in the way that they did? How do these genre features work together?

The introduction to your paper should name the article you will analyze, describe what aspects of the writing you will be focusing on, and explain the goal of your analysis—to analyze an academic article in order to see how the writer responds to a rhetorical situation. The body of your paper might be organized around the two guiding questions, or you might focus on one or two of the genre features that are of specific interest in your article. Of course, you can subdivide the features you are analyzing to address specific elements of the larger categories. For example, if you were analyzing conventions of language, you could address the use of qualifiers, the use of first person, and so on, providing examples from the article and commenting on their usefulness for the writer. In your conclusion, reflect on what you've found. Are there other issues still to be addressed? What other rhetorical strategies could be explored to analyze the work further? How effective are the strategies the author used, given the intended audience?

COMPARING SCHOLARLY ARTICLES FROM DIFFERENT DISCIPLINES

Locate two academic articles representing different disciplines. For example, you might find two articles discussing the issue of increasing taxes on the wealthy to deal with the U.S. national debt. You might find one article written by an economist that addresses the impact of the national debt and projects the feasibility of different solutions and another article written by a humanist discussing how the media has portrayed the issue.

Analyze the genre features of the articles using the questions above, and consider the choices the writers made when they wrote the article. You might focus on one genre feature or all three. Formulate a thesis that assesses the degree to which the genre features compare or contrast. Organize your analysis in a way that helps your reader follow the main points you want to make about your comparison. Throughout your paper, develop your comparisons and contrasts by illustrating your findings with examples from the texts. Consider the implications of your findings: What do the conventions say about the values of the discipline? Do not avoid discussing findings that might contradict your assumptions about writing in these two academic domains. Instead, study them closely and try to rationalize the authors' rhetorical decision making.

COMPARING A SCHOLARLY AND POPULAR ARTICLE

Choose a scholarly article and an article written for a more general audience on a common topic. You might reread the discussion of the differences between scholarly and popular articles in Chapter 5 as you're looking for articles to choose.

Once you have described the genre features of the articles using the questions above, consider how the different audiences are reflected in the writing. How do the writers handle specialized vocabulary? How much background knowledge does each writer assume? How much depth and detail does each writer offer? What differences do you perceive in sentence style? For each area of your analysis, look for examples to illustrate your points.

....

Insider Example

Student Comparative Genre Analysis

Max Bonghi, a first-year writing student, compared two articles from the scholarly casebook on love found in the Long Edition of this book (Chapter 12), with a focus on one aspect of genre expectations (language). He wrote this essay after studying writing in the humanities and natural sciences, which are topics covered in Chapters 7 and 10, respectively.

Writing about Love:

Comparing Language Differences in Two Scholarly Articles

Love is an incredibly difficult word to define, but one could summarize it as an unconditional affection you have toward someone with no limits or drawbacks, while placing your trust into another person that you would do anything for. This broad topic is approached in very different ways in the humanities and natural sciences, as the two academic articles to be analyzed demonstrate. Warren E. Milteer Jr., a historian at the University of South Carolina, looks at sexual and family relationships between white men and women of color during the antebellum period in his essay "The Strategies of Forbidden Love: Family across Racial Boundaries in Nineteenth-Century North Carolina." Through a series of historical examples, active commentary, and thorough discussions, Milteer reveals the creative and mindful techniques that these couples used to navigate a society that publicly refused to accept their relationships. Medical doctors and researchers Donatella Marazziti and Domenico Canale approach the topic of love from a natural science perspective in "Hormonal Changes When Falling in Love," analyzing the complex chemical changes that occur within romantic partners as the first step in long-term pair formation. The researchers report on a study that explored the physiology of falling in love by recording various

> Introduces the common theme and then provides a rhetorical overview of the articles being compared

hormonal levels in twenty-four subjects reported to be in love versus a control group. An analysis of the language features of these two articles reveals the contrasting values of the academic communities for which they were written.

States the focus of the analysis

The differences in how the humanities and natural sciences use language are clear from the start, beginning with the article titles. Humanities articles often employ vivid language, whereas natural science articles are typically plain and purely descriptive. Milteer's humanities article title uses the emotionally charged phrase "forbidden love," which intrigues and engages the reader, and then the subtitle delivers a more specific idea of what the article will be about. Marazziti and Canale use a rather simple title as compared to Milteer. "Hormonal Changes When Falling in Love" gets straight to the point with a phrase that represents the entire premise of the article. The scientists' title is significantly shorter with less abstract and more straightforward words than the historian's. In the historian's title, we can see how the humanities community values the artful use of language, and writers use interesting phrasing to draw readers into their essays. Milteer's title suggests to the reader that they will discover a new way of looking at a piece of American history through his analysis. In the scientists' title, we can see how the scientific community values objectivity and the unadorned presentation of facts. The reader is promised an analysis of quantifiable data that will explain a human phenomenon in terms of body chemistry.

A topic sentence introduces what is being compared in this paragraph.

Each paragraph follows a similar pattern, first discussing the humanities article and then the natural sciences article.

The language features of the two articles at the sentence level also reflect differing genre conventions in the disciplines. Humanities articles tend to include language that revolves around creativity, drama, and bringing attention to an issue. Milteer employs language to create a vivid portrait of the past in his historical essay. For example, when he discusses the dynamics of daily life between white men and women of mixed ancestry, he states that these women "ruled the domestic realm of their households and worked side by side with their white partners to make decisions about other family matters such as finances" (375). He uses dramatic words that highlight the dangers of mixed-race relationships, as when noting that cooperation between the partners was "imperative to their survival" (375). Unlike Milteer's inclusion of vivid phrasing and dramatic terms, Marazziti and Canale stick to more concrete, concise, and specific word choice, as is common in natural science writing. They employ jargon such as "the hypothalamic-pituitary-adrenal (HPA) axis" that has precise meanings within

Quotes are used to support points.

their community of scholars (393). Their sentences often use the passive voice, so that people are "subjects" who are acted upon for the purpose of measurement: "The differences in hormone levels between subjects of the two sexes who recently had or had not fallen in love were measured by means of the Student t-test (unpaired, two-tailed)" (394).

Another related aspect of the differences between the two articles has to do with the celebration versus reduction of language. Milteer and other humanities scholars celebrate the use of language through attention to style. The Milteer article's stylish syntax, diction, and flow take the reader along with the historian as he builds an argument about a particular piece of social history based on his analysis of the evidence. He frames his writing as a contribution to an ongoing conversation about the past when he says that "[s]cholars have shown that familial relationships between whites and non-whites existed despite legal prohibitions, but more work still needs to be completed in order to understand how women of color and white men managed family life in communities that refused to give legal recognition to their unions" (371). Language is central to this work of interpretation, and humanities scholars often communicate their imaginative insights in a way that celebrates language as the expression of ideas. In the natural sciences, on the other hand, writers may attempt to communicate through charts, graphs, images, and numbers rather than words to the extent possible. Marazziti and Canale's article is filled with standard deviations, equations, numerical temperatures, and more. Because natural science articles deliver information in terms of numbers and observations, they can clearly present their findings in a way that seems unbiased. Of course, clarity is a general expectation for all writing, but the desire for clarity in natural science writing can also be linked to the community's shared value of objectivity. The preference to communicate in numbers instead of words is because words can sometimes be open to interpretation. Numbers are more fixed in terms of their ability to communicate specific meaning. For example, the researchers describe their experimental subjects with numeric terms that suggest precision: "They were selected according to the criteria already applied in a previous study (Marazziti et al., 1999), in particular: the relationship was required to have begun within the previous 6 months (mean $\pm$ SD: 3 ± 1 months) and at least four hours a day spent thinking about the partner (mean $\pm$ SD: 9 ± 3 hours), as recorded by a specifically designed questionnaire" (393).

Examining the difference between genre conventions in different disciplines, such as the humanities and natural sciences, offers insights

> The conclusion summarizes the analysis and makes a larger point that is relevant beyond the two articles.

into their different values and goals. Comparing two articles on the broad topic of love, we see a historian use language to create a vivid picture of the complex dynamics among a group of mixed-race couples two centuries ago and to make an argument about the effects of institutional racism on these individuals. We see medical researchers use language and numerical data to show their colleagues how they followed scientific processes to gather data supporting the idea that falling in love creates hormonal changes. The humanities and natural sciences disciplines both address significant questions and aim to share their findings through writing, but the form that writing takes is significantly different.

Works Cited

Marazziti, Donatella, and Domenico Canale. "Hormonal Changes When Falling in Love." Miller-Cochran et al., pp. 396–402.

Miller-Cochran, Susan, et al., editors. *An Insider's Guide to Academic Writing: A Rhetoric and Reader*. 3rd ed., Bedford/St. Martin's, 2022.

Milteer, Warren E., Jr. "The Strategies of Forbidden Love: Family across Racial Boundaries in Nineteenth-Century North Carolina." Miller-Cochran et al., pp. 366–83.

Writing Project — Translating a Scholarly Article for a Public Audience

The goal of this project is to translate a scholarly article for a public audience. To do so, you will first analyze the scholarly article rhetorically and then shift the genre through which the information in your article is reported. You will produce two documents in response to this assignment:

- a translation of your scholarly article
- a written analysis of the choices you made as you wrote your translation

IDENTIFY YOUR NEW AUDIENCE, PURPOSE, AND GENRE

To get started, you'll need to identify a new audience and purpose for the information in your selected article. The goal here is to shift the audience from an academic one to a public one and to consider whether the purpose for reporting the information also shifts. You may, for instance, choose to report the findings of the article in a magazine targeted toward a general audience of people who are interested in science, or you may choose to write a newspaper article that announces the research findings. You might also choose to write a script for a news show that reports research findings to a general television audience. Notice that once the rhetorical situation shifts, a new genre with unique conventions is often called for. The genre you produce will be contingent on the audience you're targeting and the purpose for writing: magazine article, newspaper article, or news show script.

ANALYZE THE EXPECTATIONS OF YOUR GENRE

Closely analyze an example or two of the kind of genre you're attempting to create, and consider how those genre examples fulfill a particular purpose and the expectations of the target audience. Your project will be assessed according to its ability to reproduce those genre expectations, so you will need to explain, in detail, the choices you had to make in the construction of your piece. Be sure that you're able to explain those choices. In addition to thinking about the audience and purpose, consider the structure, language, and reference conventions of the genre.

CONSTRUCT THE GENRE

At this point, you're ready to begin constructing or translating the article into the new genre. The genre you're producing could take any number of forms. As such, the form, structure, and development of your ideas are contingent on the genre of public reporting you're attempting to construct. If you're constructing a magazine article, for example, then the article you produce should really look like one that would appear in a magazine. Take a look at examples of the genre as models, and consider questions such as these:

- What kind of title does the example have?
- How is information organized in the example?
- How does the example attempt to connect to its intended audience?
- How long is the example? How long are paragraphs, sentences, or other parts of the example?
- Are quotations used? If so, how often? Are they documented? If so, how?

REFLECT ON YOUR CHOICES

Once your translation is complete, compose a reflective analysis. As part of your analysis, consider the choices you made as you constructed your translation. Offer a rationale for each of your decisions that connects your translation to your larger rhetorical context and the conventions of the genre. For example, if you had to translate the title of the scholarly article for a public audience, explain why your new title is the most appropriate one for your public audience.

....

Insider Example
Student Translation of a Scholarly Article

Jonathan Nastasi, a first-year writing student, translated a scholarly article about the possible habitability of another planet from the journal *Astronomy & Astrophysics* into a press release for a less specialized audience. He condensed the information into a two-page press release for a potential audience interested in publishing these research results in news venues.

Release Date: 18 September 2014
Contact: W. von Bloh
bloh@pik-potsdam.de
Potsdam Institute for Climate Impact Research

Press release formatting is applied here.

Life May Be Possible on Other Planets

Attention-grabbing title

New data shows that a new planet found outside of our solar system may be habitable for life.

The key finding is summarized at the start for a busy audience of reporters.

RALEIGH (SEPTEMBER 18, 2014)—A study from the Potsdam Institute for Climate Impact Research shows that a planet in another solar system is in the perfect position to harbor life. Additionally, the quantity of possibly habitable planets in our galaxy is much greater than expected.

Gliese 581g is one of up to six planets found to be orbiting the low-mass star Gliese 581, hence its name. Gliese 581g and its other planetary siblings are so-called "Super Earths," rocky planets from one to ten times the size of our Earth. This entire system is about twenty light-years away from our Sun. W. Von Bloh, M. Cuntz, S. Franck, and C. Bounama from the Potsdam Institute for Climate Impact Research chose to research Gliese 581g because of its size and distance from its star, which make it a perfect candidate to support life.

Background information is provided for a non-specialist audience.

A planet must be a precise distance away from a star in order to sustain life. This distance is referred to as the habitable zone. According to Von Bloh et al., the habitable zones "are defined as regions around the central star where the physical conditions are favourable for liquid water to exist at the planet's surface for a period of time sufficient for biological evolution to occur." This "Goldilocks" zone can be affected by a number of variables, including the temperature of the star and the composition of the planet.

Simple, non-technical explanation of the research question and methods

The actual distance of Gliese 581g from its star is known; the goal of this study was to find out if the planet is capable of supporting life at that distance. The researchers began by finding the habitable zone of the star Gliese 581—specifically, the

An artist's rendition of Gliese 581g orbiting its star.

LYNETTE RENE COOK FOR NASA

zone that allowed for photosynthesis. Photosynthesis is the production of oxygen from organic life forms and is indicative of life. In order for the planet to harbor this kind of life, a habitable zone that allows for a specific concentration of CO_2 in the atmosphere as well as liquid water would have to be found.

The scientists used mathematical models based on Earth's known attributes and adjusted different variables to find out which scenarios yielded the best results. Some of these variables include surface temperature, mass of the planet, and geological activity. The scientists also considered settings where the surface of the planet was all-land, all-water, or a mix of both.

Considering all of these scenarios, Von Bloh et al. determined that the habitable zone for Gliese 581g is between 0.125 and 0.155 astronomical units, where an astronomical unit is the distance between the Earth and the Sun. Other studies conclude that the *actual* orbital distance of Gliese 581g is 0.146 astronomical units. Because Gliese 581g is right in the middle of its determined habitable zone, the error and uncertainty in the variables that remain to be determined are negligible.

> Concepts essential to understanding the results are explained for a non-specialist audience.

However, the ratio of land to ocean on the planet's surface is key in determining the "life span" of the habitable zone. The habitable zone can shift over time due to geological phenomena caused by a planet having more land than ocean. According to Von Bloh et al., a planet with a land-to-ocean ratio similar to ours would remain in the habitable zone for about seven billion years, shorter than Gliese 581g's estimated age. In other words, if Gliese 581g has an Earth-like composition, it cannot sustain life. But if the ratio is low (more ocean than land), the planet will remain in its habitable zone for a greater period of time, thus allowing for a greater chance of life to develop.

The researchers conclude that Gliese 581g is a strong candidate for life so long as it is a "water world." According to the authors, water worlds are defined as "planets of non-vanishing continental area mostly covered by oceans."

The discovery of Gliese 581g being a strong candidate for sustaining life is especially important considering the vast quantity of planets just like it. According to NASA's *Kepler Discoveries* Web page, the Kepler telescope alone has found over 4,234 planet candidates in just five years. With the collaboration of other research, 120 planets have been deemed "habitable," according to *The Habitable Exoplanets Catalog*.

Accessible quotes from the researchers are provided for reporters to use in their stories.

"Our results are another step toward identifying the possibility of life beyond the Solar System, especially concerning Super-Earth planets, which appear to be more abundant than previously surmised," say the authors. More and more scientists are agreeing with the idea that extraterrestrial life is probable, given the abundance of Earth-like planets found in our galaxy already. If this is true, humanity will be one step closer to finding its place in the universe.

"[W]e have to await future missions to identify the pertinent geodynamical features of Gl[iese] 581g . . . to gain insight into whether or not Gl[iese] 581g harbors life," write the researchers. The science community agrees: continued focus in researching the cosmos is necessary to confirm if we have neighbors.

The full journal article can be found at http://www.aanda.org.prox.lib.ncsu .edu/articles/aa/full_html/2011/04/aa16534-11/aa16534-11.html.

Reporters can find the original article easily, and the credibility of the source is established.

Astronomy & Astrophysics, published by EDP Sciences since 1963, covers important developments in the research of theoretical, observational, and instrumental astronomy and astrophysics. For more information, visit http://www.aanda.org/.

tip sheet

Reading and Writing in Academic Disciplines

- **You should not expect to master the writing of every academic discipline by reading one book,** even this one.

- **It's important to become familiar with key concepts of disciplinary writing in academic discourse communities:** *research* expectations; *conventions* (expectations) of writing; *genres* (types) of writing.

- **Genres are not always bound by discipline, although their conventions may vary somewhat from discipline to discipline.** For example, you can expect to write literature reviews in many different courses across the curriculum.

- **Analyzing academic writing is a multistep process.**
  1. Understand the rhetorical context (author, audience, topic, purpose for writing).
  2. Identify the disciplinary area and what you know about it.
  3. Identify the conventions of writing for that genre, including *structure*, *language*, and *reference* expectations.
  4. Analyze the persuasive strategies if the writer is developing an argument.

- **Remember SLR.** The acronym for *structure*, *language*, and *reference* offers categories that can help you determine genre conventions and choices appropriate for most writing situations. These categories are particularly useful in academic writing situations.
  - *Structure* concerns how texts are organized. *Example:* IMRaD—signifying Introduction, Methods, Results, and Discussion—is a common format in both the social and natural sciences.
  - *Language* encompasses conventions of style or word choice. *Example:* Active voice is typically favored in the humanities, and passive voice is more characteristic of writing in the social and natural sciences.
  - *Reference* concerns the ways writers engage source material, including their use of conventions of citation and documentation. *Example:* Many humanities scholars use MLA style; many social science scholars use APA style.

- **Academic research is important beyond the academy.** Writing that conveys academic research often must be repurposed—translated—for different venues and audiences.

Reading and Writing in the Humanities

S cholars in the **humanities** are interested in, and closely observe, human thought, creativity, and experience. The American Council of Learned Societies explains that humanistic scholars "help us appreciate and understand what distinguishes us as human beings as well as what unites us." To that end, scholars in the humanities ask questions such as these:

- What can we learn about human experience from examining the ways we think and express ourselves?
- How do we make sense of the world through various forms of expression?
- How do we interpret what we experience or make meaning for ourselves and for others?

ANDREA TSURUMI

To understand the human condition and respond to these questions, humanists often turn to artifacts of human culture that they observe and interpret for meaning. These might be films, historical documents, comic strips, paintings, poems, religious artifacts, video games, essays, photographs, and songs. They might even include graffiti on the side of a building, a social media status update, or a YouTube video.

In addition to tangible artifacts, humanist writers might turn their attention to events, experiences, rituals, or other elements of human culture to develop meaning. When Ernest Hemingway wrote *Death in the Afternoon* about the traditions of bullfighting in Spain, for instance, he carefully observed and interpreted the meaning of a cultural ritual. And when historians interpret Hemingway's text through the lens of historical context, or when literary scholars compare the book to Hemingway's fiction of a later period, they are extending that understanding of human culture. Through such examination and interpretation of specific objects of study, scholars in the humanities develop theories that explain human expression and experience or that help us understand further what it means to be human.

In this chapter, we'll often refer to artifacts and events that humanistic scholars study as **texts**. The ability to construct meaning from a text is an essential skill within the scholarship of the humanities. In high school English classes, students are often asked to interpret novels, poetry, or plays. You've likely written such analyses in the past, so you've probably developed a set of observational and interpretive skills that we'd like to build upon in this chapter. The same skills, such as the observational skills that lead you to find evidence in a literary text to develop and support an interpretation, can help you analyze other kinds of texts as well.

| Connect 7.1 | **Reflecting on Your Experience as a Writer in the Humanities** |

What experiences have you already had with the interpretation of texts in the humanities? Have you had to write a formal interpretation of a text before? If so, what questions did you ask?

Research in the Humanities

The collection of information, or data, is an integral part of the research process for scholars in all academic disciplines. The data that researchers collect form the foundation of evidence they use to answer a question. In the humanities, data are generally gathered from texts. Whether you're reading a novel, analyzing a sculpture, or speculating on the significance of a cultural ritual, your object of analysis is a text and the primary source of data you collect to use as evidence typically originates from that text.

Academic fields within the humanities have at their heart the creation and interpretation of texts. A history scholar may pore through photographs of Civil War soldiers for evidence to support a claim. An actor in a theater class might scour a script to develop an interpretation of a character to be performed onstage. And those who are primarily the creators of texts—visual artists, novelists, poets, playwrights, screenwriters, musicians—will have read widely in the field to master elements of style and content to contribute to their art in original and innovative ways. In the humanities, it's all about the text. Humanists are either creators or interpreters of texts, and often they are both.

Observation and Interpretation

To understand research and writing in a specific disciplinary area, it is important to know not only what the objects of study are but also what methods scholars in that area use to analyze and study the objects of their attention. In the humanities, just as in other disciplines, scholars begin with observation. They closely observe the texts that interest them, looking for patterns, meaning, and connections that will help generate and support an interpretation. Humanists use their observations to pose questions about the human condition, to gather evidence to help answer those questions, and to generate theories about the human experience that can extend beyond one text or set of texts.

You probably engage every day in the observation of texts, but you might not be doing it in the systematic way that humanistic scholars do. When you listen to music, how do you make meaning? Perhaps you listen to the words, the chord progressions, or repeated phrases. Or maybe you look to specific matters of context such as who wrote the song, what other music the artist has performed, and when it was recorded. You might consider how it is similar to or different from other songs. In order to understand the song's meaning, you might even think about social and cultural events surrounding the period when the song was recorded. These kinds of observational and interpretive acts are the very things humanists do when they research and write; they just use careful methods of observing, documenting, and interpreting that are generally more systematic than what most of us do when listening to music for enjoyment.

Insider's View
Historian Matthew Sakiestewa Gilbert on Research in American Indian Studies

COURTESY OF MATTHEW SAKIESTEWA GILBERT

"Trained in the field of Native American history, I spend a lot of time studying archival documents such as letters, memos, reports, photographs, and historical newspapers. As a historian, my job is to 'tell and analyze the story,' and I do this by gathering information about certain topics and interpreting their historical and cultural significance. A faculty at a large research university, I publish the bulk of my scholarship in books, journals, and in edited volumes.

"While I am expected to publish as a member of the academy, I am also a member of the Hopi community, and I have a responsibility to make my research meaningful and useful to my people. Since many on the Hopi Reservation do not have access to my academic writings, I created the weblog (blog) *Beyond the Mesas* to reach people back home. It also provides an opportunity for me to engage a broad public audience with my work. For example, sometimes I receive e-mails from young students who stumble across my website as they search for information on the Hopi for their school projects. They occasionally send me short questionnaires to fill out on Hopi history and culture, which I am happy to do.

"Hopi people also regularly engage with my blog. After I published a story about a Hopi runner named Harry Chaca who competed for Sherman Institute in the 1920s, his granddaughter, Cheryl Chaca, read my post and commented about how pleased she was to learn of her grandfather's athletic accomplishments. However, the most meaningful comment came from my oldest daughter, Hannah, who at the time was seven years old. One morning, I heard the words 'If so, please consider...' coming from our living room. I looked around the corner, and to my surprise, I saw my daughter sitting with my iPad on her lap. My blog was open on the screen. When I asked what she was doing, she simply replied, 'I'm learning about Hopi.'"

Observing and Interpreting an Image

Consider the following image, a work of graffiti, as a text that has something to say about human experience. Study the image and then write your ideas in response to the following questions:

- What effect does the text have on you? How does it make you feel, or what does it make you think about?

- How is the text constructed, or what elements make up its content?

- How do the elements of the text fit together to create a specific effect on you?

- Based on your responses to the previous questions, what does the text mean?

SKIP BOLEN/EPA/SHUTTERSTOCK

The Role of Theory in the Humanities

When scholars in the humanities analyze and interpret a text, they often draw on a specific theory of interpretation to help them make meaning. Theories in the humanities offer a particular perspective through which to understand human experience. Sometimes those perspectives are based on ideas about *how* we make meaning from a text; such theories include Formalism (sometimes called New Criticism, though it is far from new), Reader Response, and Deconstruction. Other theories, such as Feminist Theory and Queer Theory, are based more on ideas about how identity informs meaning-making. Still other theories, such as New Historicism, Postcolonialism, and Marxism, are centrally concerned with how historical, social, cultural, and other contexts inform meaning.

These are only a few of the many prominent theories of humanistic interpretation, barely scratching the surface of the theory-building work that has taken place in the humanities. Our goal is not for you to learn specific names of theories at this point, though. Rather, we want you to understand that when scholars in the humanities draw on a theory in the interpretation of a text, the theory gives them a *lens* through which to view the text and a set of questions they might ask about it. For example, they might ask:

- When was the text written, and what major social forces might have influenced the text at the time? (New Historicism)
- What characters exhibit the most power in their relationships to their partners? (Feminism)
- What kinds of tensions does the artifact create for the viewer through its use of shading and lighting? (New Criticism)

Different theories lead to different sets of questions and varying interpretations of the same text.

Engaging with Theory: A Sample Annotated Text

As in other disciplines, scholars in the humanities draw on the work of others to make sure they're contributing something new to the ongoing conversation about a text they're studying. They may also read the work of others to determine if they agree or disagree with previous interpretations of that text. Because of the importance of specific language and detail in the humanities, scholars in the humanities often quote one another's exact words, and they also quote directly from their primary sources. We'll discuss some of the reasons for these conventions, and others, later in the chapter.

In the following example of an interpretation of a text, scholar Dale Jacobs discusses how he constructs meaning from comics. He first presents his theory that interpretations of comics require more complex literacy skills than texts composed only of words (e.g., a novel or short story) because readers of comics must also interpret visual, gestural, and spatial language at work in the panels. He situates his theory in the context of the work of other scholars, quoting directly in a couple of instances. He then illustrates his theory with a close reading of a comic called *Polly and the Pirates*. This excerpt is part of a larger essay aimed at an audience of composition instructors. In it, Jacobs calls on instructors to challenge students to think critically about how they construct meaning from texts. As you read this excerpt from his article, you might reflect on this question: When reading a text, how do you make meaning?

Excerpt from **More Than Words: Comics as a Means of Teaching Multiple Literacies**

DALE JACOBS

COMICS AS MULTIMODAL LITERACY: THE THEORY

If we think about comics as multimodal texts that involve multiple kinds of meaning making, we do not give up the benefits of word-based literacy instruction but strengthen it through the inclusion of visual and other literacies. This complex view of literacy is touched on but never fully fleshed out in two excellent recent articles on comics and education: Rocco Versaci's "How Comic Books Can Change the Way Our Students See Literature: One Teacher's Perspective" and Bonny Norton's "The Motivating Power of Comic Books: Insights from Archie Comic Readers." By situating our thinking about comics, literacy, and education within a framework that views literacy as occurring in multiple modes, we can use comics to greater effectiveness in our teaching at all levels by helping us to arm students with the critical-literacy skills they need to negotiate diverse systems of meaning making.

> Jacobs presents his thesis here: his approach to teaching comics will help students develop critical-literacy skills that they can use to approach multimodal texts.

I'm going to offer an example of how comics engage multiple literacies by looking at Ted Naifeh's *Polly and the Pirates*, but first let me give a brief outline of these multiple systems of meaning making. As texts, comics provide a complex environment for the negotiation of meaning, beginning with the layout of the page itself. The comics page is separated into multiple panels, divided from each other by gutters, physical or conceptual spaces through which connections are made and meanings are negotiated; readers must fill in the blanks within these gutters and make connections between panels. Images of people, objects, animals, and settings, word balloons, lettering, sound effects, and gutters all come together to form page layouts that work to create meaning in distinctive ways and in multiple realms of meaning making. In these multiple realms of meaning making, comics engage in what the New London Group of literacy scholars calls *multimodality*, a way of thinking that seeks to push literacy educators, broadly defined and at all levels of teaching, to think about literacy in ways that move beyond a focus on strictly word-based literacy. In the

> Jacobs identifies how comics employ multiple modes of literacy through their page layout.

introduction to the New London Group's collection, *Multiliteracies: Literacy Learning and the Design of Social Futures*, Bill Cope and Mary Kalantzis write that their approach "relates to the increasing multiplicity and integration of significant modes of meaning-making, where the textual is also related to the visual, the audio, the spatial, the behavioural, and so on. . . . Meaning is made in ways that are increasingly multimodal—in which written-linguistic modes of meaning are part and parcel of visual, audio, and spatial patterns of meaning" (5). By embracing the idea of multimodal literacy in relation to comics, then, we can help students engage critically with ways of making meaning that exist all around them, since multimodal texts include much of the content on the Internet, interactive multimedia, newspapers, television, film, instructional textbooks, and many other texts in our contemporary society.

Jacobs addresses the "So what?" of his theory.

Such a multimodal approach to reading and writing asserts that in engaging with texts, we interact with up to six design elements, including linguistic, audio, visual, gestural, and spatial modes, as well as multimodal design, "of a different order to the others as it represents the patterns of interconnections among the other modes" (New London Group 25). In the first two pages from *Polly and the Pirates*, all of these design elements are present, including a textual and visual representation of the audio element. Despite the existence of these multiple modes of meaning making, however, the focus in thinking about the relationship between comics and education is almost always on the linguistic element, represented here by the words in the words balloons (or, in the conventions of comics, the dialogue from each of the characters) and the narrative text boxes in the first three panels (which we later find out are also spoken dialogue by a narrator present in the story).

Jacobs concludes the introduction to his theory by reinforcing the idea that comics are multimodal and not a simplified version of word-based texts.

As discussed earlier, comics are seen as a simplified version of word-based texts, with the words supplemented and made easier to understand by the pictures. If we take a multimodal approach to texts such as comics, however, the picture of meaning making becomes much more complex. In word-based texts, our interaction with words forms an environment for meaning making that is extremely complex. In comics and other multimodal texts, there are five other elements added to the mix. Thought about in this way, comics are not just simpler versions of word-based texts but can be viewed as the complex textual environments that they are.

COMICS AS MULTIMODAL LITERACY: *POLLY AND THE PIRATES* IN THE CLASSROOM

In this section, Jacobs uses an example to illustrate his theory of how to read comics.

In comics, there are elements present besides words, but these elements are just as important in making meaning from the text. In fact, it is impossible to make full sense of the words on the page in isolation from the audio, visual, gestural, and spatial. For example, the first page of *Polly and the Pirates* (the first issue of a six-issue miniseries) opens with three panels of words from what the reader takes to be the story's narrative voice. Why? Partially it is because of *what* the words say—how they introduce a character and begin to set up the story—but also it is because of the text boxes that enclose the words. That is, most people understand from their experiences of reading comics at some point in their history that words in text boxes almost always contain the story's narrative voice and denote a different kind of voice than do words in dialogue balloons. What's more, these text boxes deviate in shape and design from the even rectangles usually seen in comics; instead, they are depicted more like scrolls, a visual element that calls to mind both the time period and genre associated with pirates. Not only does this visual element help to place the reader temporally and generically, but it, along with lettering and punctuation, also aids in indicating tone, voice inflection, cadence, and emotional tenor by giving visual representation to the text's audio element. We are better able to "hear" the narrator's voice because we can see what words are emphasized by the bold lettering, and we associate particular kinds of voices with the narrative voice of a pirate's tale, especially emphasized here by the shape of the text boxes. Both the visual and the audio thus influence the way we read the words in a comic, as can be seen in these three opening panels.

It seems to me, however, that the key lies in going beyond the way we make meaning from the words alone and considering the other visual elements, as well as the gestural and spatial. If I were teaching this text, I would engage students in a discussion about how they understand what is going on in the story and how they make meaning from it. Depending on the level of the class, I would stress different elements at varying levels of complexity. Here I will offer an example of how I make meaning from these pages and of some of the elements I might discuss with students.

In talking about the visual, I would consider such things as the use of line and white space, shading, perspective, distance, depth of field, and composition. The gestural refers to facial expression and body posture, while the spatial refers to the meanings of environmental and architectural space, which, in the case of comics, can be conceived as the layout of panels on the page and the relation between these panels through use of gutter space. The opening panel depicts a ship, mainly in silhouette, sailing on the ocean; we are not given details, but instead see the looming presence of a ship that we are led to believe is a pirate ship by the words in the text boxes. The ship is in the center of an unbordered panel and is the only element in focus, though its details are obscured. The unbordered panel indicates openness, literally and metaphorically, and this opening shot thus acts much in the same way as an establishing shot in a film, orienting us both in terms

> Jacobs shows how he would use his theory as a lens through which to view the text.

of place and in terms of genre. The second panel pulls in closer to reveal a silhouetted figure standing on the deck of the ship. She is framed between the sails, and the panel's composition draws our eyes toward her as the central figure in the frame. She is clearly at home, one arm thrust forward while the other points back with sword in hand, her legs anchoring herself securely as she gazes across the ocean. The third panel pulls in even farther to a close-up of her face, the top half in shadow and the bottom half showing a slight smile. She is framed by her sword on the left and the riggings of the ship on the right, perfectly in her element, yet obscured from our view. Here and in the previous panel, gestural and visual design indicate who is the center of the story and the way in which she confidently belongs in this setting. At the same time, the spatial layout of the page and the progression of the panels from establishing shot to close-up and from unbordered panels to bordered and internally framed panels help us to establish the relationship of the woman to the ship and to the story; as we move from one panel to the next, we must make connections between the panels that are implied by the gutter. Linguistic, visual, audio, gestural, and spatial elements combine in these first three panels to set up expectations in the reader for the type of story and its narrative approach. Taken together, these elements form a multimodal system of meaning making.

What happens in the fourth panel serves to undercut these expectations as we find out that the narrative voice actually belongs to one of the characters in the story, as evidenced by the shift from text box to dialogue balloon even though the voice is clearly the same as in the first three panels of the page. Spatially, we are presented with a larger panel that is visually dominated by the presence of a book called *A History of the Pirate Queen*. This book presumably details the story to which we had been introduced in the first three panels. The character holding the book is presenting it to someone and, because of the panel's composition, is also effectively presenting it to us, the readers. The gesture becomes one of offering this story up to us, a story that simultaneously becomes a romance as well as a pirate story as evidenced by the words the character says and the way she says them (with the bold emphasis on *dream* and *marry*). At this point, we do not know who this character is or to whom she is speaking, and the answers to these questions will be deferred until we turn to the second page.

On the first panel of page 2, we see three girls, each taking up about a third of the panel, with them and the background in focused detail. Both the words and facial expression of the first girl indicate her stance toward the story, while the words and facial expression of the second girl indicate her indignation at the attitude of the first girl (whom we learn is named Sarah). The third girl is looking to the right, away from the other two, and has a blank expression on her face. The next panel depicts the second and third girls, pulling in to a tighter close-up that balances one girl on either side of the panel and obscures the background so that we will focus on their faces and dialogue. The unbordered panel

again indicates openness and momentary detachment from their surroundings. Polly is at a loss for words and is not paying attention to the other girl, as indicated by the ellipses and truncated dialogue balloons, as well as her eyes that are pointing to the right, away from the other girl. Spatially, the transition to panel 3 once more encloses them in the world that we now see is a classroom in an overhead shot that places the students in relation to the teacher. The teacher's words restore order to the class and, on a narrative level, name the third of the three girls and the narrative voice of the opening page. The story of the pirates that began on page 1 is now contained within the world of school, and we are left to wonder how the tensions between these two stories/worlds will play out in the remaining pages. As you can see, much more than words alone is used to make meaning in these first two pages of *Polly and the Pirates*.

Jacobs ends his close reading by connecting his observations to his thesis: comics engage multiple modes of literacy to create meaning.

CONCLUSION

In the Conclusion, Jacobs summarizes and expands upon his theory of meaning-making with multimodal texts.

My process of making meaning from these pages of *Polly and the Pirates* is one of many meanings within the matrix of possibilities inherent in the text. As a reader, I am actively engaging with the "grammars," including discourse and genre conventions, within this multimodal text as I seek to create/negotiate meaning; such a theory of meaning making with multimodal texts acknowledges the social and semiotic structures that surround us and within which we exist, while at the same time it recognizes individual agency and experience in the creation of meaning. Knowledge of linguistic, audio, visual, gestural, and spatial conventions within comics affects the ways in which we read and the meanings we assign to texts, just as knowledge of conventions within word-based literacy affects the ways in which those texts are read. For example, the conventions discussed above in terms of the grammar of comics would have been available to Naifeh as he created *Polly and the Pirates*, just as they are also available to me and to all other readers of his text. These conventions form the underlying structure of the process of making meaning, while familiarity with these conventions, practice in reading comics, interest, prior experience, and attention given to that reading all come into play in the exercise of agency on the part of the reader (and writer). Structure and agency interact so that we are influenced by design conventions and grammars as we read but are not determined by them; though we are subject to the same set of grammars, my reading of the text is not necessarily the same as that of someone else.

WORKS CITED

Cope, Bill, and Mary Kalantzis. "Introduction: Multiliteracies: The Beginnings of an Idea." *Multiliteracies: Literacy Learning and the Design of Social Futures.* Ed. Bill Cope and Mary Kalantzis. New York: Routledge, 2000. 3–8.

Naifeh, Ted. *Polly and the Pirates* 1 (Sept. 2005): 1–2.

New London Group, The. "A Pedagogy of Multiliteracies: Designing Social Futures." *Multiliteracies: Literacy Learning and the Design of Social Futures.* Ed. Bill Cope and Mary Kalantzis. New York: Routledge, 2000. 9–37.

Norton, Bonny. "The Motivating Power of Comic Books: Insights from Archie Comic Readers." *The Reading Teacher* 57.2 (Oct. 2003): 140–47.

Versaci, Rocco. "How Comic Books Can Change the Way Our Students See Literature: One Teacher's Perspective." *English Journal* 91.2 (Mar. 2001): 61–67.

Connect 7.3   Reflecting on Meaning-Making

Study one of the panels from *Polly and the Pirates* and consider how you make meaning from it. Freewrite for five minutes about your own process for making sense of what the comic means.

Strategies for Close Reading

To develop clear claims about the texts they are interpreting, scholars in the humanities must carefully observe texts to learn about them. Careful observation of a text might involve the kinds of reading strategies we discussed in Chapter 3, especially if the text is alphabetic (i.e., letter-based), such as a book, a story, or a poem. The method that humanities scholars use to engage in such careful observation of a text is often referred to as **close reading**. It's possible to do a close reading of a story, of course, but you can also do a close reading of non-alphabetic texts such as films, buildings, paintings, events, songs, or even multimodal texts, as the preceding example from Dale Jacobs illustrates.

Most college students are highly skilled at reading for content knowledge, or for information, because that's what they are most often asked to do as students. This is what a professor generally expects when assigning a reading from a textbook. As you read such texts, you're primarily trying to figure out what the text is saying rather than thinking about how it functions, why the author makes certain stylistic choices, or how others might interpret the text. As we mentioned in Chapter 3, you might also read to be entertained, to learn, or to communicate.

Close observation or reading in the humanities, however, requires our focus to shift from reading for information to reading to understand how a text functions and how we can make meaning of it. Because texts are the primary sources of data used in humanistic research, it's important for those who work in the humanities to examine how a text conveys meaning to its audience. This kind of work—observing a text critically to analyze what it means and how it conveys meaning—is what we call close reading.

Notetaking Steps

For most of us, when we observe a printed text closely, we highlight, underline, and take notes in the margins. If we're analyzing a visual or aural text, we might take notes on our thoughts, observations, and questions. We might keep a separate notebook or computer file in which we expand on our notes or clarify meaning. As with any skill, the more you practice these steps, the better you will become at interpretation. We encourage you to take detailed notes, underline passages if applicable, and actively engage with a text when conducting your observation. In all cases, we recommend two specific data-collection steps for humanistic inquiry: annotating and developing a content/form-response grid.

● **Annotating**   We suggest that you take notes in the margins for a printed text or on a separate sheet of paper as you read, view, or listen to a text to be interpreted. These notes will draw your attention to passages that may serve as direct evidence to support points you will make later. Additionally, you can elaborate in more detail when something meaningful in the text draws your attention. Jotting down page numbers, audio/video file time markers, and paragraph numbers is often helpful for cataloging your notes. The key is to commit fully to engaging with a text by systematically recording your observations.

● **Developing a Content/Form-Response Grid** We recommend that you develop a **content/form-response grid** to organize the essential stages of your interpretation. The "content" is what happens in the text, and the "form" is how the text's creator structures the piece. In the case of a painting, you might comment on the materials used, the artist's technique, the color palette and imagery choice, or the historical context of the piece. In the case of a religious or political text, you might examine style, language, and literary devices used. The "response" is your interpretation of what the elements you've identified might mean. The grid setup can be as simple as two columns, one for the content/form notes and the second for the corresponding responses.

Close Reading: Sample Annotations and Content/Form-Response Grids

Read the following opening paragraphs from "The Story of an Hour," a brief short story by Kate Chopin published in 1894 that is now recognized as a classic work of American literature. The excerpt includes a student's annotations followed by a content/form-response grid. Notice the frequency of notes the student takes in the margins and the kinds of questions she asks at this early stage. She offers a fairly equal balance of questions and claims.

Heart trouble? I wonder what kind of trouble.

The news of her husband's death is delivered by her sister.

Knowing that Mrs. Mallard was afflicted with a heart trouble, great care was taken to break to her as gently as possible the news of her husband's death. It was her sister Josephine who told her, in broken sentences; veiled hints that revealed in half concealing. Her husband's friend Richards was there, too, near her. It was he who had been in the newspaper office when intelligence of the railroad disaster was received, with Brently Mallard's name leading the list of "killed." He had only taken the time to assure himself of its truth by a second telegram, and had hastened to forestall any less careful, less tender friend in bearing the sad message.

Why would she act differently from other women hearing the same kind of news?

Interesting comparison. The storm-like quality of her grief.

She did not hear the story as many women have heard the same, with a paralyzed inability to accept its significance. She wept at once, with sudden, wild abandonment, in her sister's arms. When the storm of grief had spent itself she went away to her room alone. She would have no one follow her.

Why is she "exhausted"? Interesting word choice.

There stood, facing the open window, a comfortable, roomy armchair. Into this she sank, pressed down by a physical exhaustion that haunted her body and seemed to reach into her soul.

She could see in the open square before her house the tops of trees that were all aquiver with the new spring life. The delicious breath of rain was in the air. In the street below a peddler was crying his wares. The notes of a distant song which some one was singing reached her faintly, and countless sparrows were twittering in the eaves.

There are lots of images of life here. This really contrasts with the dark news of the story's opening.

This student's annotations can be placed into a content/form-response grid that helps her keep track of the ideas she had as she read and observed closely, both for information (*what*) and for ways the text shaped her experience of it (*how*). Notice that the student uses the Content/Form section to summarize the comments from her annotations, and then she reflects on her annotations in the Response section:

Content/Form Notes (*what* and *how*)	Response (*What effect does it have on me?*)
Heart trouble? I wonder what kind of trouble.	There's a mystery here. What's wrong with Mrs. Mallard's heart?
The news of her husband's death is delivered by her sister.	Interesting that a female relative is chosen to deliver the news. A man would be too rough?
Why would she act differently from other women hearing the same kind of news?	I wonder what is special about Mrs. Mallard that causes her reaction to be different. Is she putting on a show? Story says her reaction was "sudden" and "wild."
Why is she "exhausted"? Interesting word choice.	Maybe this has to do with her heart condition or with how physically draining her mourning is.
There are lots of images of life here. This really contrasts with the dark news of the story's opening.	This is a sudden change in feeling. Everything is so calm and pleasant now. What happened?

The purpose of this activity is to construct meaning from the text based on the student's close observation of it. This is an interpretation. We can already see that major complexities in the story are beginning to emerge in the student's response notes—such as the importance of the story's setting and the change that occurs in Mrs. Mallard.

Because content/form-response grids like the one above allow you to visualize both your ideas and how you arrived at those ideas, we recommend using this activity any time you have to observe a text closely in order to interpret its meaning. For a non-alphabetic text, start with the content/form-response grid and use it to log your initial notes as you observe; then reflect later. In the end, such an activity provides a log of details that can help explain how you arrived at a particular conclusion or argument about the text.

Close Reading Practice: Analyzing a Short Story

Now it's your turn. Read the whole text of Kate Chopin's "The Story of an Hour" below, and then annotate the text as you read, paying particular attention to the following elements:

- **Content**   What is being said (the facts, the events, and who the characters are)
- **Form**   How it is being said (the style, language, literary techniques, and narrative perspective)

A follow-up Connect activity at the conclusion of the story asks you to draw a content/form-response grid like the example above. It's important to take extensive marginal notes (perhaps one or two comments per paragraph) and highlight and underline passages as you read the story. These notes will help shape your content/form-response grid and will strengthen your interpretation. We encourage you to expand on your notes on a separate sheet of paper while you read the story.

The Story of an Hour

KATE CHOPIN

Knowing that Mrs. Mallard was afflicted with a heart trouble, great care was taken to break to her as gently as possible the news of her husband's death.

It was her sister Josephine who told her, in broken sentences; veiled hints that revealed in half concealing. Her husband's friend Richards was there, too, near her. It was he who had been in the newspaper office when intelligence of the railroad disaster was received, with Brently Mallard's name leading the list of "killed." He had only taken the time to assure himself of its truth by a second telegram, and had hastened to forestall any less careful, less tender friend in bearing the sad message.

She did not hear the story as many women have heard the same, with a paralyzed inability to accept its significance. She wept at once, with sudden, wild abandonment, in her sister's arms. When the storm of grief had spent itself she went away to her room alone. She would have no one follow her.

There stood, facing the open window, a comfortable, roomy armchair. Into this she sank, pressed down by a physical exhaustion that haunted her body and seemed to reach into her soul.

She could see in the open square before her house the tops of trees that 5 were all aquiver with the new spring life. The delicious breath of rain was in the air. In the street below a peddler was crying his wares. The notes of a distant song which some one was singing reached her faintly, and countless sparrows were twittering in the eaves.

There were patches of blue sky showing here and there through the clouds that had met and piled one above the other in the west facing her window.

She sat with her head thrown back upon the cushion of the chair, quite motionless, except when a sob came up into her throat and shook her, as a child who has cried itself to sleep continues to sob in its dreams.

She was young, with a fair, calm face, whose lines bespoke repression and even a certain strength. But now there was a dull stare in her eyes, whose gaze was fixed away off yonder on one of those patches of blue sky. It was not a glance of reflection, but rather indicated a suspension of intelligent thought.

There was something coming to her and she was waiting for it, fearfully. What was it? She did not know; it was too subtle and elusive to name. But she felt it, creeping out of the sky, reaching toward her through the sounds, the scents, the color that filled the air.

Now her bosom rose and fell tumultuously. She was beginning to recognize 10
this thing that was approaching to possess her, and she was striving to beat it back with her will—as powerless as her two white slender hands would have been.

When she abandoned herself a little whispered word escaped her slightly parted lips. She said it over and over under her breath: "free, free, free!" The vacant stare and the look of terror that had followed it went from her eyes. They stayed keen and bright. Her pulses beat fast, and the coursing blood warmed and relaxed every inch of her body.

She did not stop to ask if it were or were not a monstrous joy that held her. A clear and exalted perception enabled her to dismiss the suggestion as trivial.

She knew that she would weep again when she saw the kind, tender hands folded in death; the face that had never looked save with love upon her, fixed and gray and dead. But she saw beyond that bitter moment a long procession of years to come that would belong to her absolutely. And she opened and spread her arms out to them in welcome.

There would be no one to live for during those coming years; she would live for herself. There would be no powerful will bending hers in that blind persistence with which men and women believe they have a right to impose a private will upon a fellow-creature. A kind intention or a cruel intention made the act seem no less a crime as she looked upon it in that brief moment of illumination.

And yet she had loved him—sometimes. Often she had not. What did it 15
matter! What could love, the unsolved mystery, count for in face of this posses-sion of self-assertion which she suddenly recognized as the strongest impulse of her being!

"Free! Body and soul free!" she kept whispering.

Josephine was kneeling before the closed door with her lips to the keyhole, imploring for admission. "Louise, open the door! I beg, open the door—you will make yourself ill. What are you doing, Louise? For heaven's sake open the door."

"Go away. I am not making myself ill." No; she was drinking in a very elixir of life through that open window.

Her fancy was running riot along those days ahead of her. Spring days, and summer days, and all sorts of days that would be her own. She breathed a quick prayer that life might be long. It was only yesterday she had thought with a shudder that life might be long.

She arose at length and opened the door to her sister's importunities. There was a feverish triumph in her eyes, and she carried herself unwittingly like a goddess of Victory. She clasped her sister's waist, and together they descended the stairs. Richards stood waiting for them at the bottom.

Some one was opening the front door with a latchkey. It was Brently Mallard who entered, a little travel-stained, composedly carrying his grip-sack and umbrella. He had been far from the scene of accident, and did not even know there had been one. He stood amazed at Josephine's piercing cry; at Richards' quick motion to screen him from the view of his wife.

But Richards was too late.

When the doctors came they said she had died of heart disease—of joy that kills.

> ### Connect 7.4   Preparing a Content/Form-Response Grid
>
> Based on your annotations and notes, construct a content/form-response grid modeled after the example in "Close Reading: Sample Annotations and a Content/Form-Response Grid" (p. 134). Be sure to include your responses to the items you identify in the Content/Form column. Remember that in this case "content" relates to what happens in the story, and "form," in the context of a literary text, relates to how the writer makes the story function through style, narrative perspective, and literary techniques.
>
> Once you've completed your close reading, you might pair up with a classmate or two and share your content/form-response grids. When doing so, consider the following questions as part of your discussion:
>
> - What facts or events did you note about the story?
>
> - What did you notice about the ways Chopin shapes your experience of the story? What style or literary techniques did you note?
>
> - What patterns do you see in the notes you've taken in the Form column? What repeated comments did you make, or what elements strike you in a similar way? How would you explain the meaning of those patterns?

As a last step in interpreting Chopin's story, you might draw on the work of other scholars to build and support your interpretations. For example, you might review the notes you made in your content/form-response grid, search for interesting patterns, and then see if other scholars have noticed the same things. You might look for an element of the story that doesn't make sense to you and see if another scholar has already offered an interpretation. If you agree with the interpretation, you might cite it as support for your own argument. If you disagree, you might look for evidence in the story to show why you disagree and then offer your own interpretation.

Structural Conventions in the Humanities

Some writing conventions are shared across different fields in the humanities. Because the kinds of texts humanistic scholars examine can vary so much, though, there are also sometimes distinctions in writing conventions among its various fields. One of the challenges of learning the conventions of a disciplinary discourse community is figuring out the specific expectations for communicating with a specific academic audience. In the following sections, we turn our attention from the nature of research in the humanities to *strategies of rhetorical analysis* that help us examine how scholars in the humanities write about their insights.

Many scholars learn about disciplinary writing conventions through imitation and examination of articles in their fields. Recall that in Chapter 6 we introduced a three-part method for analyzing texts by examining the conventions of structure, language, and reference. Applying this analytical framework to professional writing in the various humanities fields may facilitate your success in writing in those contexts. In this section, we will examine structural conventions—that is, conventions governing how writing is organized. Rather than trying to master the conventions of every type of writing in the humanities, your goal is to understand the general principles underlying writing conventions in the humanities and to practice applying an analytical framework to any writing assignment you encounter.

From your experience in high school, you might already be familiar with common structural features of writing in the humanities. Arguments in the humanities are generally "thesis-driven"; that is, they make an interpretive claim about a text and then support that claim with specific evidence from the text and sometimes with material from other sources that support the interpretation. By contrast, arguments in the social sciences and the natural sciences are usually driven by a hypothesis that must be tested in order to come to a conclusion, which encourages a different structure. First, we'll talk about how humanistic scholars develop research questions and thesis statements. Then we'll turn our attention to a common structure that many students learn in secondary school to support their thesis statements with evidence, which is loosely based on the structure of the thesis-driven argument, and we'll compare it with published scholarship in the humanities.

Using Research Questions to Develop a Thesis

An important part of the interpretation process is using observations to pose questions about a text. From these close observations, humanists develop research questions that they answer through their research. A **research question** in the humanities is the primary question a scholar asks about a text or set of texts. It is the first step in interpretation because questions grow out of our observations and the patterns or threads that we notice. A **thesis statement** is an answer to a research question and is most persuasive when supported by logical evidence. Thesis statements are discussed in more detail in Chapter 4 as the central claim of an argument. It's important to note that developing a research question works best when it is generated prior to writing a thesis statement. Novice writers can sometimes overlook this crucial step in the writing process and attempt to make a thesis statement without formulating a well-realized research question first.

Some of the most important questions for humanists begin by asking, "Why?" Why does George befriend Lenny in John Steinbeck's novella *Of Mice and Men*? Why did Frida Kahlo present a double self-portrait in her painting *The Two Fridas* (1939)? Why did Ava DuVernay open her film *Selma* (2014) with Dr. Martin Luther King Jr.'s acceptance of the Nobel Peace Prize in

1964? To answer such questions, humanistic scholars collect evidence, and in the humanities, evidence often originates from texts.

Many students confess to struggling with the process of writing a good thesis statement. A key to overcoming this hurdle is to realize that a good thesis statement comes first from asking thoughtful questions about a text and searching for answers to those questions through observation.

Examples of Research Questions and Corresponding Thesis Statements

Research Question   What does the recurring motif of Janie's hair represent in her journey throughout Zora Neale Hurston's *Their Eyes Were Watching God?*

Thesis Statement   In Zora Neale Hurston's *Their Eyes Were Watching God*, Janie's hair represents three distinct stages—from innocence to conflict to experience—that parallel her development of identity and voice throughout the novel.

Research Question   What is the significance of light and dark in John Gast's *American Progress?*

Thesis Statement   John Gast's 1872 painting *American Progress* reflects the nineteenth-century American idea of manifest destiny in its depiction of settlers from the east bringing the light of "civilization" to the west.

Once you have carefully observed a text, gathered thorough notes, and developed a content/form-response grid as discussed earlier in the chapter, you will be in a great position to begin brainstorming and drafting research questions. We encourage open-ended questions (*why*, *what*, and *how*) as opposed to closed questions (questions that can be answered with a *yes* or *no*) as a pivotal step before drafting a thesis statement. Scholars in the humanities often start by asking questions that begin with *why*, but you might also consider questions that begin with *what* and *how*.

Connect 7.5   **Developing *Why*, *What*, and *How* Questions**

The process of asking questions after conducting a close reading of a text is part of interpretation, and it can help you generate effective research questions to guide the development of a thesis. In this activity, we walk you through developing research questions from your notes on "The Story of an Hour." You could easily follow these steps after observing another kind of text as well.

1. Review your notes on "The Story of an Hour," and develop three questions about the story's content and form using *why* as a starter word.

2. Next, develop three questions using *what* as your starter word. Try to focus your questions on different aspects of the story's characters, language, style, literary techniques, or narrative perspective.

3. Then use *how* as a starter word to develop three more questions. Again, write your questions with a different aspect of the story as the central focus for each—that is, don't just repeat the same questions from your *what* or *why* list by inserting *how* instead. Think of different questions that can help address the story's meaning.

Try sharing your questions with a fellow student and discuss which ones might lead to promising thesis statements to ground an extended interpretation. Effective research questions are ones that can be answered with evidence and not just feelings or emotions.

Developing Effective Thesis Statements

The thesis statement, or the central claim, asserts *what* the author intends to prove, and it may also provide insight into *how* it will be proven. Providing both of these elements in a thesis allows writers to establish a blueprint for the structure of their entire argument—what we describe as a complex thesis statement in Chapter 4. Based on the thesis alone, a reader can determine the central claim and see how the writer intends to go about supporting it.

In the following example, Sarah Ray provides a thesis for her interpretation of Chopin's "The Story of an Hour" that responds to her original research question about the story: "How does Mrs. Mallard's marriage function in the story?" Notice that she includes clues as to how she will prove her claim in the thesis statement itself:

> Through Mrs. Mallard's emotional development and the concomitant juxtaposition of the vitality of nature to the repressive indoors, Chopin exposes the role of marriage in the oppression of one's true self and desires.

Blueprint for how Sarah will prove her claim

Sarah's interpretation of the story, provided as a clear claim

Although it's not uncommon for thesis statements in humanistic scholarship to remain implied, as opposed to being stated explicitly, most interpretations explicitly assert a claim close to the beginning of the argument, often in the introductory paragraph (or, in a longer piece, paragraphs). Thesis statements may appear as single-sentence statements or may span multiple sentences.

Another example of a thesis statement comes from a scholarly article by Christopher Collins, "Final Meals: The Theater of Capital Punishment." Collins explicitly poses a research question: "If food functions as 'a way of getting at some essential truth about each other,' what truths are revealed in the final meals of inmates?" (p. 89). He then provides a plan for how he will develop his analysis of the final meals of inmates as part of the unifying thesis of his article:

> This article analyzes the prisoner's final meals through three perspectives. Dwight Conquergood provides a framework for understanding executions as theatrical performance. Terri Gordon complements Conquergood's work by explaining the final meals within the sacred, the spectacle, and the profane. Finally, Barbara Kirshenblatt-Gimblett provides a method for understanding food as a performance medium. This article aims to achieve an understanding of food as a performance object in order to understand the link between the condemned and the system of capital punishment. (p. 89)

Collins provides a roadmap for how he will develop his argument, building off the scholarship of others to establish his own argument.

Collins offers a clear statement of thesis.

When you develop your own thesis statements, you will want to focus on the content as much as the form. The following checklist will help you determine if you have a strong thesis:

- **Is the thesis debatable?** Claims in the humanities are propositions, not statements of fact. For example, the assertion that "The Story of an Hour" deals with a wife's response to the news of her husband's death is a fact. It is not, therefore, debatable and will not be a very useful thesis. If, however, we assert that the wife's response to her husband's death demonstrates some characteristic of her relationship with her husband and with the institution of marriage, then we're proposing a debatable claim. This is a proposition we can try to prove, instead of a fact that is already obviously true.

- **Is the thesis significant?** Claims about texts should offer substantial insight into the meaning of the artifacts. They should account for as much of the artifacts as possible and avoid reducing their complexity. Have you paid attention to all of the evidence you collected, and have you looked at it in context? Are you considering all of the possible elements of the text that might contribute to your interpretation?

- **Does the thesis contribute to an ongoing scholarly conversation?** Effective thesis statements contribute to an ongoing conversation without repeating what others have already said about the text. How does the claim extend, contradict, or affirm other interpretations of the text?

Connect 7.6   Drafting Thesis Statements

Review the questions and responses you drafted in Connect 7.5, "Developing *Why*, *What*, and *How* Questions." Structure your responses to any two of your questions as separate thesis statements, using an "I" statement in the following form:

Template: By examining *x* (*x* = the evidence you have found), I argue that *y* (*y* = your claim).

Example: By examining Mrs. Mallard's emotional development and the juxtaposition of the vitality of nature to the repressive indoors in the story, I argue that Chopin exposes the role of marriage in the story to show the oppression of a person's true self and desires.

Note that some scholars avoid using "I" in thesis statements. You can always edit the thesis statement later to take out "I" if your instructor discourages its use. We find that even if the "I" will need to be changed, it helps when figuring out what you want to say to include yourself in the statement.

- Now test the appropriateness of your claim by asking: Is the thesis debatable? Is the thesis significant? Does the thesis contribute to an ongoing scholarly conversation?
- Once you've analyzed Chopin's story and constructed two separate thesis statements, consider sharing them with a classmate, identifying strengths and weaknesses in both. How is your claim both argumentative and significant? How many direct quotes from the story would help support your points? Which of the two thesis statements offers a more significant insight into the story's meaning?

Thesis-Driven Structural Templates

Many students learn to write academic arguments in primary and secondary school following a template known as the five-paragraph essay. This template places a thesis, or claim, near the beginning of an argument (often at the end of an introductory paragraph), devotes the body of the essay to supporting the thesis, and then offers a final paragraph of conclusion that connects all the parts of the argument by summarizing the main points and reminding readers of the argument's overall significance.

While the premise behind this structure is based on some conventions of the humanities, following the template too closely could get you into trouble. For example, not every thesis has three points to prove. And sometimes an introduction needs to be longer than one paragraph. Instead, we suggest a flexible thesis-driven essay structure that guides the reader through the parts of your argument with appropriate transitional words and phrases.

● **A Flexible Thesis-Driven Template**   The elements of a thesis-driven template that tend to be consistent in scholarship in the humanities are the following:

- Thesis statements generally appear toward the beginning of the argument in an introduction that explains the scope and importance of the topic.

- The body of the argument presents evidence gathered from the text to support the thesis.

- The conclusion connects the parts of the argument together to reinforce the thesis, summarizing the argument's important elements and reminding readers of its overall significance.

A template such as this one can provide a useful place to start as you organize your argument, but be careful not to allow a template to restrict your argument by oversimplifying your understanding of how humanistic scholars structure their writing.

● **Paragraphs and Transitions**   In arguments in the humanities, paragraphs tend to link back to the thesis by developing a reason and providing evidence. The paragraphs are often connected through **transitional words and phrases** (e.g., *similarly, in addition, in contrast, for example*) that guide readers by signaling shifts between and among the parts of an argument. These words and phrases help the reader understand the order in which the reasons are presented and how one paragraph connects to the preceding one. Notice, for example, how Christopher Collins moves between ideas using the transitional phrase "On the other end of the spectrum" (underlined here) in this excerpted section of his article:

> Thomas Grasso, executed by Oklahoma in 1995, wanted Spaghetti-Os. . . . Instead Grasso received a can of Franco-American spaghetti. Grasso complained in his final statement "I did not get my Spaghetti-Os. I got spaghetti. I want the press to know this!" Grasso, in his last words, found it extremely important to communicate that the proper ritual of the final meal, and thus of the execution, was not followed. The final meal request form serves as a behavioral performance of food.

On the other end of the spectrum, some individuals use the request slip as a metaphorical performance. Alyda Faber, drawing on Catherine Bell's *Ritual Theory, Ritual Practice*, discusses the potential political weight of such food performances. . . . The state uses the final meal ritual as an embodied practice that orders and illustrates its sovereignty. (p. 96)

● **Titles**   Scholars in the humanities value the artistic and creative use of language, and titles of their work often reflect that value. In contrast to articles in the social sciences and the natural sciences, which often have descriptive titles that directly state the topic of study and leave little room for interpretation, articles in the humanities tend to have titles that play with language in creative ways, sometimes incorporating quotations from a text in an interesting way. Such titles are meant to engage readers by piquing their interests. Occasionally, such creative titles may have the effect of entertaining an intended audience. Humanistic scholars are also notorious for their love of subtitles. Here are a few examples:

Reforming Bodies: Self-Governance, Anxiety, and Cape Colonial Architecture in South Africa, 1665–1860

Resident Franchise: Theorizing the Science Fiction Genre, Conglomerations, and the Future of Synergy

---

Connect 7.7   **Observing Structural Features in the Humanities**

Although we've discussed some common structural features for scholarly articles in the humanities, we'd like to stress that writers might choose to depart from these conventional expectations if they don't serve the writers' particular aims. Find a scholarly article from the humanities, and examine it in terms of these structural features. If the article deviates from the conventions we've described, what might be the writer's reasons?

- **Title**   Does the title seek to entertain, to challenge, or to intrigue the reader?
- **Thesis**   Can you identify a clear statement of thesis? Where is it located? Does the thesis explicitly or implicitly provide a "blueprint" for guiding the reader through the rest of the paper?
- **Paragraphs and Transitions**   Look closely at four successive body paragraphs in the paper. Explain how each paragraph relates to the paper's guiding thesis. How does the writer transition between each of the paragraphs?

Language Conventions in the Humanities

Writing in the humanities generally follows several conventions of language use that might sound familiar because they're often taught in English classes. Keep in mind, though, that even though these conventions are common in the humanities, they aren't necessarily conventional in other disciplinary areas.

Descriptive and Rhetorical Language

Writers in the humanities often use language that is creative or playful, not only when producing artistic texts but sometimes also when writing interpretations of texts. For example, you might notice that writing in the humanities uses figurative language and rhetorical devices (similes, metaphors, and alliteration, for example) more often than in other disciplines. Because writers in the humanities are studying texts so closely, they often pay similarly close attention to the text they're creating, and they take great care to choose precise, and sometimes artistic, language. In many cases, the language not only conveys information; it also engages in rhetorical activity of its own.

Active Voice

Writing in the humanities tends to privilege the use of the active voice rather than the passive voice. Sentences written in the **active voice** clearly state the subject of the sentence, the agent, as the person or thing doing the action. By contrast, the **passive voice** inverts the structure of the sentence, obscuring or eliminating mention of the agent. Let's look at three simple examples.

Active Voice: The girl chased the dog.

Passive Voice (agent obscured): The dog was chased by the girl.

Passive Voice (agent not mentioned): The dog was chased.

In the first example, the girl is the subject of the sentence and the person (the agent) doing the action — chasing. In the second sentence, the girl is still there, but her presence is less prominent because the dog takes the subject's position at the beginning of the sentence. In the final sentence, the girl is not mentioned at all.

Now let's look at an example from a student paper in the humanities to understand why active voice is usually preferred. In her interpretation of "The Story of an Hour," Sarah Ray writes this sentence in the introduction, using active voice:

Active Voice: Kate Chopin presents a completely different view of marriage in "The Story of an Hour," published in 1894.

If Sarah were to write the sentence in the passive voice, eliminating the agent, it would look like this:

Passive Voice: A completely different view of marriage is presented in "The Story of an Hour," published in 1894.

In this case, the active voice is preferred because it gives credit to the author, Kate Chopin, who created the story and the character. Scholars in the humanities value giving credit to the person doing the action, conducting the study, or creating a text. Active voice also provides the clearest, most transparent meaning—another aspect of writing that is valued in the humanities.

Hedging

In the humanities, writers sometimes *hedge*, or qualify, the claims that they make when interpreting a text, called **hedging**, even though they are generally quite fervent about defending their arguments once established. In fact, the beginning of the sentence that you just read contains not one but three **hedges**. Take a look:

> In the humanities, writers sometimes *hedge*, or qualify, the claims that they make when interpreting a text.

Each underlined phrase limits the scope of the claim in a way that is important to improve accuracy and to allow for other possibilities. In contrast, consider the next claim:

> Writers hedge the claims that they make.

If we had stated our claim that way, not only would it not be true, but you would immediately begin to think of exceptions. Even if we had limited the claim to writers in the humanities, you still might find exceptions to it. As the original sentence is written, we've allowed for other possibilities while still identifying a predominant trend in humanities writing. Hedging phrases include *they tend to*, *they might*, *it appears that*, and *it is likely to*, along with modifiers such as *some*, *often*, *perhaps*, and *maybe*.

Humanistic scholars hedge their claims for several reasons. The disciplines of the humanities do not tend to claim objectivity or neutrality in their research as other disciplines do, so they allow for other interpretations of and perspectives on texts. As an example, take a look at the opening and closing sentences of the first paragraph of Dale Jacobs's "Conclusion" from his article printed earlier in the chapter:

> My process of making meaning from these pages of *Polly and the Pirates* is one of many meanings within the matrix of possibilities inherent in the text. (par. 16)
>
> Structure and agency interact so that we are influenced by design conventions and grammars as we read but are not determined by them; though we are subject to the same set of grammars, my reading of the text is not necessarily the same as that of someone else. (par. 16)

In these sentences, Jacobs not only hedges the interpretation he offers, but he explicitly states that there are many possible meanings of the text he has just analyzed.

Insider's View
Cristina Ramírez, Writing Studies Scholar, on Writing in the Humanities

COURTESY OF CRISTINA RAMÍREZ

"I've seen a lot of different kinds of writing in the humanities. Personal essays are common, and scholars in my field often relate their work to their personal experience. Humanities scholars will also draw on familial knowledge about their culture and heritage. I've also seen poetry in scholarly writing in the humanities, sometimes on its own and sometimes embedded within a larger scholarly piece that is multi-genre. Other scholars will use song lyrics, recipes, photographs, or other media in their work in a multi-genre approach. I remember a humanities article I read that had a photograph of all of the shoes collected at the Mexico-U.S. border. Using these kinds of media in scholarly work can evoke an emotional response in the reader.

"Writing in the humanities is becoming more accessible, and academics are beginning to understand that they are not only writing to the academy, but they are also writing with and to the communities and people they are writing about. For example, I just wrote a chapter in a book titled *Revolutionary Women of Texas and Mexico: Portraits of Soldaderas, Saints, and Subversives*. All of the chapters in the book are written so that they are very accessible. The language did not sound as academic and jargon-filled as scholarly writing sometimes can; even though the book was published by a university press, it was clearly written for a broader audience, and the language used in the chapters was embedded in the communities that the chapters were written for and with."

Connect 7.8   Observing Language Features in the Humanities

Continue your examination of the article you selected for Connect 7.7, using the questions below as a guide. If the article deviates from the conventions we've described, what might be the writer's reasons?

- **Descriptive and Rhetorical Language**   Is the language of the text meant only to convey information, or does it engage in rhetorical activity? In other words, do similes, metaphors, or other rhetorical devices demonstrate attempts to be creative with language?

- **Voice**   Is the voice of the text primarily active or passive?

- **Hedging**   Is there evidence of hedging? That is, does the writer qualify statements with words and phrases such as *tend, suggest, may, it is probable that,* or *it is reasonable to conclude that*? What is the significance of hedging?

Reference Conventions in the Humanities

Scholars in the humanities frequently cite the work of others in their scholarship, especially when supporting an interpretation of a text. They often quote the language from their primary sources exactly instead of summarizing or paraphrasing, because the exact words or details included in the primary source might be important to the argument.

Values Reflected in Citations

When humanistic scholars cite the work of other scholars, they show how their research contributes to ongoing conversations about a subject—whether they're agreeing with a previous interpretation, extending someone else's interpretation, or offering an alternative one. These citations can strengthen their own argument and provide direct support by showing that another scholar had a similar idea or by demonstrating how another scholar's ideas are incorrect, imprecise, or not fully developed.

As we mentioned in Chapter 5, you can integrate the work of others into your writing by paraphrasing, summarizing, or quoting directly. Scholars in the humanities use all these options, but they quote directly more often than scholars in other disciplines because the exact language or details from their primary sources are often important to their argument.

Take a look at this example from Collins's "Final Meals: The Theater of Capital Punishment." In it, Collins establishes a comparison ("A similar idea") between his own interpretation of prisoners' final meals and the work of another scholar, Bordo, whose ideas on anorexia are explored in a scholarly book by Deane Curtin and Lisa Heldke:

> The final meal serves to reinforce the dichotomy of body and mind through the supposed death of the body and continuation of the mind or soul. A similar idea can be found in Bordo's understanding of anorexia. Bordo notes that starvation of the body is motivated by the dream to be "without a body," to achieve "absolute purity, hyperintellectuality and transcendence of the flesh." The last meal is not a hunger for food as much as it is a gesture towards purity and transcendence of the flesh. (p. 98)

Most scholars in the humanities include references to the work of others early in their writing to establish what the focus and stance of their own research will be. Because abstracts appear in humanities scholarship less frequently than in social sciences and natural sciences research, the introduction to an article in the humanities provides a snapshot of how the researcher is positioning himself or herself in the ongoing conversation about an object of study.

As you read scholarship in the humanities, notice how frequently the text references or cites secondary sources in the opening paragraphs. Here is an example from the beginning of Dale Jacobs's article on teaching literacy through the use of comics (not included in the excerpt in this chapter). Jacobs situates his work historically among work published about comics in the 1950s, and he also references the research of other scholars who had already written about that history in more detail:

> Prior to their current renaissance, comics were often viewed, at best, as popular entertainment and, at worst, as a dangerous influence on youth. Such attitudes were certainly prevalent in the early 1950s when comics were at their most popular, with critics such as Fredric Wertham voicing the most strenuous arguments against comics in his 1954 book *Seduction of the Innocent* (for an extended discussion of this debate, see Dorrell, Curtis, and Rampal).

In these two sentences, Jacobs positions his work within that of other scholars, showing how it's connected to and distinct from it. Also, by citing the work of Dorrell, Curtis, and Rampal, Jacobs doesn't have to write a lengthy history about a period that's tangentially related to his argument but not central to it.

Documentation Styles: MLA and CMS

A few documentation styles are prevalent in the humanities, and those styles highlight elements of a source that are important in humanistic study. Many scholars in the humanities, especially in literature and languages, tend to follow the documentation style of the Modern Language Association (MLA). Scholars in history and some other disciplines of the humanities may rely on the *Chicago Manual of Style* (CMS). When using CMS, scholars can choose between two systems of citations: the notes and bibliography system or the author-date system. In the humanities, researchers generally use the notes and bibliography system, in which numbered footnotes or endnotes are used to cite sources, and then the full publication data for those sources is provided at the end of the paper, in a list alphabetically organized by author. This source list is referred to as "Works Cited" in MLA style and "Bibliography" in CMS.

The values of the humanities are reflected in their citation systems. In MLA, in-text citations appear in parenthetical references that include the author's last name and a page number, with no comma in between; for example: (Miller-Cochran et al. 139). If the author's name is included in the body of the sentence, then only the page number appears in parentheses.

The page number is included regardless of whether the cited passage was paraphrased, summarized, or quoted — unlike in other common styles like APA, where page numbers are usually given only for direct quotations. One reason for including the page number in the MLA in-text citation is that humanistic scholars highly value the original phrasing of an argument or passage and might want to look at the original source. The page number makes searching easy for the reader, facilitating the possibility of examining the original context of a quotation or the original language of something that was paraphrased or summarized.

CMS style also supports looking for the information in the original source by giving the citation information in a footnote on the same page as the referenced material. Additionally, CMS allows authors to include descriptive details in a footnote that provides more information about where a citation came from in a source.

For an example of a paper in MLA format, see Insider Example: Student Interpretation of a Literary Text (pp. 154–60). For a discussion of the elements of citations and Works Cited lists, see "Modern Language Association (MLA) Style" in the Appendix.

Connect 7.9   **Observing Reference Features in the Humanities**

Conclude your examination of the article you selected for Connect 7.7, using the questions below as a guide:

- **Engagement with Other Scholars**   Does the writer refer to other scholars' words or ideas? If so, in what ways? Are other scholars' words or ideas used to support the writer's argument, or do they serve to contrast with what the writer has to say? Does the writer quote directly from other writers?

- **Documentation**   Look closely at examples of how the writer cites the work of other scholars. What form of documentation applies? What type of information is valued?

Genres: Textual Interpretation

Similar to scholars in the social sciences and the natural sciences, scholars in the humanities often present their research at conferences and publish their work in journal articles and books. In some fields of the humanities, books are highly valued, and scholars here tend to work individually more frequently than scholars in the social sciences and the natural sciences. Also, many scholars in the humanities engage in creative work and might present it at an art installation, reading, or exhibit.

In this section, we offer the opportunity to analyze and practice one of the most common genres required of students in introductory-level courses in the humanities: textual interpretation, whether the text is a work of literature, art, film, music, theater, dance, or some other creative form of expression.

What Is the Rhetorical Context for This Genre?

A **textual interpretation** (also referred to as an "analysis") offers a close reading of a text that shows how the elements of the text work together to create meaning. While works of art such as literature, film, music, and visual art have multiple meanings and there is no one "right" interpretation of a text, a strong interpretation is insightful, convincing, and grounded in evidence derived from the text itself.

Students and scholars may compose a textual interpretation to come to a better understanding of a text and how it contributes to a larger understanding of the human experience. In college, students might be writing for their instructor and peers, and using the interpretation to apply what they are learning about the elements of an art form (such as *mise en scene* in film or *meter* in poetry) to a specific work. The writer can assume that their audience has seen, heard, or read the text being interpreted. A **textual interpretation** makes a clear claim about the object of study and may use evidence drawn from the interpretations of other scholars as support.

Strategies for Writing a Textual Interpretation

● **Observe closely and make notes in the way that works best for the medium you are exploring.**   As you read, view, listen to, and/or study the text and make notes, consider the ways you are interacting with the text by creating a content/form-response grid: *What* are you learning, and *how* is the text itself shaping your experience of it?

● **Formulate a thesis.**   Once your close reading is complete, formulate a thesis (or a claim) about the text. You'll need to provide evidence to support your thesis from the text itself. You might make your reader aware of how your claim about the work is different from that of other scholars, signaling what new insights you bring to the conversation. If you choose to situate your text in a historical context, you will need to do additional research to gather the facts.

● **Remember SLR as you draft and revise.**   The Writing Project that follows suggests a structure for your interpretation. Apply what you've learned in this chapter about writing conventions in the humanities as you draft each section of your textual analysis. Focus on developing your interpretation and supporting your points in the first draft, and then use the revision to further clarify your points and work on style.

Writing Project   **Textual Interpretation/Analysis**

Your goal in this writing project is to offer an interpretation of a text or a set of texts for an audience of your peers. Begin by selecting a text or texts that you find particularly interesting, and then work through the process of close reading described in the chapter.

THE INTRODUCTION

The introductory paragraph of your paper should include information to help the audience understand what your argument is about: the title of the work and name of its creator, a few sentences of background information on the work and/or creator, and a thesis that makes a clear and insightful claim about the meaning of the work.

THE BODY

The body of the argument should present evidence gathered from the text to support the thesis. It should offer an analysis of the work, not simply a summary or description. Select the best evidence from your form/content grid, using quotes, images, paraphrases, and descriptions as appropriate. Each paragraph should make a point that advances the argument, with clear topic sentences and transitions that show the relationships among your ideas.

THE CONCLUSION

The conclusion should connect the parts of the argument together to reinforce the thesis, summarizing the argument's important elements and reminding readers of its overall significance.

TECHNICAL CONSIDERATIONS

Construct a Works Cited page in MLA format that includes the name of the work and any secondary sources you use. Be certain that you include in-text citations throughout your project whenever you quote, summarize, reference, or paraphrase information from source material.

....

Insider Example
Student Interpretation of a Literary Text

In the following essay, "Till Death Do Us Part: An Analysis of Kate Chopin's 'The Story of an Hour,'" Sarah Ray offers an interpretation of Chopin's story that relies on close observation of the text for support. Read her essay below, and pay particular attention to her thesis statement and to her use of evidence. Note how her thesis responds to the question, "How does Mrs. Mallard's marriage function in the story?" Sarah didn't use outside scholars to support her interpretation, so you could also consider how secondary sources might have provided additional support for her claim. ▶

Sarah Ray

Professor Stamper

ENG 101

10 April 2021

Till Death Do Us Part: An Analysis of Kate Chopin's

"The Story of an Hour"

The nineteenth century saw the publication of some of the most renowned romances in literary history, including the novels of Jane Austen and the Brontë sisters, Charlotte, Emily, and Anne. While their stories certainly have lasting appeal, they also inspired an unrealistic and sometimes unattainable ideal of joyful love and marriage. In this romanticized vision, a couple is merely two halves of a whole; one without the other compromises the happiness of both. The couple's lives, and even destinies, are so intertwined that neither individual worries about what personal desires and goals are being forsaken by commitment to the other. By the end of the century, in her "The Story of an Hour" (1894), Kate Chopin presents a completely different view of marriage. Through the perspective of a female protagonist, Louise Mallard, who believes her husband has just died, the author explores the more challenging aspects of marriage in a time when divorce was rare and disapproved of. Through Mrs. Mallard's emotional development and the concomitant juxtaposition of the vitality of nature to the repressive indoors, Chopin explores marriage as the oppression of one's true self and desires.

"The Story of an Hour" begins its critique of marriage by ending one, when the news of Brently Mallard's death is gently conveyed to his wife, Louise. Chopin then follows Mrs. Mallard's different emotional stages in response to her husband's death. When the news is initially broken to Louise, "[s]he did not hear the story as many women have heard the same, with a paralyzed inability to accept its significance"

FORM: Ray uses a common line from marriage vows to indirectly indicate that she will focus on the role of marriage in her interpretation.

CONTENT: Ray clearly states her thesis and provides a preview about how she will develop and support her claim.

CONTENT: In this paragraph, Ray develops the first part of her thesis, the stages of Mrs. Mallard's emotional development.

(Chopin, par. 3). She instead weeps suddenly and briefly, a "storm of grief" that passes as quickly as it had come (par. 3). This wild, emotional outburst and quick acceptance says a great deal about Louise's feelings toward her marriage. "[S]he had loved [her husband]—sometimes," but a reader may infer that Louise's quick acceptance implies that she has considered an early death for her spouse before (par. 15). That she even envisions such a dark prospect reveals her unhappiness with the marriage. She begins to see, and even desire, a future without her husband. This desire is expressed when Louise is easily able to see past her husband's death to "a long procession of years to come that would belong to her absolutely" (par. 13). Furthermore, it is unclear whether her "storm of grief" is genuine or faked for the benefit of the family members surrounding her. The "sudden, wild abandonment" with which she weeps almost seems like Louise is trying to mask that she does not react to the news as a loving wife would (par. 3). Moreover, the display of grief passes quickly; Chopin devotes only a single sentence to the action. Her tears are quickly succeeded by consideration of the prospects of a future on her own.

Chopin uses the setting to create a symbolic context for Louise's emotional outburst in response to the news of her husband's death. Louise is informed of Brently's death in the downstairs level of her home: "It was her sister Josephine who told her, in broken sentences; veiled hints that revealed in half concealing" (par. 2). No mention is made of windows, and the only portal that connects to the outside world is the door that admits the bearers of bad news. By excluding a link to nature, Chopin creates an almost claustrophobic environment to symbolize the oppression Louise feels from her marriage. It is no mistake that this setting plays host to Mrs. Mallard's initial emotional breakdown. Her desires have been suppressed

FORM: Ray primarily uses active voice to clarify who is doing the action in her sentences.

throughout her relationship, and symbolically, she is being suffocated by the confines of her house. Therefore, in this toxic atmosphere, Louise is only able to feel and show the emotions that are expected of her, not those that she truly experiences. Her earlier expression of "grief" underscores this disconnect, overcompensating for emotions that should come naturally to a wife who has just lost her husband, but that must be forced in Mrs. Mallard's case.

Chopin continues Mrs. Mallard's emotional journey only after she is alone and able to process her genuine feelings. After her brief display of grief has run its course, she migrates to her upstairs bedroom and sits in front of a window looking upon the beauty of nature. It is then and only then that Louise gives in not only to her emotions about the day's exploits, but also to those feelings she could only experience after the oppression of her husband died with him — dark desires barely explored outside the boundaries of her own mind, if at all. They were at first foreign to her, but as soon as Louise began to "recognize this thing that was approaching to possess her . . . she [strove] to beat it back with her will" (par. 10). Even then, after the source of her repression is gone, she fights to stifle her desires and physical reactions. The habit is so engrained that Louise is unable to release her emotions for fear of the unknown, of that which has been repressed for so long. However, "her bosom rose and fell tumultuously…When she abandoned herself a little whispered word escaped her slightly parted lips. She said it over and over under her breath: 'free, free, free!' . . . Her pulses beat fast, and the coursing blood warmed and relaxed every inch of her body" (pars. 10, 11). When she's allowed to experience them, Louise's feelings and desires provide a glimpse into a possible joyous future without her husband, a future where "[t]here would be no powerful will bending hers in that blind persistence with which men

> **FORM:** Ray uses transitions between paragraphs that indicate her organization and connect different ideas.

and women believe they have a right to impose" (par. 14). Her marriage is over, and Louise appears finally to be able to liberate her true identity and look upon the future with not dread but anticipation.

The author's setting for this scene is crucial in the development of not only the plot but also her critique of marriage. Chopin sought to encapsulate the freedom Louise began to feel in her room with this scene's depiction of nature. For example, Chopin describes the view from Louise's bedroom window with language that expresses its vitality: "She could see in the open square before her house the tops of trees that were all aquiver with the new spring life" (par. 5). She goes on to say, "The delicious breath of rain was in the air. In the street below a peddler was crying his wares ... and countless sparrows were twittering in the eaves" (par. 5). The very adjectives and phrases used to describe the outdoors seem to speak of bustling activity and life. This is in stark contrast to the complete lack of vivacity in the description of downstairs.

The language used in the portrayal of these contrasting settings is not the only way Chopin strives to emphasize the difference between the two. She also uses the effect these scenes have on Mrs. Mallard to convey their meaning and depth. On the one hand, the wild, perhaps faked, emotional outburst that takes place in the stifling lower level of the house leaves Louise in a state of "physical exhaustion that haunted her body and seemed to reach into her soul" (par. 4). On the other hand, Louise "[drank] in a very elixir of life through that open window" of her bedroom through which nature bloomed (par. 18). Because the author strove to symbolize Mrs. Mallard's marriage with the oppressive downstairs and her impending life without her husband with the open, healing depiction of nature, Chopin suggests that spouses are sometimes better off

FORM: When making assumptions about the author's intentions, Ray sometimes uses hedging words—in this case, "seem to."

without each other because marriage can take a physical toll on a person's well-being while the freedom of living for no one but one's self breathes life into even the most burdened wife. After all, "[w]hat could love, the unsolved mystery, count for in face of this possession of self-assertion" felt by Mrs. Mallard in the wake of her emancipation from oppression (par. 15)?

Chopin goes on to emphasize the healing capabilities and joy of living only for one's self by showing the consequences of brutally taking it all away, in one quick turn of a latchkey. With thoughts of her freedom of days to come, "she carried herself unwittingly like a goddess of Victory. She clasped her sister's waist, and together they descended the stairs" (par. 20). Already Chopin is preparing the reader for Mrs. Mallard's looming fate. Not only is she no longer alone in her room with the proverbial elixir of life pouring in from the window, but also she is once again sinking into the oppression of the downstairs, an area that embodies all marital duties as well as the suffocation of Louise's true self and desires. When Brently Mallard enters the house slightly confused but unharmed, the loss of her newly found freedom is too much for Louise's weak heart to bear. Chopin ends the story with a hint of irony: "When the doctors came they said she had died of heart disease—of joy that kills" (par. 23). It may be easier for society to accept that Mrs. Mallard died of joy at seeing her husband alive, but in all actuality, it was the violent death of her future prospects and the hope she had allowed to blossom that sent Louise to the grave. Here lies Chopin's ultimate critique of marriage: when there was no other viable escape, only death could provide freedom from an oppressive marriage. By killing Louise, Chopin solidifies this ultimatum and also suggests that even death is kinder when the only other option is the slow and continuous addition of the crushing weight of marital oppression.

CONTENT: Ray provides a broad summary of her argument in the concluding paragraph.

In "The Story of an Hour," Kate Chopin challenges the typical, romanticized view of love and marriage in the era in which she lived. She chooses to reveal some of the sacrifices one must make in order to bind oneself to another in matrimony. Chopin develops these critiques of marriage through Louise Mallard's emotional responses to her husband's supposed death, whether it is a quick, if not faked, outburst of grief, her body's highly sexualized awakening to the freedoms to come, or the utter despair at finding that he still survives. These are not typical emotions for a "grieving" wife, and Chopin uses this stark contrast as well as the concomitant juxtaposition of nature to the indoors to further emphasize her critique. Louise Mallard may have died in the quest to gain independence from the oppression of her true self and desires, but now she is at least "[f]ree! Body and soul free!" (par. 16).

CONTENT: In her last sentence, Ray reveals a portion of the significance of the story to an understanding of marital oppression.

Work Cited

FORM: Ray cites her source using MLA format.

Chopin, Kate. "The Story of an Hour." 1894. Ann Woodlief's Web Study Texts, www.vcu.edu/engweb/webtexts/hour.

Reading and Writing in the Humanities

- **In the humanities, scholars seek to understand and interpret human experience.** To do so, they often create, analyze, and interpret texts.

- **Scholars in the humanities often conduct close readings of texts** to interpret and make meaning from them, and they might draw on a particular theoretical perspective to ask questions about those texts.

- **Keeping a content/form-response grid can help you track important elements of a text** and your response to them as you complete a close reading.

- **Writing in the humanities often draws on the interpretations of others,** either as support or to position an interpretation within prior scholarship.

- **Arguments in the humanities typically follow a thesis-driven *structure*.** They often begin with a thesis statement that asserts what the author intends to prove, and it may also provide insight into how the author will prove it. Each section of the argument should provide support for the thesis.

- **Rhetorical language, active voice, and hedging are uses of *language*** that characterizes writing in the humanities.

- **MLA and CMS styles are commonly used for *reference*** in the fields of the humanities.

- **Textual interpretation is a common *genre*** in the humanities.

8

Reading and Writing in the Social Sciences

Scholars in the fields of the **social sciences** study human behavior and inter-action along with the systems and social structures we create to organize our world. Their work helps us understand why we do what we do as well as how processes (political, economic, personal, etc.) contribute to our lives. The social sciences encompass a broad area of academic inquiry that comprises numerous fields of study. These include sociology, psychology, anthropology, economics, communication studies, and political science, among others.

Maybe you've observed a friend or family member spiral into addictive or self-destructive behavior, and you've struggled to understand how it happened. Maybe you've spent time wondering how cliques were formed and maintained among students in your high school, or how friends are typically chosen. Perhaps larger social problems like poverty or famine concern you the most. If you've ever stopped to consider any of these kinds of issues, then you've already begun to explore the world of the social sciences.

ANDREA TSURUMI

As a social scientist, you might study issues like therapy options for autism, the effects of racism on people of color, peer pressure, substance abuse, social networking websites, stress, or commu-nication practices and gender equality. You might study family counseling techniques or the effects of divorce on teens. Or perhaps you might wonder (as the authors of examples in this chapter do) about the effects of differing educational environments on student satisfaction and success. Your work would make a difference in peo-ple's lives by informing practices, therapies, and policies that could alleviate social problems.

Whatever the case may be, if you're interested in studying human behavior and understanding why we do what we do, you'll want to consider further how social scientists conduct research and how they present their results in writing. As in all the academic domains, progress in the social sciences rests upon researchers' pri-mary skills at making observations of the world around them.

In this chapter, you'll look at some of the observational methods used by social scientists and see how their ways of researching are reflected in their academic writing.

Connect 8.1 **Observing Behavior**

For this activity, pick a place to sit and observe people. You can choose a place that you enjoy going to regularly, but make sure you can observe and take notes without being interrupted or distracted. Try to avoid places where you might feel compelled to engage in conversation with people you know.

For ten minutes, freewrite about the people around you and what they're doing. Look for the kinds of interactions and engagements that characterize their behavior. Then draft some questions that you think a social scientist observing the same people might ask about them.

For example, if you wrote about behaviors you observed at a public library, you might draft questions such as these: How are people seated around the space in the library? What does the seating arrangement look like? Are some places to sit more popular than others? What different types of activities are people doing in the library? Are people interacting with one another, and, if so, how? How are they positioned when they interact? What do you notice about the volume of their voices? What happens if someone (a child, perhaps) disrupts that volume?

See how many different behaviors, people, and interactions you can observe and how many questions you can generate. You might do this activity in the same place with a partner and then compare notes. What did you or your partner find in common? What did you each observe that was unique? Why do you think you noticed the things you did? What was the most interesting thing you observed?

Research in the Social Sciences

The social sciences comprise a diverse group of academic fields that aim to understand human behavior and systems. But despite the differences in the types of behavior they study and the theories that inform their work, we can link various disciplines in the social sciences and the values they share by considering how social scientists conduct and report their research.

The Role of Theory in the Social Sciences

Unlike in the natural sciences, where research often takes place in a laboratory setting under controlled conditions, research in the social sciences is necessarily "messier." The reason is fairly simple: human beings and the systems they organize cannot generally be studied in laboratory conditions, where variables are controlled. For this reason, social scientists do not generally establish fixed laws or argue for absolute truths, as natural scientists sometimes do. For instance, while natural scientists are able to argue, with certainty, that a water molecule contains two atoms of hydrogen and one of oxygen, social scientists cannot claim to know the absolute fixed nature of a person's psychology (why a person does what she does in any particular instance, for example) or that of a social system or problem (why homelessness persists, for instance).

Much social science research is therefore based on theories of human behavior and human systems, which are propositions that scholars use to explain specific phenomena. Theories can be evaluated on the basis of their ability to explain why or how or when a phenomenon occurs, and they generally result from research that has been replicated time and again to confirm their accuracy, appropriateness, and usefulness. Still, it's important to understand that theories are not laws; they are not absolute, fixed, or perfect explanations. Instead, social science theories are always being refined as research on particular social phenomena develops. The study by Rathunde and Csikszentmihalyi used as an example later in the chapter, for instance, makes use of goal theory and optimal experience theory as part of the research design to evaluate the type of middle school environment that best contributes to students' education.

Research Questions and Hypotheses

As we've noted throughout this book, research questions are typically formulated on the basis of observations. In the social sciences, such observations focus on human behavior, human systems, and/or the interactions between the two. Observations of a social phenomenon can give rise to questions about how a phenomenon operates or what effects it has on people or how it could be changed to improve individuals' well-being. For example, in their social science study "'Under the Radar': Educators and Cyberbullying in Schools," W. Cassidy, K. Brown, and M. Jackson (2012) offer the following as guiding research questions for their investigation:

> Our study of educators focused on three research questions: Do they [educators] consider cyberbullying a problem at their school and how familiar are they with the extent and impact among their students? What policies and practices are in place to prevent or counter cyberbullying? What solutions do they have for encouraging a kinder online world? (p. 522)

Research that is designed to inform a theory of human behavior or to provide data that contributes to a fuller understanding of some social or political structure (i.e., to answer a social science research question) also often begins with the presentation of a hypothesis. As we saw in Chapter 4, a **hypothesis** is a testable proposition that provides an answer or predicts an outcome in response to the research question(s) at hand. Generally, a hypothesis is formed based on prior knowledge, research, or experience that would help the researcher predict the outcome of a study. C. Kerns and K. Ko (2009) present the following hypothesis, or predicted outcome, for their social science study "Exploring Happiness and Performance at Work." The researchers make a prediction concerning what they believed their research would show before presenting their findings later in their research report:

> The intent of this analysis was to review how happiness and performance related to each other in this workplace. It is the authors' belief that for performance to be sustained in an organization, individuals and groups within that organization need to experience a threshold level of happiness. It is difficult for unhappy individuals and work groups to continue performing at high levels without appropriate leadership intervention. (p. 5)

It's important to note that not all social science reports include a statement of hypothesis. Some social science research establishes its focus by presenting the questions that guide researchers' inquiry into a particular phenomenon instead of establishing a hypothesis.

Hypotheses differ from *thesis statements*, which are more commonly associated with arguments in the humanities. While thesis statements offer researchers' final conclusions on a topic or issue, hypothesis statements offer a predicted outcome. The proposition expressed in a hypothesis may be either accepted or rejected based on the results of the research. For example, a team of educational researchers might hypothesize that teachers' use of open-ended questioning increases students' level of participation in class. However, the researchers would not be able to confirm or reject such a hypothesis until the completion of their research.

Connect 8.2   Developing Hypotheses

- For five minutes, brainstorm *social science* topics or issues that have affected your life. One approach is to consider issues that are causing you stress in your life right now. Examples might include peer pressure, academic performance, substance abuse, dating, or a relative's cancer treatment.

- Once you have a list of topics, focus on one that you believe has had the greatest impact on you personally. Generate a list of possible research questions concerning the topic that, if answered, would offer you a greater understanding of it. Examples: What triggers most people to try their first drink of alcohol? What types of therapies are most effective for working with children on the autism spectrum? What kinds of technology actually aid in student learning?

- Now propose a hypothesis, or testable proposition, as an answer to one of the research questions you've posed. For example, if your research question is "What triggers most people to try their first drink of alcohol?" then your hypothesis might be "Peer pressure generally causes most people to try their first drink of alcohol, especially for those who try their first drink before reaching the legal drinking age."

Methods

Research in the diverse fields of the social sciences is, as you probably suspect, quite varied, and social scientists collect data to answer their research questions or test their hypotheses in several different ways. Their choice of methods is directly influenced by the kinds of questions they ask in any particular instance, as well as by their own disciplinary backgrounds. In his Insider's View, Kevin Rathunde highlights the connection between the kinds of research questions a social scientist asks and the particular methods the researcher uses to answer those questions.

Insider's View
Psychologist Kevin Rathunde on Research Questions

COURTESY OF KEVIN RATHUNDE

"I have strong interests in how people experience their lives and what helps them stay interested, engaged, and on a path of lifelong learning and development. I tend to ask questions about the quality of life and experience. How are students experiencing their time in class? When are they most engaged? How does being interested affect the learning process? How can

parents and teachers create conditions in homes and families that facilitate interest?

"The fields of developmental psychology and educational psychology are especially important to my work. The questions I ask, therefore, are framed the way a developmental or educational psychologist might ask them. Social scientists from other disciplines would probably look at the same topic (i.e., human engagement and interest) in a different way. My daughter is studying anthropology in graduate school. She would probably approach this topic from a cultural perspective. Where I might design a study using questionnaires that are administered in family or school contexts, she might focus on interviews and cultural frameworks that shed light on the meaning and organization of educational institutions. Although my research is primarily quantitative and uses statistical analysis to interpret the results, I have also used a variety of qualitative techniques (i.e., interviews and observations) over the years. A good question is usually worth looking at from multiple perspectives."

We can group most of the research you're likely to encounter in the fields of the social sciences into three possible types: quantitative, qualitative, and mixed methods. Researchers make choices about which types of methods they will employ in any given situation based on the nature of their line of inquiry. A particular research question may very well dictate the methods used to answer that question. If you wanted to determine the number of homeless veterans in a specific city, for instance, then collecting numerical, or quantitative, data would likely suffice to answer that question. However, if you wanted to know what factors affect the rates of homelessness among veterans in your community, then you would need to do more than tally the number of homeless veterans. You would need to collect a different type of data to help construct an answer—perhaps responses to surveys or interview questions.

● **Quantitative Methods**   Quantitative studies include those that rely on collecting numerical data and performing statistical analyses to reveal findings in research. Basic statistical data, like those provided by *means* (averages), *modes* (most often occurring value), and *medians* (middle values), are fundamental to quantitative social science research. More sophisticated statistical procedures commonly used in professional quantitative studies include correlations, chi-square tests, analysis of variance (ANOVA), and multivariate analysis of variance (MANOVA), as well as regression model testing, just to name a few. Not all statistical procedures are appropriate in all situations, however, so researchers must carefully select procedures based on the nature of their data and the kinds of findings they seek. Researchers who engage in advanced statistical procedures as part of their methods are typically highly skilled in such procedures. At the very least, these researchers consult or work in cooperation with statisticians to design their studies and/or to analyze their data.

You may find, in fact, that a team of researchers collaborating on a social science project often includes individuals who are also experienced statisticians. Obviously, we don't expect you to be familiar with the details of statistical procedures, but it's important that you be able to notice when researchers rely on statistical methods to test their hypotheses and to inform their results.

Also, take note of how researchers incorporate discussion of such methods into their writing. In the following example, we've highlighted a few elements in the reporting that you'll want to notice when reading social science studies that make use of statistical procedures:

- **Procedures**   What statistical procedures are used?
- **Variables**   What variables are examined in the procedures?
- **Results**   What do the statistical procedures reveal?
- **Participants**   From whom are the data collected, and how are those individuals chosen?

In their study, Rathunde and Csikszentmihalyi report on the statistical procedures they used to examine different types of schools:

> The first analysis compared the main motivation and quality-of-experience variables across school type (Montessori vs. traditional) and grade level (sixth vs. eighth) using a two-way MANCOVA with parental education, gender, and ethnic background as covariates. Significant differences were found for school context (Wilks's lambda = .84, $F(5, 275) = 10.84, p < .001$), indicating that students in the two school contexts reported differences in motivation and quality of experience. After adjusting for the

Variables examined, participants or populations involved in the study, and statistical procedure employed—MANCOVA, or a multivariate analysis of covariance—are identified.

Results of the statistical procedure are identified.

covariates, the multivariate eta squared indicated that 17 percent of the variance of the dependent variables was associated with the school context factor. The omnibus test for grade level was not significant (Wilks's lambda = .99, $F(5, 275)$ = .68, p = .64) indicating that students in sixth and eighth grade reported similar motivation and quality of experience. Finally, the omnibus test for the interaction of school context x grade level was not significant (Wilks's lambda = .97, $F(5, 275)$ = 2.02, p = .08). None of the multivariate tests for the covariates—parental education, gender, and ethnic background—reached the .05 level. (p. 357)

● **Qualitative Methods**   Qualitative studies generally rely on language, observation, and reporting of individual human experiences to reveal findings in research. Research reports often communicate these methods through the form of a study's results, which rely on in-depth narrative reporting. Methods for collecting data in qualitative studies include interviews, document analysis, surveys, and observations.

We can see examples of these methods put into practice in Barbara Allen's "Environmental Justice, Local Knowledge, and After-Disaster Planning in New Orleans" (2007), published in the academic social science journal *Technology and Society*. In this example, we've highlighted a few elements in the reporting that you'll want to notice when reading qualitative research methods:

- **Method**   What method of data collection is used?
- **Data**   What data are gathered from that method?
- **Results**   What are the results? What explanation do the researchers provide for the data, or what meaning do they find in the data?
- **Participants**   From whom are the data collected, and how are these individuals chosen?

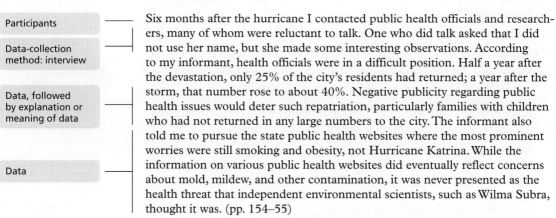

Participants

Data-collection method: interview

Data, followed by explanation or meaning of data

Data

Six months after the hurricane I contacted public health officials and researchers, many of whom were reluctant to talk. One who did talk asked that I did not use her name, but she made some interesting observations. According to my informant, health officials were in a difficult position. Half a year after the devastation, only 25% of the city's residents had returned; a year after the storm, that number rose to about 40%. Negative publicity regarding public health issues would deter such repatriation, particularly families with children who had not returned in any large numbers to the city. The informant also told me to pursue the state public health websites where the most prominent worries were still smoking and obesity, not Hurricane Katrina. While the information on various public health websites did eventually reflect concerns about mold, mildew, and other contamination, it was never presented as the health threat that independent environmental scientists, such as Wilma Subra, thought it was. (pp. 154–55)

. . .

About five months after Hurricane Katrina, I received an e-mail from a high school student living in a rural parish west of New Orleans along the Mississippi River (an area EJ advocates have renamed Cancer Alley). After Hurricane Katrina, an old landfill near her house was opened to receive waste and began emitting noxious odors. She took samples of the "black ooze" from the site and contacted the Louisiana Department of Environmental Quality, only to be told that the landfill was accepting only construction waste, and the smell she described was probably decaying gypsum board. I suspect her story will be repeated many times across south Louisiana as these marginal waste sites receive the debris from homes and businesses ruined by the hurricane. The full environmental impact of Hurricane Katrina's waste and its hastily designated removal sites will not be known for many years. (p. 155)

> Participant

> Explanation or meaning of data

● **Mixed Methods**   Studies that make use of both qualitative and quantitative data-collection techniques are generally referred to as mixed-methodology studies. Rathunde and Csikszentmihalyi's study used mixed methods: the authors report findings from both qualitative and quantitative data. In this excerpt, they share results from qualitative data they collected as they sought to distinguish among the types of educational settings selected for participation in their study:

After verifying that the demographic profile of the two sets of schools was similar, the next step was to determine if the schools differed with respect to the five selection criteria outlined above. We used a variety of qualitative sources to verify contextual differences, including observations by the research staff; teacher and parent interviews; school newsletters, information packets, mission statements, and parent teacher handbooks; summaries from board of education and school council meetings; and a review of class schedules and textbook choices discussed in strategic plans. These sources also provided information about the level of middle grade reform that may or may not have been implemented by the schools and whether the label "traditional" was appropriate. (p. 64)

However, Rathunde and Csikszentmihalyi's central hypothesis, "that students in Montessori middle schools would report more positive perceptions of their school environment and their teachers, more often perceive their classmates as friends, and spend more time in collaborative and/or individual work rather than didactic educational formats such as listening to a lecture" (p. 68), was tested by using quantitative methods:

The main analyses used two-way multivariate analysis of covariance (MANCOVA) with school type (Montessori vs. traditional) and grade level (sixth vs. eighth) as the two factors. Gender, ethnicity, and parental education were covariates in all of the analyses. Overall multivariate F tests (Wilks's lambda) were performed first on related sets of dependent variables. If an overall F test was significant, we performed univariate ANOVAs as follow-up tests to the MANCOVAs. If necessary, post hoc analyses were done using Bonferroni corrections to control for Type I errors. Only students with at least 15 ESM signals were included in the multivariate analyses, and follow-up ANOVAs used students who had valid scores on all of the dependent variables. (p. 68)

● **Addressing Bias**   Because social scientists study people and organizations, their research is considered more valuable when conducted within a framework that minimizes the influence of personal or researcher bias on the study's outcome(s). When possible, social scientists strive for objectivity (in quantitative research) or neutrality (in qualitative research) in their research. This means that researchers undertake all possible measures to reduce the influence of biases on their research. Bias is sometimes inevitable, however, so social science research places a high value on honesty and transparency in the reporting of data. Each of the methods outlined above requires social scientists to engage in rigorous procedures and checks (e.g., ensuring appropriate sample sizes and/ or using multiple forms of qualitative data) to ensure that the influence of any biases is as limited as possible.

The IRB Process and Use of Human Subjects

All research, whether student or faculty initiated and directed, must treat its subjects, or participants, with the greatest of care and consider the ethical implications of all its procedures. Although institutions establish their own systems and procedures for verifying the ethical treatment of subjects, most of these include an **institutional review board (IRB)**, or a committee of individuals whose job is to review research proposals in light of ethical concerns for subjects and applicable laws. Such proposals typically include specific forms of documentation that identify a study's purpose; rigorously detail the research procedures to be followed; evaluate potential risks and rewards of a study, especially for study participants; and ensure (whenever possible) that participants are fully informed about a study and the implications of their participation in it.

We encourage you to learn more about the IRB process at your own institution and, when appropriate, to consider your own research in light of the IRB policies and procedures established for your institution. Many schools maintain informational, educational, and interactive websites. You'll notice similarities in the mission statements of institutional review boards from a number of colleges and universities, as the following examples illustrate:

Duke University: To ensure the protection of human research subjects by conducting scientific and ethical review of research studies while providing leadership and education for the research community

George Washington University: To support [the] research community in the conduct of innovative and ethical research by providing guidance, education, and oversight for the protection of human subjects

Maricopa County Community College District: [T]o review all proposed research involving human subjects to ensure that subjects are treated ethically and that their rights and welfare are adequately protected

Structural Conventions in the Social Sciences

In light of the variety of research methods used by social scientists, it is not surprising that there are also a number of ways social scientists report their research findings. In this section, we turn to strategies of rhetorical analysis that help us examine how scholars in the social sciences communicate their research to one another. Understanding how certain writing conventions support the work of social scientists, we believe, can help foster your understanding of this academic domain more broadly. Recall that in Chapter 6 we introduced a three-part method for analyzing texts by examining the conventions of structure, language, and reference. This section will focus on structural conventions, and the sections that follow will address language and reference. Rather than trying to master the conventions of every type of writing in the social sciences, your goal is to understand the general principles underlying social science writing conventions and to practice applying an analytical framework to any writing assignment you encounter.

Aya Matsuda is a linguist and social science researcher at Arizona State University, where she studies the use of English as an international language, the integration of a "World Englishes" perspective into U.S. education, and the ways bilingual writers negotiate identity. In her Insider's View, Matsuda explains that she learned the conventions of writing as a social scientist, and more particularly as a linguist, "mostly through writing, getting feedback, and revising."

As Matsuda also suggests, reading can be an important part of understanding the writing of a discipline. Furthermore, reading academic writing with a particular focus on the rhetorical elements used is a powerful way to acquire insight into the academic discipline itself, as well as a way to learn the literacy practices that professional writers commonly follow in whatever academic domain you happen to be studying.

Insider's View
Linguist Aya Matsuda on Learning Academic Writing Conventions

COURTESY OF AYA MATSUDA

"In undergraduate and graduate courses, I had writing assignments that are similar to the kind of writing I do now. For those, I wrote (often using the published materials as a model) and got feedback from the professors. Sometimes I had a chance to revise according to those comments. Other times I didn't, but used the comments when I had to do a similar writing assignment in later courses. As I became more advanced in my academic career (starting in graduate school), I started submitting my papers for publication. I would draft my manuscript and then share it with my professors or fellow students (when I was in graduate school) or with my colleagues (now) to get their feedback. I also got comments from reviewers and editors. The process of writing, getting feedback, and revising helped me not only learn about but also learn to follow and negotiate the conventions.

"Reading the kind of writing I needed to do (e.g., journal articles) helped me learn about the conventions, but that alone did not help me learn to follow them. I needed to write and use what I learned in order to feel I had actually added it to my writing repertoire."

IMRaD Format

Structural conventions within the fields of the social sciences can vary quite dramatically, but the structure of a social science report should follow logically from the type of study conducted or the methodological framework (quantitative, qualitative, or mixed methods) it employs. The more quantitative a study is, the more likely its reporting will reflect the conventions for scientific research, using IMRaD (Introduction, Methods, Results, and Discussion) format.

● **Introduction**   The introduction of a social science report establishes the context for a study, providing appropriate background on the issue or topic under scrutiny. The introduction is also where you're likely to find evidence of researchers' review of previous scholarship on a topic. As part of these reviews, researchers typically report what's already known about a phenomenon or what's relevant in the current scholarship for their own research. They may also situate their research goals within some gap in the scholarship—that is, they explain how their research contributes to the growing body of scholarship on the phenomenon under investigation. If a theoretical perspective drives a study, as often occurs in more qualitative studies, then the introduction may also contain an explanation of the central tenets or the parameters of the researchers' theoretical lens. Regardless, an introduction in the social sciences generally builds to a statement of specific purpose for the study. This may take the form of a hypothesis or thesis, or it may appear explicitly as a general statement of the researchers' purpose, perhaps including a presentation of research questions. The introduction to Rathunde and Csikszentmihalyi's study provides an example:

> The difficulties that many young adolescents encounter in middle school have been well documented (Carnegie Council on Adolescent Development 1989, 1995; Eccles et al. 1993; U.S. Department of Education 1991). During this precarious transition from the elementary school years, young adolescents may begin to doubt the value of their academic work and their abilities to succeed (Simmons and Blyth 1987; Wigfield et al. 1991). A central concern of many studies is motivation (Anderman and Maehr 1994); a disturbingly consistent finding associated with middle school is a drop in students' intrinsic motivation to learn (Anderman et al. 1999; Gottfried 1985; Harter et al. 1992).

Provides an introduction to the topic at hand: the problem of motivation for adolescents in middle school. The problem is situated in the scholarship of others.

> Such downward trends in motivation are not inevitable. Over the past decade, several researchers have concluded that the typical learning environment in middle school is often mismatched with adolescents' developmental needs (Eccles et al. 1993). Several large-scale research programs have focused on the qualities of classrooms and school cultures that may enhance student achievement and motivation (Ames 1992; Lipsitz et al. 1997; Maehr and Midgley 1991). School environments that provide a more appropriate developmental fit (e.g., more relevant tasks, student-directed learning, less of an emphasis on grades and competition, more collaboration, etc.) have been shown to enhance students' intrinsic, task motivation (Anderman et al. 1999).

Reviews relevant scholarship: the researchers review previous studies that have bearing on their own aims—addressing the decline in motivation among students.

> The present study explores the issues of developmental fit and young adolescents' quality of experience and motivation by comparing five Montessori middle schools to six "traditional" public middle schools. Although the Montessori educational philosophy is primarily associated with early childhood education, a number of schools have extended its core principles to early adolescent education. These principles are in general agreement with the reform proposals associated with various motivation theories (Anderman et al. 1999; Maehr and Midgley 1991), developmental fit theories (Eccles et al. 1993), as well as insights from various recommendations for middle school reform (e.g., the Carnegie Foundation's "Turning Points" recommendations; see Lipsitz et al. 1997). In addition, the Montessori philosophy is consistent with the theoretical and practical implications of optimal experience (flow) theory (Csikszentmihalyi and Rathunde 1998). The present study places a special emphasis on students' quality of experience in middle school. More specifically, it uses the Experience Sampling Method (ESM) (Csikszentmihalyi and Larson 1987) to compare the school experiences of Montessori middle school students with a comparable sample of public school students in traditional classrooms. (pp. 341–42)

Identifies researchers' particular areas of interest

Although the introductory elements of Rathunde and Csikszentmihalyi's study actually continue for a number of pages, these opening paragraphs reveal common rhetorical moves in social science research reporting: establishing a topic of interest, reviewing the scholarship on that topic, and connecting the current study to the ongoing scholarly conversation on the topic.

● **Methods**   Social science researchers are very particular about the precise reporting of their methods of research. No matter what the type of study (quantitative, qualitative, or mixed methods), researchers are very careful not only to identify the methods used in their research but also to explain why they chose certain ones in light of the goals of their study. Because researchers want to reduce the influence of researcher bias and to provide enough context so others might replicate or confirm their findings, social scientists make sure that their reports thoroughly explain the kinds of data they have collected and the precise procedures they used to collect that data (interviews, document analysis, surveys, etc.). Also, there is often much discussion of the ways the data were interpreted or analyzed (using case studies, narrative analysis, statistical procedures, etc.).

An excerpt from W. Cassidy, K. Brown, and M. Jackson's study on educators and cyberbullying provides an example of the level of detail at which scholars typically report their methods:

Provides highly specific details about data collection methods, and emphasizes researchers' neutral stance

> Each participant chose a pseudonym and was asked a series of 16 in-depth, semi-structured, open-ended questions (Lancy, 2001) and three closed-category questions in a private setting, allowing their views to be voiced in confidence (Cook-Sather, 2002). Each 45- to 60-minute audiotaped interview was conducted by one of the authors, while maintaining a neutral, nonjudgmental stance in regards to the responses (Merriam, 1988).

Provides detailed explanation of procedures used to support the reliability of the study's findings

> Once the interviews were transcribed, each participant was given the opportunity to review the transcript and make changes. The transcripts were then reviewed and re-reviewed in a backward and forward motion (Glaser & Strauss, 1967; McMillan & Schumacher, 1997) separately by two of the three researchers to determine commonalities and differences among responses as well as any salient themes that surfaced due to the frequency or the strength of the response (Miles & Huberman, 1994). Each researcher's analysis was then compared with the other's to jointly determine emergent themes and perceptions.

Connects the research to the development of theory

> The dominant themes were then reviewed in relation to the existing literature on educators' perceptions and responses to cyberbullying. The approach taken was "bottom-up," to inductively uncover themes and contribute to theory, rather than apply existing theory as a predetermined frame for analysis (Miles & Huberman, 1994). (p. 523)

You'll notice that the researchers do not simply indicate that the data were collected via interviews. Rather, they go to some lengths to describe the kinds of interviews they conducted and how they were conducted, as well as how those interviews were analyzed. This level of detail supports the writers' ethos, and it further highlights their commitment to reducing bias in their research. Similar studies might also report the interview questions at the end of the report in an appendix. Seeing the actual questions helps readers interpret the results on their own and also provides enough detail for readers to replicate the study or test the hypothesis with a different population, should they desire to do so. Readers of the study need to understand as precisely as possible the methods for data collection and analysis.

● **Results**   There can be much variety in the ways social science reports present the results, or findings, of a study. You may encounter a section identified by the title "Results," especially if the study follows IMRaD format, but you may not find that heading at all. Instead, researchers often present their results by using headings and subheadings that reflect their actual findings. As examples, we provide here excerpts from two studies: (1) Rathunde and Csikszentmihalyi's 2005 study on middle school student motivation, and (2) Cassidy, Brown, and Jackson's 2012 study on educators and cyberbullying.

In the Results section of their report, Rathunde and Csikszentmihalyi provide findings from their study under the subheading "Motivation and Quality-of-Experience Differences: Nonacademic Activities at School." Those results read in part:

> Follow-up ANCOVAs were done on each of the five ESM variables. Table 3 summarizes the means, standard errors, and significance levels for each of the variables.

Table 3

Univariate F-Tests for Quality of Experience in Nonacademic Activities at School by School Context

| | School Context | | | |
	Montessori ($N = 131$)	Traditional ($N = 150$)	F-test	p
ESM Measure				
Flow (%)	11.0 (1.7)	17.3 (1.6)	7.19	.008
Affect	.32 (.05)	.14 (.05)	6.87	.009
Potency	.22 (.05)	.16 (.05)	1.90	NS
Motivation	−.03 (.05)	−.12 (.05)	1.70	NS
Salience	−.38 (.04)	−.19 (.04)	11.14	.001

Means are z-scores (i.e., zero is average experience for the entire week) and are adjusted for the covariates gender, parental education, and ethnicity. Standard errors appear in parentheses. Flow percent indicates the amount of time students indicated above-average challenge and skill while doing nonacademic activities.

Result — Consistent with the relaxed nature of the activities, students in both school contexts reported higher levels of affect, potency, and intrinsic motivation in nonacademic activities, as well as lower levels of salience and flow (see table 2).

Result — In contrast to the findings for academic work, students in both groups reported similar levels of intrinsic motivation and potency. In addition, students in the traditional group reported significantly more flow in nonacademic activities,

Result — although the overall percentage of flow was low. Similar to the findings for academic activities, the Montessori students reported better overall affect,

Result — and despite the fact that levels of salience were below average for both student groups, the traditional students reported that their activities were more important. (pp. 360–61)

You'll notice that in this section, the researchers remain focused on reporting their findings. They do not, at this point, go into great detail about what those findings mean or what the implications are.

Cassidy, Brown, and Jackson also report their findings in a Results section, and they subdivide their findings into a number of areas of inquiry (identified in the subheadings) examined as part of their larger study. Only the results are presented at this point in the article; they are not yet interpreted:

RESULTS

Familiarity with technology

Results — Despite the district's emphasis on technology, the educators (except for two younger teachers and one vice-principal) indicated that they were not very familiar with chat rooms and blogs, were moderately familiar with YouTube and Facebook and were most familiar with the older forms of communication—email and cellular phones.

Cyberbullying policies

Result — We asked respondents about specific cyberbullying policies in place at their school and their perceived effectiveness. Despite the district's priorities around technology, neither the school district nor either school had a specific cyberbullying policy; instead educators were supposed to follow the district's bullying policy. When VP17-A was asked if the district's bullying handbook effectively addressed the problem of cyberbullying, he replied: "It effectively addresses the people that are identified as bullying others [but] it doesn't address the educational side of it . . . about what is proper use of the Internet as a tool."

Result — P14-B wanted to see a new policy put in place that was flexible enough to deal with the different situations as they arose. VP19-B thought that a cyberbullying policy should be separate from a face-to-face bullying policy since the impact on students is different. He also felt that there should be a concerted district policy regarding "risk assessment in which you have a team that's trained at determining the level of threat and it should be taken very seriously whether it's a phone threat, a verbal threat, or a cyber threat." Participants indicated that they had not considered the idea of a separate cyberbullying policy before the interview, with several commenting that they now saw it as important. (pp. 524, 526–27)

Visual Representations of Data The Results section of a report may also provide data sets in the form of tables and/or figures. Figures may appear as photos, images, charts, or graphs. When you find visual representations of data in texts, it's important that you pause to consider these elements carefully. Researchers typically use *tables* when they want to make data sets, or raw data, available for comparisons. These tables, such as the one Rathunde and Csikszentmihalyi include in their study of middle school students' motivation, present variables in columns and rows.

In this instance, the "background variable[s]" used to describe the student populations are listed in the column, and the rows compare values from two "school context[s]," Montessori and traditional schools. The table's title reveals its overall purpose: to compare "Montessori and Traditional Middle School Samples on Various Background Variables." Rathunde and Csikszentmihalyi describe the contents of their table this way:

> Table 1 summarizes this comparison. The ethnic diversity of the samples was almost identical. Both shared similar advantages in terms of high parental

Table 1

Comparison of Montessori and Traditional Middle School Samples on Various Background Variables

Background Variable	School Context	
	Montessori	Traditional
Ethnicity (%):		
European American	72.6	74.9
Asian American	10.2	7.8
Latino	1.9	3.4
African American	12.7	12.6
Other	2.6	1.2
Parental education	5.5	5.4
Home resources	29.6	29.5
School-related:		
Parental discussion	2.41	2.49
Parental involvement	2.11	2.10
Parental monitoring	1.69	1.66
Number of siblings	1.8	2.0
Mother employment (%)	71.6	74.1
Father employment (%)	83.7	88.1
Intact (two-parent) family (%)	81.0	84.0
Grade point average	1.97	1.93

Note. None of the differences reported in the table were statistically significant.

education (baccalaureate degree or higher), high rates of two-parent families, high family resources, and other indicators of strong parental involvement in their children's education. Although only one-third of the Montessori students received grades, *t*-tests indicated that both samples were comprised of good students (i.e., they received about half As and half Bs). (p. 356)

Researchers use *figures* when they want to highlight the results of research or the derived relationships between data sets or variables. *Graphs*, a type of figure, contain two axes—the horizontal x-axis and the vertical y-axis. The relationship between variables on these axes is indicated by the cells of overlap between the two axes in the body of the figure. Conventionally, the *x-axis* identifies an independent variable, or a variable that can be controlled; by contrast, the *y-axis* identifies the dependent variable, which is dependent on the variable identified in the x-axis. Here's a figure from Rathunde and Csikszentmihalyi's study:

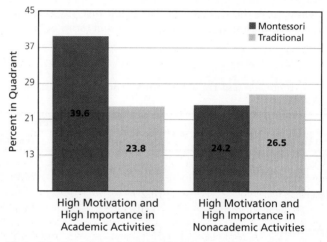

Figure 8.1 Percentage of undivided interest in academic and nonacademic activities

As with tables, the titles of figures reveal their overall purpose. In this case, the researchers demonstrate the "[p]ercentage of undivided interest in academic and nonacademic activities." Reading the figure, in this instance, comes down to identifying the percentage of "undivided interest" that students in Montessori and traditional middle schools (revealed in different colors, as the legend indicates) expressed in the quadrants "High Motivation and High Importance in Academic Activities" and "High Motivation and High Importance in Nonacademic Activities." Colored cells in the body of the graph reveal the percentages. Rathunde and Csikszentmihalyi note about this figure: "[O]n the key variable undivided interest, students in the traditional group reported a slightly higher percent of high-motivation and high-importance activities; this noteworthy change from academic activities is illustrated in figure 2" (p. 361).

Whenever you see charts or figures in social science reports, you should take time to do the following:

- Study the titles carefully.
- Look for legends, which provide keys to understanding elements in the chart or figure.
- Identify the factors or variables represented, and understand how those factors or variables are related, as well as how they are measured.
- Look closely for possible patterns.

● Discussion   The Discussion section of a social science report explains the significance of the findings in light of the study's aims. This is also where researchers reflect on the study more generally, highlight ways their study could be improved (often called "limitations"), and/or identify areas of further research that the study has brought to light. Researchers sometimes lay out the groundwork for continued research, based on their contribution, as part of the ongoing scholarly conversation on the topic or issue at hand. A few excerpts from the Discussion section of Rathunde and Csikszentmihalyi's study reveal their adherence to these conventional expectations:

DISCUSSION

Given the well-documented decline in students' motivation and engagement in middle school, and the ongoing emphasis on middle school reform (Cross 1990; Eccles et al. 1993; Lipsitz et al. 1997), an increasing number of studies have explored how to change classroom practices and school cultures in ways that provide a healthier fit for young adolescents (Ames 1992; Eccles et al. 1993; Felner et al. 1997; Maehr and Midgley 1991). The present study adds to this area of research by comparing the motivation and quality of experience of students from five Montessori middle schools and six traditional middle schools. (p. 362)

Reveals why their study is important to the ongoing conversation on this topic

. . .

Results from the study showed that while engaged in academic work at school, Montessori students reported higher affect, potency (i.e., feeling alert and energetic), intrinsic motivation (i.e., enjoyment, interest), and flow experience than students from traditional middle schools. (p. 363)

Discusses important findings

. . .

The present study did not look at whether such experiential differences translated into positive achievement and behavioral outcomes for the students. This is an important topic for future research. (p. 363)

Identifies limitations in the study and an area for possible future research

Following are some additional structural conventions to consider when you are reading or writing in the fields of the social sciences.

Abstracts and Other Structural Conventions

● **Abstracts**   Another structural feature of reports in the social sciences is the abstract. Abstracts typically follow the title of the report and the identification of the researchers. They provide a brief overview of the study, explaining the topic or issue under study, the specific purpose of the study and its methods, and offering a concise statement of the results. These elements are usually summarized in a few sentences. Abstracts can be useful to other researchers who want to determine if a study might prove helpful for their own work or if the methods might inform their own research purposes. Abstracts thus serve to promote collaboration among researchers. Though abstracts appear at the beginning of research reports, they're typically written after both the study and the research report are otherwise completed. Abstracts reduce the most important parts of a study into a compact space.

The following example from Rathunde and Csikszentmihalyi illustrates a number of the conventions of abstracts:

The study's purpose is identified.

Methods are briefly outlined.

Results are provided.

Implications of the research findings are noted.

This study compared the motivation and quality of experience of demographically matched students from Montessori and traditional middle school programs. Approximately 290 students responded to the Experience Sampling Method (ESM) and filled out questionnaires. Multivariate analyses showed that the Montessori students reported greater affect, potency (i.e., feeling energetic), intrinsic motivation, flow experience, and undivided interest (i.e., the combination of high intrinsic motivation and high salience or importance) while engaged in academic activities at school. The traditional middle school students reported higher salience while doing academic work; however, such responses were often accompanied by low intrinsic motivation. When engaged in informal, nonacademic activities, the students in both school contexts reported similar experiences. These results are discussed in terms of current thought on motivation in education and middle school reform.

● **Conclusion**   On occasion, researchers separate out coverage of the implications of their findings (as part of a Discussion section) from other elements in the Discussion. When this occurs, these researchers typically construct a separate Conclusion section in which they address conventional content coverage of their study's limitations, as well as their findings' implications for future research.

● **Acknowledgments**   Acknowledgment sections sometimes appear at the end of social science reports. Usually very brief, they offer a quick word of thanks to organizations and/or individuals who have helped to fund a study, collect data, review the study, or provide another form of assistance during the production of the study. This section can be particularly telling if you're interested in the source of a researcher's funding.

● **Appendices**   Social science research reports sometimes end with one or more appendices. Items here are often referenced within the body of the report itself, as appropriate. These items may include additional data sets, calculations, interview questions, diagrams, and images. The materials typically offer context or support for discussions that occur in the body of a research report.

● **Titles**   Research reports in the social sciences, as in the natural sciences, tend to have rather straightforward titles that are concise and that contain key words highlighting important components of the study. Titles in the social sciences tend not to be creative or rhetorical, although there is a greater tendency toward creativity in titles in qualitative studies, which are more typically language driven than numerically driven. The title of Barbara Allen's study reported in the academic journal *Technology in Society*, for instance, identifies the central issues her study examined as well as the study location: "Environmental Justice, Local Knowledge, and After-Disaster Planning in New Orleans." Similarly, the title of Rathunde and Csikszentmihalyi's article is concise in its identification of the study's purpose: "Middle School Students' Motivation and Quality of Experience: A Comparison of Montessori and Traditional School Environments."

Connect 8.4   Observing Structural Features in the Social Sciences

Although we've discussed a number of structural expectations for reports in the social sciences, we'd like to stress again that these expectations are conventional. As such, you'll likely encounter studies in the social sciences that rely on only a few of these structural features or that alter the conventional expectations in light of the researchers' particular aims. Find a scholarly article from the social sciences, either from Part Three or your own research, and examine it in terms of these structural features. If the article deviates from the conventions we've described, what might be the writers' reasons for any deviations?

- **IMRaD Format**   Does the report have a section labeled "Introduction" that establishes the context for the study and offers a review of the literature? Is there a "Methods" section that thoroughly explains the kinds of data the researchers have collected and the precise procedures they used? Are "Results" discussed and data presented? Is there a "Discussion" section that explains the significance of the researchers' findings?

- **Abstract**   Does the report begin with a brief summary of the study?

- **Title**   Does the title contain key words that highlight important components of the study?

Language Conventions in the Social Sciences

As with structural conventions, the way social scientists use language can vary widely with respect to differing audiences and/or genres. Nevertheless, we can explore several language-level conventional expectations for writing in the social sciences. In the following sections, we consider the use of both active and passive voice, as well as the use of hedging (or hedge words) to limit the scope and applicability of assertions.

Active and Passive Voice

Many students have had the experience of receiving a graded paper back from an English teacher in high school and discovering that a sentence or two was marked for awkward or inappropriate use of the passive voice. This does not mean that the passive voice is always to be avoided. As we discussed in Chapter 7, writers in English and other fields of the humanities often prefer the active voice, but writers in the social sciences and natural sciences often prefer the passive voice, and with good purpose.

To review, in the **active voice**, the subject of the sentence is the agent—the person or thing doing the action. By contrast, in the **passive voice**, the subject of the sentence has something done to them by an agent. The agent is either omitted or downplayed.

You may wonder why anyone would want to remove altogether the actor/agent from a sentence. The passive voice is often preferable in writing in the social sciences and natural sciences because it can foster a sense that researchers are acting objectively or with neutrality. This does not mean that natural or social scientists are averse to the active voice. However, in particular instances, the passive voice can go a long way toward supporting an ethos of objectivity, and its use appears most commonly in the Methods section of social science reports. Consider these two sentences that might appear in the Methods section of a hypothetical social science report:

Active Voice	We asked participants to identify the factors that most influenced their decision.
Passive Voice	Participants were asked to identify the factors that most influenced their decision.

In the example above, the action is "asking" and the agents are the researchers, "we." The passive voice construction deemphasizes the researchers conducting the study. In this way, the researchers maintain more of a sense of objectivity or neutrality and keep the focus on the study's subjects.

Hedging

Another language feature common to writing in the social sciences is **hedging**—limiting a claim by conditions or exceptions rather than making a definitive statement. Hedging typically occurs when researchers want to make a claim or propose an explanation but also want to be extremely careful not to overstep the scope of their findings based on their actual data set. Consider the following sentences:

Participants seemed to be anxious about sharing their feelings on the topic.

Participants were anxious about sharing their feelings on the topic.

When you compare the two, you'll notice that the first sentence "hedges" against making a broad or sweeping claim about the participants. The use of *seemed to be* is a hedge against overstepping, or saying something that may or may not be absolutely true in every case. Other words or phrases that are often used to hedge include the following, just to name a few:

apparently	perhaps
it appears that	possibly
likely	probably
might	some
partially	sometimes

Considering that social scientists make claims about human behavior, and that participants in a study may or may not agree with the conclusions, it's perhaps not surprising that writers in these fields often make use of hedging.

Connect 8.5   **Observing Language Features in the Social Sciences**

Continue your examination of the article you selected for Connect 8.4 using the questions below as a guide. If the article deviates from the conventions we've described, what might be the writers' reasons?

- **Voice**   Is the voice of the text primarily active or passive?

- **Hedging**   Is there evidence of hedging? That is, do the researchers limit claims about human behavior by conditions or exceptions rather than making definitive statements?

Reference Conventions in the Social Sciences

Scholars in the social sciences cite the work of others when establishing a context for their own research. Their use of sources establishes that they are aware of the latest research and thinking in the area of their own research, and it indicates that they are advancing the conversation around this research area. Most scholars in the social sciences follow the documentation style of the American

Psychological Association (APA) when crediting their sources. The values of the social sciences are reflected in this citation system, as we will explain.

Scholars use the APA method for documenting sources that are paraphrased, summarized, or cited as part of their reports. In APA style, in-text citations not only include the author's last name but also provide the year of publication. Page numbers are included for direct quotations, but more often social science writers paraphrase information, so the use of page numbers is infrequent. Full publication data for the sources is provided in the References section at the end of the paper, in a list alphabetically organized by author.

We can compare APA in-text citations to the MLA documentation system described in Chapter 6 through the following examples:

MLA A recent study of slave narratives and contemporary events "links the current use of visual technologies and biometrics in racial profiling to the surveillance of enslaved people in the nineteenth century" (Ross 300).

Through an examination of slave narratives and contemporary events, Ross argues that the "persistence of racial hypervisibility links the current use of visual technologies and biometrics in racial profiling to the surveillance of enslaved people in the nineteenth century" (300).

APA The study reports that individuals who engage in perspective taking are more likely to benefit from feedback than those who do not (Sherf and Morrison, 2020).

Sherf and Morrison (2020) report that individuals who engage in perspective taking are more likely to benefit from feedback than those who do not.

Although these examples by no means illustrate all the differences between MLA and APA styles of documentation, they do highlight the elevated importance that social science fields place on the year of a source's publication. Why? Imagine that you're reading a sociological study conducted in 2020 that examines the use of tobacco products among teenagers. The study references the finding of a similar study from 1990. By seeing the date of the referenced study in the in-text citation, readers can quickly consider the usefulness of the 1990 study for the one being reported on. Social scientists value recency, or the most current data possible, and their documentation requirements reflect this preference.

Another distinction that we've noted is that social scientists quote researchers in other fields far less frequently than scholars in the humanities do. Why is this so? For humanist scholars, language is of the utmost importance, and how someone conveys an idea can seem almost inseparable from the idea being conveyed. Additionally, for humanists, language is often the "unit of measure"—that is, *how* someone says something (like a novelist or a poet) is actually *what* is being studied. Typically, this is not the case for social science researchers (with the exception of fields such as linguistics and communication, although they primarily address how study participants say something and not how prior research reported its findings). Instead, social scientists tend to be much more interested in other researchers' methodology and findings than they are in the language through which those methods or finding are conveyed. As a result, social scientists are more likely to summarize or paraphrase source materials than to quote them directly.

For an example of papers in APA format, see Insider Example: Student Literature Review (pp. 190–98) and Insider Example: Student Theory Response Paper (pp. 201–9). For a discussion of the elements of citations and References lists, see "American Psychological Association (APA) Style" in the Appendix.

Connect 8.6   **Observing Reference Features in the Social Sciences**

Conclude your examination of the article you selected for Connect 8.4, using the questions below as a guide:

- **Engagement with Other Scholars**   Does the writer refer to other scholars' words or ideas? If so, in what ways? Are other scholars' words or ideas used to support the writer's argument, or do they serve to contrast with what the writer has to say? Does the writer quote directly from other writers?

- **Documentation**   Look closely at examples of how the writer cites the work of other scholars. What form of documentation applies? What type of information is valued?

Genres: Literature Review

Scholars in the social sciences share the results of their research in various ways. They might, for instance, compose a talk for a conference or publish a research report in a journal or a book. In the sections that follow, you'll have the opportunity to analyze and practice several common genres that you're likely to encounter in social sciences courses, beginning with the literature review.

A *literature review* (also referred to as a *review of scholarship*) is an analysis of published resources related to a specific topic. It is not a "review" in the sense of a critique (as in a movie review) but rather as an assessment of the current state of scholarship. The literature review is one of the most common genres you will encounter in academic writing. Though the genre occurs quite frequently in the social sciences, you can find evidence of reviews of scholarly literature in virtually every academic field—including the humanities, the natural sciences, and applied fields. It is so common because all scholars build on the work of others.

What Is the Rhetorical Context for This Genre?

Students and researchers may conduct a review of scholarship simply to establish what research has already been conducted on a topic, or the review may make a case for how new research can fill in gaps or advance knowledge about a topic. In the former situation, the resulting literature review may appear as a freestanding piece of writing; in the latter, a briefer review of scholarship may be embedded at the start (usually in the introduction) of a research study. In fact, most published scholarly articles include a review of literature in the introduction. For an example, see the Introduction to Mihaly Csikszentmihalyi and Kevin Rathunde's report within the discussion of IMRaD format on page 173.

Besides serving as a means to identify a gap in the scholarship or a place for new scholarship, a literature review helps to establish researchers' credibility by demonstrating their awareness of what has been discovered about a particular topic or issue. It further respectfully acknowledges the hard work of others within the community of scholarship. Equally important, the literature review illustrates how previous studies interrelate. A good literature review may examine how prior research is similar and different, or it may suggest how a group of researchers' work developed over several years and how scholars have advanced the work of others.

Strategies for Writing a Literature Review

● **Narrow the focus of your topic and determine the scope of your research.** The scope of a freestanding literature review can vary greatly, depending on the knowledge and level of interest of the investigator conducting the review. For instance, you may have very little knowledge about autism, so your review of the scholarship might be aimed at learning about various aspects of the condition and issues related to it. If this is the case, your research would cast a pretty wide net. However, let's say you're quite familiar with certain critical aspects of issues related to autism and are interested in one aspect in particular—for example, the best therapies for addressing autism in young children. If this is the case, then you could conduct a review of scholarship with a more focused purpose, narrowing your net to only the studies that address your specific interest.

Regardless of the scope of your research interest, literature reviews should begin with a clear sense of your topic. One way to narrow the focus of your topic is by proposing one or more research questions about it (*What are researchers studying with regard to autism?*) or a narrower one (*What are the best therapies for addressing autism in young children?*). (See Chapter 5 for more support for crafting such research questions.)

● **Conduct your search for relevant studies.** Once you've clearly established your topic, the next step is to conduct your research. The research you discover and choose to read, which may be quite substantial for a literature review, is chosen according to the scope of your research interest. (For help in narrowing a search based on key terms in your research question, see Chapter 5.) As you search for and review possible sources, pay particular attention to the *abstracts* of studies, as they may help you quickly decide if a study is right for your purposes. And unless your review of scholarship targets the tracing of a particular thread of research across a range of years, you should probably focus on the most current research available.

● **Organize your sources.** After you've examined and gathered a range of source materials, determine the best way to keep track of the ideas you discover. Many students find this is a good time to produce an annotated bibliography as a first step in creating a literature review. (See Chapter 5 for more help on constructing annotated bibliographies.)

Another useful strategy for organizing your sources is a source synthesis chart. We recommend this as a way to visualize the areas of overlap in your research, whether for a broad focus (*What are researchers studying with regard to autism?*) or a more narrow one (*What are the best therapies for addressing autism in young children?*). Here's an abbreviated example of a source synthesis chart for a broad review of scholarship on autism:

	Topics We Expect to Emerge in Scholarship			
Authors of Study	*Issues of Diagnosis*	*Treatments*	*Debate over Causes*	*Wider Familial Effects*
Solomon et al. (2012)	pp. 252–55 Notes: emphasizes problems families face with diagnosis	pp. 257–60 Notes: examines and proposes strategies for family therapists	p. 253 Notes: acknowledges a series of possible contributing factors	
Vanderborght et al. (2012)		pp. 359–67 (results) Notes: examines use of robot for storytelling		
Grindle et al. (2012)		pp. 208–313 (results) Notes: school-based behavioral intervention program (ABA)		p. 229 Notes: home-based therapy programs
Lilley (2011)	pp. 135–37 Notes: explores the roles of mothers in diagnosis processes	pp. 143–51 Notes: explores rationales and lived experiences of ABA and non-ABA supporters		

In this case, the studies that we read are named in the column under "Authors of Study." The topics or issues that we anticipated would emerge from our review of the sources are shown in the top row. Based on our reading of a limited number of studies, four at this point, we can already discern a couple of areas of overlap in the scholarship: the diagnosis of autism in children and intervention programs for children with autism. We can tell which researchers talked about what issues at any given time because we've noted the areas (by page number, along with some detail) where they addressed these issues. The empty cells in the synthesis chart reveal that our review of the sources, thus far at least, suggests there is less concern for those topics. We should note, however, that our review of sources is far from exhaustive. If you're able to create a visual representation of your research such as this one, then you're well on your way to creating a successful literature review. Keep in mind that the more detailed you can make your synthesis chart, the easier your process may be moving forward.

● **Synthesize your sources.**   Synthesizing sources is the process of identifying and describing the relationships between and among researchers' ideas or approaches. What trends emerge? Does the Grindle et al. study say something similar to the Lilley study about behavioral interventions? Something different? Do they share methods? Do they approach the issue of behavioral interventions similarly or differently? Defining the relationships between the studies and making these relationships explicit is critically important to your success. As you read the sources, you'll likely engage in an internal process of comparing and contrasting the researchers' ideas. You might even recognize similarities and differences in the researchers' approaches to the topic. Many of these ideas will probably be reflected in your synthesis chart, and you might consider color-coding (or highlighting in different colors) various cells to indicate types of relationships among the researchers you note.

A quick review of the abstract to "The Experience of Infertility: A Review of Recent Literature," a freestanding literature review published in the academic journal *Sociology of Health and Illness*, demonstrates the areas of synthesis that emerged from the professionals' examination of recent research on infertility:

About 10 years ago Greil published a review and critique of the literature on the socio-psychological impact of infertility. He found at the time that most scholars treated infertility as a medical condition with psychological consequences rather than as a socially constructed reality. This article examines research published since the last review. More studies now place infertility within larger social contexts and social scientific frameworks, although clinical emphases persist. Methodological problems remain, but important improvements are also evident. We identify two vigorous research traditions in the social scientific study of infertility. One tradition uses primarily quantitative techniques to study clinic patients in order to improve service delivery and to

Four synthesis points: (1) more recent studies approach the topic of infertility differently; (2) there remains a focus on examining infertility from a clinical viewpoint; (3) there are still questions about research methods, but there have also been "important improvements" in methods; (4) two trends emerged from these scholars' review of the current research.

assess the need for psychological counseling. The other tradition uses primarily qualitative research to capture the experiences of infertile people in a sociocultural context. We conclude that more attention is now being paid to the ways in which the experience of infertility is shaped by social context. We call for continued progress in the development of a distinctly sociological approach to infertility and for the continued integration of the two research traditions identified here.

Presents conclusions reached as a result of the literature review project

Another example, this one a brief excerpt from the introduction to Csikszentmihalyi and Hunter's "Happiness in Everyday Life: The Uses of Experience Sampling," demonstrates the kind of synthesis that typically appears in reviews of scholarship when they're embedded as part of a larger study:

> Cross-national comparisons suggest that macro-social conditions such as extreme poverty, war, and social injustice are all obstacles to happiness (Inglehart & Klingemann, 2000; Veenhoven, 1995). Chance events like personal tragedies, illness, or sudden strokes of good fortune may drastically affect the level of happiness, but apparently these effects do not last long (Brickman et al., 1978; Diener, 2000).

The writers indicate that there is agreement between researchers: both Inglehart & Klingemann (2000) and Veenhoven (1995) have confirmed the finding in "cross-national comparisons."

Again, the writers indicate there is agreement between researchers: both Brickman et al. (1978) and Diener (2000) have confirmed this finding.

● **Remember SLR as you draft and revise.** The Writing Project that follows suggests a structure for your literature review. Apply what you've learned in this chapter about writing conventions in the social sciences as you draft each section of your literature review. Focus on developing your ideas and supporting your points in the first draft, and then use the revision to further clarify your points and work on style. When you proofread, be sure to check for typos in the source names and dates.

Writing Project   Literature Review

Your goal in this writing project, a freestanding literature review, is to provide an overview of the research that has been conducted on a topic of interest to you.

THE INTRODUCTION

The opening of your literature review should introduce the topic you're exploring and assess the state of the available scholarship on it: What are the current areas of interest? What are the issues or elements related to a particular topic being discussed? Is there general agreement? Are there other clear trends in the scholarship? Are there areas of convergence and divergence?

THE BODY

Paragraphs within the body of your literature review should be organized according to the issues or synthesized areas you're exploring. For example, based on the synthesis chart shown earlier, we might suggest that one of the body sections of a broadly focused review of scholarship on autism should concern issues of diagnosis. We might further reveal, in our topic sentence to that section of the literature review, that we've synthesized the available research in this area and that it seems uniformly to suggest that although many factors have been studied, no credible studies establish a direct link between any contributing factor and the occurrence of autism in children. The rest of that section of our paper would explore the factors that have been examined in the research to support the claim in our topic sentence.

Keep in mind that the body paragraphs should be organized according to a claim about the topic or ideas being explored. They should not be organized merely as successive summaries of the sources. Such an organization does not promote effective synthesis.

THE CONCLUSION

Your conclusion should reiterate your overall assessment of the scholarship. Notify your readers of any gaps you've determined in the scholarship, and consider suggesting areas where future scholarship can make more contributions.

TECHNICAL CONSIDERATIONS

Keep in mind the conventions of writing in the social sciences that you've learned about throughout this chapter. Use APA documentation procedures for in-text documentation of summarized, paraphrased, and cited materials, as well as for the References page at the end of your literature review.

Insider Example
Student Literature Review

William O'Brien, a first-year writing student who had a particular interest in understanding the effects of sleep deprivation, composed the following literature review. As you read, notice how William's text indicates evidence of synthesis both between and among the sources he used to build his project. Notice also that he follows APA style conventions in his review. ▶

Effects of Sleep Deprivation: A Literature Review

William O'Brien

Department of English, North Carolina State University

Comp II: Writing in the Disciplines

Prof. Roy Stamper

October 29, 2015

Effects of Sleep Deprivation: A Literature Review

Everybody knows the feeling of having to struggle through a long day after a night of poor sleep, or sometimes even none at all. You may feel groggy, cloudy, clumsy, or unable to think of simple things. Sometimes you may even feel completely fine but then get angry or frustrated easily. These effects are amplified when poor sleep continues for a long period of time. In a society with an ever-increasing number of distractions, it is becoming harder for many people to get the recommended amount of sleep. Sleep issues plague the majority of the U.S. population in one way or another. The Centers for Disease Control recognizes insufficient sleep as a public health epidemic.

A lot of research is being conducted relating to sleep and sleep deprivation, and for good reason. Most researchers seem to agree that short-term sleep deprivation has purely negative effects on mental functioning in general. However, the particular types of effects caused by poor sleep are still being debated, as are the long-term implications of sleep deprivation. The questions for researchers, then, are under what circumstances do these negative effects begin to show, to what extent do they show, and most significant, what exactly are these negative effects?

Short-Term Effects of Sleep Deprivation

In order to examine the direct and immediate effects of sleep deprivation, numerous researchers rely on experimentation, which allows them to control for variables. Minkel et al. (2012) identified a gap in the research relating to how sleep deprivation affects the stress response (p. 1015). To investigate this connection, the researchers divided healthy adults into two groups. Participants in the first group acted as the control and were allowed a 9-hour sleeping opportunity during the night. The second group was not allowed to

The writer establishes the general topic, sleep deprivation, in the opening paragraph.

SYNTHESIS POINT: scholars agree on the negative effects of short-term sleep deprivation.

SYNTHESIS POINT: questions remain about the effects of long-term sleep deprivation.

Focuses on scholarship that uses experimental studies to examine the effects of short-term sleep deprivation.

sleep at all during that night. The next day, the participants completed stressful mental tasks (primarily math) and were asked to report their stress levels and mood via visual scales (Minkel et al., 2012, pp. 1016–1017). The researchers hypothesized that the participants who did not sleep would have higher stress responses than the rested group, and that sleep loss would increase the stress response in proportion to the severity of the stressor (p. 1016). Their findings, however, showed that while the negative response to stressors was more profound for the sleep-deprived group, the differences in stress response between groups were not significant for the high-stressor condition. Still, the research clearly showed that sleep-deprived people have "significantly greater subjective stress, anger, and anxiety" in response to low-level stressors (p. 1019).

Research by Jugovac and Cavallero (2012) focused on the immediate effects of sleep deprivation on attention through three attentional networks: phasic alerting, covert orienting, and executive control (Jugovac & Cavallero, 2012, p. 115). The study tested 30 young adults using the Attention Network Test (ANT), the Stanford Sleepiness Scale (SSS), and the Global Vigor-Affect Scale (GVA) before and after a 24-hour sleep deprivation period (p. 116). (All participants were subjected to sleep deprivation, because the tests before the sleep deprivation served as the control.) The findings built upon the idea that sleep deprivation decreases vigilance and that it impairs the "executive control" attentional network, while appearing to leave the other components (alerting and orienting) relatively unchanged (pp. 121–122). These findings help explain how one night of missed sleep negatively affects a person's attention, by distinguishing the effects on each of the three particular attentional networks.

Links the two studies reviewed according to their similar focus on short-term effects of sleep deprivation

The writer links this study to the continuing discussion of short-term effects of sleep deprivation but also notes a difference.

Research by Giesbrecht et al. (2013) focused on the effects that short-term sleep deprivation has on dissociation. This research connects sleep deprivation to mental illness rather than just temporarily reduced mental functioning. The researchers used 25 healthy undergraduate students and kept all participants awake throughout one night. Four different scales were used to record their feelings and dissociative reactions while being subjected to two different cognitive tasks (Giesbrecht et al., 2013, pp. 150–152). The cognitive tasks completed before the night of sleep deprivation were used to compare the results of the cognitive tasks completed after the night of sleep deprivation. Although the study was small and the implications are still somewhat unclear, the study showed a clear link between sleep deprivation and dissociative symptoms (pp. 156–158).

This paragraph provides a summative synthesis, or an overview of the findings among the sources reviewed.

It is clear that sleep deprivation negatively affects people in many different ways. These researchers each considered a different type of specific effect, and together they form a wide knowledge base supporting the idea that even a very short-term (24-hour) loss of sleep for a healthy adult may have multiple negative impacts on mental and emotional well-being. These effects include increased anxiety, anger, and stress in response to small stressors (Minkel et al., 2012), inhibited attention—the executive control attentional network more specifically (Jugovac & Cavallero, 2012)—and increased dissociative symptoms (Giesbrecht et al., 2013).

Long-Term Effects of Sleep Deprivation

The writer shifts to an examination of the long-term effects of sleep deprivation and acknowledges a shift in the methods for these studies.

Although the research on short-term effects of sleep deprivation reveals numerous negative consequences, there may be other, less obvious, implications that studies on short-term effect cannot illuminate. In order to better understand these other implications, we must examine research relating to the possible long-term effects of limited sleep. Unfortunately, long-term sleep deprivation experiments do not seem to have been done and are probably not possible (due to ethical reasons and safety reasons, among other factors). A study by Duggan, Reynolds, Kern, and Friedman (2014) pointed out the general lack of previous research into the long-term effects of sleep deprivation, but it examined whether there was a link between average sleep duration during childhood and life-long mortality risk (p. 1195). The researchers analyzed data from 1,145 participants in the Terman Life Cycle Study from the early 1900s, which measured bedtime and wake time along with year of death. The amount of sleep was adjusted by age in order to find the deviations from average sleep time for each age group. The data were also separated by sex (Duggan et al., 2014, pp. 1196–1197). The results showed that, for males, sleeping either more or less than the regular amount of time for each age group correlated with an increased life-long mortality risk (p. 1199). Strangely, this connection was not present for females. For males, however, this is a very important finding. Since we can surmise that the childhood sleep patterns are independent of and unrelated to any underlying health issues that ultimately cause the deaths later on in life, it is more reasonable to assume causation rather than simply correlation. Thus, the pattern that emerged may demonstrate that too little, or too much, sleep during childhood can cause physiological issues, leading to death earlier in life, reaffirming the importance of sleep for well-being.

While this study examined the relationship between sleep duration and death, a study by Kelly and El-Sheikh (2014) examined the relationship between sleep and a slightly less serious, but still very important, subject: the adjustment and development of children in school over a

> Establishes one of the study's central findings related to long-term effects of sleep deprivation.

period of time. The study followed 176 third grade children (this number dropped to 113 by the end of the study) as they progressed through school for five years, recording sleep patterns and characteristics of adjustment (Kelly & El-Sheikh, 2014, pp. 1137–1139). Sleep was recorded both subjectively through self-reporting and objectively though "actigraphy" in order to assess a large variety of sleep parameters (p. 1137). The study results indicated that reduced sleep time and poorer-quality sleep are risk factors for problems adjusting over time to new situations. The results also indicate that the opposite effect is true, but to a lesser extent (p. 1146).

Provides a summative synthesis that examines relationships between the sources and considers implications of findings

The negative impact of poor sleep on a person's ability to adjust to new situations is likely due to the generally accepted idea that sleep deprivation negatively affects cognitive performance and emotional regulation, as described in the Kelly and El-Sheikh article (2014, pp. 1144–1145). If cognitive performance and emotional regulation are negatively affected by a lack of sleep, then it makes sense that the sleep-deprived child would struggle to adjust over time as compared to a well-rested child. This hypothesis has important implications. It once again affirms the idea that receiving the appropriate amount of quality sleep is very important for developing children. This basic idea does not go against the research by Duggan et al. (2014) in any way; rather, it complements it. The main difference between each study is that the research by Duggan et al. shows that too much sleep can also be related to a greater risk of death earlier in life. Together, both articles provide evidence that deviation from the appropriate amount of sleep causes very negative long-term effects, including, but certainly not limited to, worse adjustment over time (Kelly & El-Sheikh, 2014) and increased mortality rates (Duggan et al., 2014).

Conclusion

This research provides great insight into the short-term and long-term effects of sleep deprivation. Duggan et al. (2014) showed increased mortality rates among people who slept too much as well as too little. This result could use some additional research. Through the analysis of each article, we see just how damaging sleep deprivation can be, even after a short period of time, and thus it is important to seriously consider preventative measures. While sleep issues can manifest themselves in many different ways, especially in legitimate sleep disorders such as insomnia, just the simple act of not allowing oneself to get enough sleep every night can have significant negative effects. Building on this, there seems to be a general lack of discussion on *why* people (who do not have sleep disorders) do not get enough time to sleep. One possible reason is the ever-increasing number of distractions, especially in the form of electronics, that may lead to overstimulation. Another answer may be that high demands placed on students and adults through school and work, respectively, do not give them time to sleep enough. The most probable, yet most generalized, answer, however, is that people simply do not appropriately manage their time in order to get enough sleep. People seem to prioritize everything else ahead of sleeping, thus causing the damaging effects of sleep deprivation to emerge. Regardless, this research is valuable for anyone who wants to live a healthy lifestyle and function at full mental capacity. Sleep deprivation seems to have solely negative consequences; thus, it is in every person's best interests to get a full night of quality sleep.

> Conclusion acknowledges what appears as a gap in the scholarship reviewed.

References

Duggan, K., Reynolds, C., Kern, M., & Friedman, H. (2014). Childhood sleep duration and lifelong mortality risk. *Health Psychology, 33*(10), 1195–1203. https://doi.org/10.1037/hea0000078

Giesbrecht, T., Smeets, T., Leppink, J., Jelicic, M., & Merckelbach, H. (2013). Acute dissociation after one night of sleep loss. *Psychology of Consciousness: Theory, Research, and Practice, 1*(S), 150–159. https://doi.org/10.1037/2326-5523.1.S.150

Jugovac, D., & Cavallero, C. (2012). Twenty-four hours of total sleep deprivation selectively impairs attentional networks. *Experimental Psychology, 59*(3), 115–123. https://doi.org/10.1027/1618-3169/a000133

Kelly, R., & El-Sheikh, M. (2014). Reciprocal relations between children's sleep and their adjustment over time. *Developmental Psychology, 50*(4), 1137–1147. https://doi.org/10.1037/a0034501

Minkel, J., Banks, S., Htaik, O., Moreta, M., Jones, C., McGlinchey, E., Simpson, N., & Dinges, D. (2012). Sleep deprivation and stressors: Evidence for elevated negative affect in response to mild stressors when sleep deprived. *Emotion, 12*(5), 1015–1020. https://doi.org/10.1037/a0026871

Genres: Theory Response Essay

In a theory response essay, students apply a social science theory to personal experiences. They may use a psychological, sociological, or communication theory as a lens through which to explain their own or others' behaviors. Whether they are using elements of Freud's dream theories to help understand their own dreams or using an interpersonal communication theory to understand why people so easily engage with them, the theory they're working with provides the frame for their analysis of some event or action. The theory is the core of any theory response.

What Is the Rhetorical Context for This Genre?

A theory response essay is an academic assignment that helps students learn to think like social scientists. The audience for this assignment is the instructor, and sometimes the audience is peers as well. The assignment has several purposes: (1) it allows students to engage with the fundamental elements of social sciences (theories), (2) it allows students to attend to the basic processes of data collection that are common in the social sciences, and (3) it often is quite engaging for faculty to read and interesting for students to write.

Strategies for Writing a Theory Response Essay

● **Identify a workable theory.**   Precisely because a theory is the core of a theory response essay project, it's crucial that in the beginning stage of such a project, you work with a theory that is actually applicable to the event, action, or phenomenon you want to understand better. You also want to choose a theory that genuinely interests you. Luckily, theories of human behavior and human system interactions abound. If you are not assigned a theory for the project, then consider the places where you might go about locating a workable theory. Textbooks in the social sciences frequently make reference to theories, and numerous academic websites maintain lists and explanations of social science theories. Here are a few categories of theories that students often find interesting:

addiction theories	parenting style theories
birth order theories	stages of grieving theories
friendship theories	

If you're unable to locate a workable theory that's "ready-made" for application to some experience(s), then consider building a theory based on your reading of a social science study. Though this certainly makes completing the assignment challenging, it is not without rewards.

● **Recall and describe events that you could view through the theory's lens.** Regardless of whether you're working with a particular theory or constructing a theory of behavior based on one or more studies, consider making a list of the "moments" or events in your life that the theory might help you understand further. Your next step might be to write out detailed descriptions of those events as you see or remember them. Capture as much detail as you can, especially if you're writing from memory.

● **Conduct research if necessary.**   Some instructors might ask you to collect and analyze the experiences of others. If you're assigned to do this, then you'll need to consider a data-collection method very carefully and ask your instructor if there are specific procedures at your institution that you should follow when collecting data from other people. We recommend, for now, that you think about the methods most commonly associated with qualitative research: observations, interviews, and open-ended surveys. These rich data-producing methods are most likely to provide the level of detail about others' experiences needed to evaluate the elements of your theory.

● **Apply and analyze the theory.**   Whether you are working with your own experiences or others', apply the theory (all of its component parts) to the experiences you've collected to see what it can illuminate: Where does it really help you understand something? Where does it fail to help? How might the theory need to change to account for your or others' experiences?

Writing Project   Theory Response Essay

The goal of this writing project is to apply a theoretical framework from an area of the social sciences to your own experiences, to the experiences of others, or to both. The first step is to choose a theoretical framework that has some relevance to you, providing ample opportunity to reflect on and write about your own experiences in relation to the theory.

THE INTRODUCTION

The introduction to your study should introduce readers to the theory and explain all of its essential elements. You should also be clear about whether you're applying the theory to your own experiences, to the experiences of others, or to both. In light of the work you did applying the theory, formulate a thesis that assesses the value of the theory for helping to understand the "moments," events, or phenomena you studied.

THE BODY

The body can be organized in a number of ways. If your theory has clear stages or elements, then you can explain each one and apply it to relevant parts of your experiences or those of others. If the theory operates in such a way that it's difficult to break into parts or stages or elements, then consider whether or not it's better to have subheadings that identify either (1) the themes that emerged from your application or (2) your research subjects (by pseudonym). In this case, your body sections would be more like case studies. Ultimately, the organization strategy you choose will depend on the nature of the theory you're applying and the kinds of events you apply it to. The body of your project should establish connections among the theory's component elements.

THE CONCLUSION

The conclusion of your study should assert your overall assessment of the theory's usefulness. Reiterate how the theory was useful and how it wasn't. Make recommendations for how it might need to be changed in order to account for the experiences you examined in light of the theory.

TECHNICAL CONSIDERATIONS

Keep in mind the conventions of writing in the social sciences that you've learned about throughout this chapter. Use APA documentation procedures for in-text documentation of summarized, paraphrased, and cited materials, as well as for the References page at the end of your study.

....

Insider Example

Student Theory Response Paper

Matt Kapadia, a first-year writing student, was interested in understanding the ways people rationalize their own successes and failures. In the following paper, he analyzes and evaluates a theory about the social science phenomenon of attribution (as described at changingminds.org) through the lenses of both his own and others' experiences. As you read Matt's paper, pay close attention to the moments when he offers evaluation of the theory. Ask yourself if his evaluation in each instance makes sense to you, based on the evidence he provides. Notice also that he follows APA style conventions in his paper. ▶

Evaluation of the Attribution Theory

Matt Kapadia

Department of English, North Carolina State University

Comp II: Writing in the Disciplines

Dr. Caroline Ruiz

October 29, 2016

2

Evaluation of the Attribution Theory

In an attempt to get a better sense of control, human beings are constantly attributing cause to the events that happen around them (Straker, 2008). Of all the things people attribute causes to, behavior is among the most common. The attribution theory aims to explain how people attribute the causes of their own behaviors compared to the behaviors of those around them. Behaviors can be attributed to both internal and external causes. Internal causes are things that people can control or are part of their personality, whereas external causes are purely circumstantial and people have no control over the resulting events (Straker, 2008). The attribution theory uses these internal and external causes to explain its two major components: the self-serving bias and the fundamental attribution error. The self-serving bias evaluates how we attribute our own behaviors, whereas the fundamental attribution error evaluates how we attribute the behaviors of those around us (Straker, 2008). This paper evaluates how applicable the attribution theory and its components are, using examples from personal experience as well as data collected from others. Based on the findings of this evaluation, I believe the attribution theory holds true on nearly all accounts; however, the category of the self-serving bias might need revision in the specific area dealing with professionals in any field of study or in the case of professional athletes.

Attribution Theory: An Explanation

The foundation of the attribution theory is based in the nature of the causes people attribute behaviors to, whether it be internal or external. A person has no control over an external cause (Straker, 2008). An example would be a student failing a math test because the instructor used the wrong answer key. In this case, the student had no control

> The writer establishes a thesis that includes an evaluation of the theory's usefulness in various contexts.

> In this paragraph and the next two, the writer reviews and exemplifies the component parts of the theory. That is, the writer offers an explanation of the theory, with examples to illustrate points, as appropriate.

over the grade he received, and it did not matter how much he had studied. A bad grade was inevitable. A person can also attribute behavioral causes to internal causes. Internal causes are in complete control of the person distributing the behavior and are typically attributed to part of the individual's personality (Straker, 2008). An example would be a student getting a poor grade on his math test because he is generally lazy and does not study. In this case, the student had complete control of his grade and chose not to study, which resulted in the poor grade. These two causes build up to the two major categories within the attribution theory.

The first major category of the attribution theory is that of self-serving bias. This category explores how people attribute causes to their own behaviors. It essentially states that people are more likely to give themselves the benefit of the doubt. People tend to attribute their poor behaviors to external causes and their good behaviors to internal causes (Straker, 2008). An example would be a student saying he received a poor grade on a test because his instructor does not like him. In this case, the student is attributing his poor behavior, making a poor grade on the test, to the external cause of his instructor not liking him. However, following the logic of the theory, if the student had made a good grade on the test, then he would attribute that behavior to an internal cause such as his own good study habits.

The second category of the attribution theory, the fundamental attribution error, states the opposite of the self-serving bias. The fundamental attribution error talks about how people attribute cause to the behaviors of those around them. It states that people are more likely to attribute others' poor behaviors to internal causes and their good behaviors to external causes (Straker, 2008). An example would be a student saying his friend got a better grade on the math test than him because the instructor likes his friend more. The student jumps to the conclusion that his friend's good grade was due to the external cause of the instructor liking the friend more. Moreover, if his friend had done poorly on the test, the student would most likely attribute the poor grade to an internal factor, such as his friend not studying for tests.

Personal Experiences

A situation from my personal experiences that exemplifies the ideas of the attribution theory is my high school golfing career. For my first two years of high school, I performed relatively poorly on the golf course. My team consistently placed last in tournaments, and I ranked nowhere near the top golfers from neighboring high schools. I blamed my performance on factors such as the wind and flat-out bad luck. At the same time, I attributed my teammates' poor performances to factors such as not practicing hard enough to compete in tournament play. In doing this, I became no better a golfer because I was denying that the true cause of my poor scores was the fact that I was making bad swings and not putting in the hours of work needed to perform at a higher level. I finally recognized this during my junior year of high school. I started to realize that blaming everything but myself was getting me nowhere and that the only way to improve was to take responsibility for my own play. I started practicing in areas where my game needed improvement and putting in hours at the driving range to improve my swing memory. In doing this, I became a much better player; by the time my senior season came around, I was ranked one of the top golfers in my conference and one of the best amateur players in the state of North Carolina. However, my team still did not perform well due to my teammates' performance, which I continued to attribute to their poor practice habits.

This experience reflects the attribution theory in several ways. I displayed self-serving bias in my early years of high

> The writer details a particular personal experience that he'll later analyze through the lens of the theory.

> In this section, the writer analyzes his experiences through the lens of the theory.

school golf. I attributed all of my poor performances to external causes, such as the wind, that I could not control. At the same time, I was displaying the fundamental attribution error in attributing my teammates' poor performances to internal causes such as not practicing hard enough. Throughout my high school golf career, I displayed the ideas of the attribution theory's category of the fundamental attribution error. However, during my junior and senior seasons my attributions moved away from the attribution theory's category of the self-serving bias. I began to attribute my poor performance to internal causes instead of the external causes I had previously blamed for my mishaps.

I believe that this is generally true for any athlete or professional seeking improvement in his or her prospective field. If a person continues to follow the ideas discussed in the category of the self-serving bias, he is not likely to improve at what he is trying to do. If Tiger Woods had constantly attributed his bad play to external causes and not taken responsibility for his actions as internal causes, he would have never become the best golfer in the world. Without attributing his poor behaviors to internal causes, he would have never gained the motivation to put in the hours of work necessary to make him the best. This observation can be applied to any other professional field, not only athletics. Personal improvement is only likely to take place when a person begins to attribute his or her poor behaviors to internal causes. I believe athletes and professionals represent problem areas for the theory of self-serving bias. However, the ideas of the fundamental attribution error generally hold true.

Experiences of Others

To evaluate the attribution theory, I conducted an experiment to test both the fundamental attribution error and the self-serving bias. The test subjects were three friends in the same class at North Carolina State University: MEA101,

The writer provides some insight into his methods for collecting data on the experiences of others.

Introduction to Geology. The students were asked to write down if their grades were good or bad on the first test of the semester ("good" meant they received an 80 or higher on the test, and "bad" meant they received below an 80). After the three students had done this for themselves, they were asked to attribute the grades of the others to a cause. This activity provided a clear sample of data that could test the validity of the self-serving bias and the fundamental attribution error. The reason I chose a group of friends versus a group of random strangers was that when people know each other they are more likely to attribute behavioral causes truthfully, without worrying about hurting anyone's feelings.

For the purposes of this experiment, the test subjects will be addressed as Students X, Y, and Z to keep their names confidential. The results of the experiment were as follows. The first student, Student X, received a "bad" grade on the test and attributed this to the instructor not adequately explaining the information in class and not telling the students everything the test would ultimately cover. However, Students Y and Z seemed to conclude that the reason Student X got a "bad" grade was because he did not study enough and is generally lazy when it comes to college test taking. Student Y received a "good" grade on the test and attributed this to studying hard the night before and to the fact that the test was relatively easy if one studied the notes. Students X and Z seemed to conclude that Student Y is a naturally smart student who usually receives good grades on tests regardless of how much he or she studies. Finally, Student Z received a "bad" grade on the test and attributed this to the instructor not covering the material on the test well enough for students to do well, a similar response to Student X. However, Students X and Y attributed Student Z's poor grade to bad study habits and not taking the class seriously.

In this section, the writer provides the results of his data collection.

In this section, the writer discusses the implications of his findings for his overall evaluation of the theory.

These results tend to prove the ideas of both of the attribution theory's categories. Student X attributed his poor grade to the external cause of the instructor not covering the material well enough, demonstrating the self-serving bias. Students Y and Z attributed Student X's poor grade to the internal cause of Student X not studying hard enough and being a generally lazy college student, exemplifying the ideas of the fundamental attribution error. Student Y attributed her good grade to the internal cause of good study habits, also exemplifying the self-serving bias. However, Students X and Z felt that the reason for Student Y's success was the external cause of being a naturally good student who does well with or without studying, reflecting the ideas of the fundamental attribution error. Student Z's results also hold true to the theory. Student Z attributed his poor grade to the external cause of the instructor not covering the material adequately, a belief shared by Student X. Also holding true to the fundamental attribution error, both Students X and Y attributed Student Z's failure to the internal cause of poor study habits. Based on the findings of this experiment, I can say that both the fundamental attribution error and the self-serving bias hold true on all accounts.

Conclusion

The writer concludes his response paper by reviewing his overall evaluation of the theory in light of his own and others' experiences he analyzed.

Overall, I believe the attribution theory's categories of the self-serving bias and the fundamental attribution error are very applicable to everyday life. Based on the data gathered through personal experiences and the experiences of others through the experiment described in this analysis, I believe the theory holds true in the vast majority of situations where people attribute causes to behaviors and/or actions. The only area needing revisions is the self-serving bias when applied to the specific situations of professionals in a field of study or in the case of professional athletes. In both situations, improvement must occur in order to become a professional, and the only way this is likely to happen is by accepting internal fault for poor behaviors. By accepting internal fault, a person gains the motivation to put in the hours of work necessary to learn and improve at what he or she is trying to do. Without this improvement and learning, the ability to reach the professional level is slim to none. This displays the exact opposite of the attribution ideas that are described in the self-serving bias. With the exception of this small niche of situations that falsify the self-serving bias, the validity of the attribution theory is confirmed on all accounts.

Reference

Straker, D. (2008). *Attribution theory*. Retrieved from changingminds.org: http://changingminds.org/explanations/theories/attribution_theory.htm

Genres: Poster Presentation

A poster presentation is a visual representation of the findings of a research study, and it is a common written genre in the social sciences and natural sciences. Social scientists often organize their posters using IMRaD as an organizing strategy, and they make the poster visually appealing to highlight the findings that might be most interesting to the audience.

What Is the Rhetorical Context for This Genre?

Poster presentations are often designed for professional and academic conferences where multiple people will be presenting the results of research at the same time. The audience is typically other researchers in the same field, although that might differ depending on the type of event at which the poster is being displayed. Often the researcher or research team stand with their poster and answer questions from audience members as they walk around to view the posters. The poster, therefore, is intended as a starting point for conversation, but it also should stand on its own by highlighting important findings.

Strategies for Designing a Poster Presentation

● **Identify important elements of the study.** A poster has limited space, so the first task of the author is to determine what is most important to highlight on the poster. Many researchers will use IMRaD as an organizing frame, so they might include a brief description of the study (Introduction); the research methods used; the results of the study; and the discussion, application, or interpretation of the results. Of these four parts of the IMRaD format, the most attention is usually given to the results in a poster presentation, and they are often presented in a visually appealing way—perhaps through a graph or chart to visually demonstrate the most important findings or a table to compare and contrast more than one group. The most effective poster presentations consider the interests and needs of the specific audience who will be viewing the poster, and the researcher focuses on highlighting those elements.

● **Develop an organizational strategy that is visually appealing.** Successful poster presentations are visually appealing. Specifically, they pay attention to white space, they don't use too many words, they use large font sizes so that the audience can understand the results, and they use visual images and graphics to help the reader quickly interpret what they are reading on the poster. They also consider the layout of the information, keeping in mind that readers tend to start at the top and left-hand side of a poster to find information, working their way down and to the right. Some poster presentations even provide visual cues for readers so they know where to go next in their viewing of the poster (with the use of headings, numbers, or arrows, for example).

● **Consider any requirements from event organizers.** When a poster is being presented at an event, the event organizers typically provide specifications about the size of the poster and how it will be presented. Some questions you might consider are the following:

- Do you need to print the poster on a certain type of material? For example, should it be on posterboard, or on paper? Or will it be displayed digitally?
- What size/dimensions do the event organizers request for your poster?
- Do you need to bring a stand or other materials to display the poster, or will that be provided?
- Will you have a table to provide materials or handouts to those viewing your poster?

In addition to these questions, you will also need to consider how to transport your poster to the event. Make sure you have a plan and give yourself plenty of time to get your poster printed and packed for transportation, should that be applicable.

Writing Project   Poster Presentation

The goal of this writing project is to design a poster that presents the results of research that you have conducted. The poster might present data that you have collected, or it might present findings from a review of literature you have conducted.

THE CONTENT

The content of your poster should include the title of your study, your name, a basic introduction to the study, and major findings. If there are sources that you cite in the content of your poster, you will also want to consider how and where to include references.

VISUAL DESIGN

As you present your findings, consider how to place elements in a visually logical and appealing way. Consider the use of white space on your poster so that your audience is not overwhelmed by the content. What information could be presented visually to help your audience quickly interpret the importance of your findings?

TECHNICAL CONSIDERATIONS

As you design your poster, work in a software program that will allow you to move visual elements around with ease. Many students have found PowerPoint, Google Slides, Keynote, and other slide presentation programs to be the best way to design a poster.

Insider Example

Professional Poster Presentation

Researchers Dana Gierdowski and Susan Miller-Cochran created this poster titled "Diversifying Design: Understanding Multilingual Perceptions of Learning in a Flexible Classroom" for the annual conference of the International Society for the Scholarship of Teaching and Learning. The poster was designed to engage conference attendees in a discussion with the authors about their work on the kinds of writing classroom designs that multilingual students preferred to support their learning.

Diversifying Design: Understanding Multilingual Perceptions of Learning in a Flexible Classroom

Researchers: Dana Gierdowski & Susan Miller-Cochran

The "Flexible" Classroom

- Situated in NCSU's First-Year Writing (FYW) Program
- Designed to engage students more in the writing process
- Designed to give instructors more pedagogical variety
- Outfitted with mobile furnishings, mobile whiteboards, & multiple fixed LCDs
- Student-owned laptop computers used in the space
- Collected data from ESL students in a FYW course

To begin to understand how ESL students responded to the flex room, data were collected that focused on student preferences for room layout and perceptions of their ideal writing classroom.

Methods

Data were collected from nine students in a first-year writing class for ESL writers. The student participants shared their perspectives by completing:

- Interviews about their perceptions of learning in the flex room
- Maps of their "ideal" writing classrooms
- Charrette-style placement of the furnishings in the room

Data were coded for consistency of patterns and themes. Inter-rater reliability was tested with Cohen's Kappa, with a Kappa strength of .805 (very good) for the ideal classroom design and a Kappa strength of .625 (good) for the charrette.

Student	Gender	Age	Native Language
1	F	23	Korean
2	F	19	Mandarin Chinese
3	F	19	Indonesian
4	M	20	Arabic/English
5	M	20	Arabic
6	M	20	French
7	M	21	German
8	M	18	Telugu
9	F	20	Mandarin Chinese

Sample Patterns of Arrangement

Students were given maps of their current classroom and were asked to layout the existing furniture in their preferred arrangement.

"I put them next to each other because I felt that if they were alone in one space they would be too isolated. I didn't feel comfortable when I was sitting alone at one of these tables. I like to be a part of a group and work together." –Student 7

"It's more organized instead of just having a lot of furniture thrown around the room." –Student 3

"The desks would be nearby the LCDs so you can connect to them, maybe we could have something that can connect to the iPad so we don't have to bring a computer. For a 50-minute class, I would rather bring my iPad than a heavy laptop." –Student 3

Sample Conceptual Maps

Students were asked to design an ideal writing classroom if given an unlimited budget.

"The furniture should be easy to move. I think that if you move a group of three or four, you should have tables that when you put them together they become organized into triangle or something." –Student 3

"I'm not sure I like the set-up groups that you always have to sit with and work with. I kind of liked the other class I was in before (with) big tables." –Student 4

"I would like to have a big screen (in the front of the room) for the whole class because everybody's looking at the teacher" –Student 7

Preliminary Results

Placement of the Instructor

- 5 students placed the teacher at the front of the class
- 2 students placed the instructor in the center of the class
- **7 students out of 9 (77%) designed an ideal classroom that remained instructor-centered**

Placement of the Students

- Overall, students placed the fewest furnishings in the quarter of the room with the teacher's computer
- Overall, students placed the highest number of furnishings in the quarter of the room opposite the teacher's computer
- **7 students (77%) placed students in groups in their ideal classrooms**

Student Technology

- 6 students included LCDs in their ideal classrooms
- 3 students indicated that student computers would be provided by the institution
- **6 students included writing technology for students in their ideal classrooms (laptops or desktops)**

Questions for Discussion

- What influence does experience in *prior* learning environments have on student preferences?
- What influence does experience in *current* learning environments have on student preferences?
- How might this type of research impact your own teaching?
- What constraints do you have to work with/around in your own instructional environment?
- If given an unlimited budget, what is the one feature you would like to have in your classroom that you don't currently have?

Relevant Resources

Bechner, R., Bernold, L., Burniston, E., Dail, P., Felder, R., Gastineau, J., et al. (1999). Case study of the physics component of an integrated curriculum. *American Journal of Physics, 67*(S1), S16-S24.

Berner, A. M., Moeller, R. M., & Ball, C. E. (2009). Designing collaborative learning spaces: Where material culture meets mobile writing processes. *Programmatic Perspectives, 1*(2), 139-166.

Boys, J. (2011). *Towards creative learning spaces.* London: Routledge.

Matsuda, P. (2006). The myth of linguistic homogeneity in U.S. college composition. *College English, 68* (6), 637-651.

Mintz, R. M. (2004). The inertia of classroom furniture. Unshackling the classroom. In E. Nagelhout & C. Rutz (Eds.), *Classroom spaces and writing instruction* (pp. 13-28). Cresskill, NJ.

Taylor, S. S. (2009). Effects of studio space on teaching and learning: Preliminary findings from two case studies. *Innovative Higher Education, 33*(4), 217-228.

- **Observation plays a critical role in the social sciences.** The academic fields of the social sciences, including sociology, psychology, anthropology, communication studies, and political science, among others, make observations about human behavior and interactions, as well as the systems and social structures we create to organize the world around us.

- **Social science research rests on theories of human behavior and human systems,** propositions that are used to explain specific phenomena. Social science research contributes to the continual process of refining these theories.

- **Researchers in the social sciences typically establish a hypothesis,** or a testable proposition that provides an answer or predicts an outcome in response to the research question(s) at hand, at the beginning of a research project.

- **Social science researchers must make choices about the types of methods they use** in any research situation, based on the nature of their line of inquiry and the kind of research question(s) they seek to answer. They may use a quantitative, qualitative, or mixed-methods research design to collect data for analysis.

- **Social scientists must guard against bias in their research.** They rely on rigorous procedures and checks (e.g., ensuring appropriate sample sizes and/ or using multiple forms of qualitative data) to ensure that the influence of any biases is as limited as possible.

- **IMRaD format—Introduction, Methods, Results, and Discussion—is a common structure used for the organization of research reports in the social sciences.** Although research reports in the social sciences may appear in any number of forms, much of the scholarship published in these fields appears in the IMRaD format.

- **The passive voice and hedging are uses of *language*** that characterize, for good reason, social scientific writing.

- **APA style is the most common documentation style used for *reference*** in the fields of the social sciences.

- **The genres of the literature review, the theory response paper, and the poster presentation are often produced in the fields of the social sciences.**

9 Reading and Writing in the Natural Sciences

Each of us has likely observed something peculiar in the natural world and asked, "Why does it do that?" or "Why does that happen?" Perhaps you've observed twinkling stars in the night sky and wanted to know why such distant light seems to move and pulse. Or perhaps you've wondered why, as you drive, trees closer to your car appear to rush by much faster than trees in the distance. Maybe you can recall the first time you looked at a living cell under a microscope in a biology course and wondered about the world revealed on the slide.

Scholars who work in the **natural sciences** study observable phenomena in the natural world and search for answers to the questions that spark their interests about these phenomena. Their work contributes to solutions to problems facing individuals and societies, from improving crop yields to the search for a coronavirus vaccine. The disciplines of the natural sciences include a wide array of fields of academic research, from agricultural and life sciences to physical sciences. Examples of disciplines within these fields include biology, botany, zoology, astronomy, physics, chemistry, and geology.

Interdisciplinary research is quite common in the natural sciences. An

ANDREA TSURUMI

interdisciplinary field is an area of study in which different disciplinary perspectives or methods are combined into one. In such instances, methods for data collection often associated with one field may be used within another field of study. Consider biochemistry—a combination of biology and chemistry. In biochemistry, methods often associated with chemistry research are useful in answering questions about living organisms and biological systems. A biochemist may study aspects of a living organism such as blood alkalinity and its impact on liver function.

No matter the specific fields in which scientists work, they all collect, analyze, and explain data. Scientists tend to embrace a shared set of values, and as a result they typically share similar desires about how best to conduct research. The importance of any scientific study and its power to explain a natural phenomenon, then, are largely based on how well a researcher or research team designs and carries out a study in light of the shared values and desires of the community's members.

In this chapter, we describe a process of writing activities involved in scientific research. We present a four-step scientific writing process that maps onto the elements of the scientific method. The process begins with careful observation of natural phenomena and leads to the development of research questions. This step is followed by an investigation that culminates in the reporting or publication of the research. You'll have the opportunity to examine several academic genres and learn the principles underlying genre conventions in the natural sciences.

Research in the Natural Sciences

For most social scientists, observation of natural phenomena is the first step in the process of conducting research. Something in the natural world captures their attention and compels them to pose questions. Some moments of scientific observation are iconic—such as Newton's observation of an apple falling from a tree as inspiration for his theory of gravity.

The search for understanding of natural phenomena can take scientists to many different places, and there is much variety in the ways they engage in research. One aspect that holds this diverse group of disciplines together, though, is a set of common values and procedures used in conducting research.

You're probably already familiar with or at least have heard about the scientific method, a protocol for conducting research in the sciences. The following table illustrates how the elements of the scientific method map onto a scientific writing process:

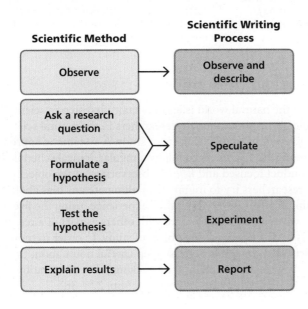

Completing the steps of a research project in a logical order and reporting the results accurately are keys to mastering research and writing in the natural sciences. You must observe and describe an object of study before you can speculate as to what it is or why it does what it does. Once you've described and speculated about a particular phenomenon and posed a research question and a hypothesis about it, then you're positioned well to construct an experiment (if appropriate) and collect data to test whether your hypothesis holds true. When you report the results of your research, you must describe these steps and the data collected accurately and clearly. These research and writing steps build on one another, and we explore each step in more detail moving forward.

Insider's View
Geologist Sian Proctor on the Diversity of Work within a Scientific Discipline

COURTESY OF SIAN PROCTOR

"Geology is an extremely diverse discipline encompassing specialties such as planetary geology, geochemistry, volcanology, paleontology, and more. The goal of a general geologist is to develop understanding of Earth processes such as the formation of mineral or energy resources, the evolution of landscapes, or the cause of natural disasters. Geologists work out in the field, in labs, in educational institutions, and in the corporate world. They collect data, analyze samples, generate maps, and write reports. Geology instructors teach students how to conceptualize all the information and processes mentioned above. It is our job to get students to think like a geologist (if you are teaching majors) or gain an appreciation for the Earth and Earth processes (if you are teaching non-majors)."

Observation and Description

Observation in the natural world is an important first step in scientific inquiry. Beyond simple observation, though, researchers in the natural sciences conduct systematic observations of their objects of study. A systematic approach to observation requires researchers to follow a regular, logical schedule of observation and to conduct focused and *neutral* observations of the object of study. In other words, researchers try to minimize or eliminate any bias about the subject matter and simply record everything they experience, using the five senses. These observations, when written up to share with others as part of a research report, form the basis of description of the object of study. In order to move from observation to description, researchers must keep careful notes about their systematic observations. We discuss one method of tracking those observations later in the chapter (see "Genres: Observation Logbook," pp. 228–38).

Connect 9.1   **Thinking about Systematic Observation in the Sciences**

Read student Kedric Lemon's logbook account of his observations of various batteries (see Insider Example: Student Observation Logbook, pp. 230–38). Then answer the following questions:

- What type of data was Lemon collecting every day? How was he able to quantify his observations?
- Which of his senses was he relying on?
- Was he able to remain neutral, or do you detect any biases? Explain.

From Description to Speculation

The distinction between description and speculation is a subtle but important one to understand as it relates to scientific inquiry. While descriptive writing gives a *who*, *what*, *where*, and/or *when* account of an observable phenomenon, speculative writing seeks to explain *how* or *why* something behaves the way that it does. Speculative writing is most commonly associated with asking a research question and formulating a hypothesis — the second and third steps of the scientific method.

The process of articulating an explanation for an observed phenomenon and speculating about its meaning is an integral part of scientific discovery. By collecting data on your own and then interpreting that data, you're engaging in the production of knowledge even before you begin testing a proposed hypothesis. In this respect, scientific discovery is similar to writing in the humanities and the social sciences. Scientists interpret data gained through observation, modeling, or experimentation much in the same way that humanists interpret data collected through observation of texts. The ability to *observe systematically* and *make meaning* is the common thread that runs through all academic research.

Descriptive writing seeks to define an object of study, and it functions like a photograph. Speculative writing engages by asking *how* or *why* something behaves the way that it does, and in this sense it triggers a kind of knowledge production that is essential to scientific discovery. Following a writing process that moves a researcher from describing a phenomenon to considering *how* or *why* something does what it does is a great strategy for supporting scientific inquiry.

To this end, we encourage you to collect original data as modeled in the Insider Examples presented at the end of this chapter — the observation logbook, the research proposal, and the lab report. Your view on the natural world is your own, and the data you collect and how you interpret that data are yours to decide. The arguments you form based on your data and your interpretation of that data can impact your world in small or very large ways.

> ### Connect 9.2   Describing and Speculating
>
> Go outdoors and locate any type of animal (a squirrel, bird, butterfly, frog, etc.) as an object of study. Decide beforehand the amount of time you'll spend observing your subject (five minutes may be enough), and write down in a notebook as many observable facts as possible about your subject and its behavior. Consider elements of size, color, weight, distance traveled, and interaction with other animals or physical objects. If you're able to make a video or take a picture (e.g., with a cell phone camera), please do so. Then write a paragraph under each of these two headings:
>
> - **Description**   Write all the observable facts about your subject, as if you were reporting it to someone who had never seen this animal before.
>
> - **Speculation**   Offer your theory about why the animal appears or behaves the way you observed it.

From Speculation to Research Questions and Hypothesis

You can move on to formalize your speculation by writing research questions, formulating a hypothesis, and designing a research study. In all these stages, writing helps you clarify your thinking and solidify your plans. Writing research questions and hypotheses in the natural sciences is a process similar to those activities in the social sciences (see Chapter 8). Devoting time to several days of focused observation, collecting data, and writing and reflecting on your object of study should trigger questions about what you're observing.

● **Open-Ended and Closed-Ended Questions**   As you write research questions, you might consider the difference between open-ended and closed-ended research questions. A **closed-ended question** can be answered by *yes* or *no*. By contrast, an **open-ended question** provokes a fuller response. Here are two examples:

Closed-Ended Question	Is acid rain killing off the Fraser fir population near Mount Mitchell in North Carolina?
Open-Ended Question	What factors contribute to killing off the Fraser fir population near Mount Mitchell in North Carolina?

Scientists use both open-ended and closed-ended questions. Open-ended questions usually begin with *What, How,* or *Why.* Closed-ended questions can be appropriate in certain instances, but they can also be quite polarizing. They often begin with *Is* or *Does.* Consider the following two questions:

Closed-Ended Question	Is global warming real?
Open-Ended Question	What factors contribute to global warming?

Rhetorically, the closed-ended question divides responses into *yes* or *no* answers, whereas the open-ended question provokes a more thoughtful response. Neither form of question is better per se, but the forms do function differently. If you're engaging in a controversial subject, a closed-ended research question might serve your purpose. If you're looking for a more complete answer to a complex issue, an open-ended question might serve you better.

● **Hypotheses**   Once you've established a focused research question, informed by or derived on the basis of your observation and speculation about a natural science phenomenon, then you're ready to formulate a **hypothesis**. This will be a testable proposition that provides an answer or that predicts an outcome in response to the research question(s) at hand.

Research Question	Do female house finches remove eggs from their own nests?
Hypothesis	Our hypothesis is that female house finches remove eggs from their own nests.

Connect 9.3   **Developing Research Questions and a Hypothesis**

Review the observation notes and the descriptions and explanations you produced in Connect 9.2. What potential research questions emerged? Write down at least two research questions that emerged from your observations, and then attempt to answer each question in the form of a hypothesis. You also have the option of writing research questions and hypotheses about another phenomenon that you've observed and are more interested in.

Research Study Design

Natural scientists collect evidence through systematic observation and experimentation, and they value methods that are quantifiable and replicable. In some instances, the natural sciences are described as "hard" sciences and the social sciences as "soft." This distinction stems from the tendency for natural scientists to value quantitative methods over qualitative methods, whereas social scientists often engage in both forms of data collection and sometimes combine quantitative and qualitative methods in a single study. (See "Methods" in Chapter 8 for more on quantitative and qualitative methods.) Natural scientists value experiments and data collection processes that can be repeated to achieve the same or similar results, often for the purposes of generalizing their findings. Social scientists acknowledge the fluidity and variability of social systems and therefore also highly value qualitative data, which helps them to understand more contextual experiences.

● **Testing Hypotheses**   In the previous two sections, we discussed how to conduct systematic observation that leads to the description of a phenomenon, and then we explored processes for speculating about what you observed in order to construct a research question and a hypothesis. One way to test a hypothesis is to engage in a systematic observation of the target of your research phenomenon. Imagine that you're interested in discovering factors that affect the migration patterns of bluefin tuna, and you've hypothesized that water temperature has some effect on those patterns. You could then conduct a focused observation to test your hypothesis. You might, for instance, observe bluefin tuna in their migration patterns and measure water temperatures along the routes.

Another way to test a hypothesis, of course, is to design an experiment. Experiments come in all shapes and sizes, and one way to learn about the experimental methods common to your discipline is by reading the "Methods" sections of peer-reviewed scholarly articles in your field. Every discipline has slightly different approaches to experimental design. Some disciplines, such as astronomy, rely almost exclusively on non-experimental systematic observation, while others rely on highly controlled experiments. Chemistry is a good example of the latter.

● **Comparative Experiments**   One of the most common forms of experimental design is the *comparative experiment*, in which a researcher tests two or more types of objects and assesses the results. For example, an engineering student may want to test different types of skateboard ball bearings. She may design an experiment that compares a skateboard's distance rolled when using steel versus ceramic bearings. She could measure distances rolled, speed, or the time it takes to cover a preset distance when the skateboard has steel bearings and when it has ceramic bearings.

In some disciplines of the natural sciences, it is common practice to test different objects against a control group. A *control group* is used in a comparative experimental design to act as a baseline with which to compare other objects. For example, a student researcher might compare how subjects score on a memorization test after having consumed (a) no coffee, (b) two cups of decaf coffee, or (c) two cups of caffeinated coffee. In this example, the group of subjects consuming no coffee would function as a control group.

The IRB Process and Use of Human Subjects

Regardless of a study's design, it is important to realize that academic institutions have very clear policies regarding experimental designs that involve human subjects, whether that research is being conducted by individuals in the humanities, the social sciences, or the natural sciences. Both professional and student researchers are required to submit proposals through an *institutional review board*, or IRB. In the United States, institutional review boards operate under federal law to ensure that any experiment involving humans is ethical. This is often something entirely new to undergraduate students, and it should be taken seriously. No matter how harmless a test involving human subjects may seem, you should determine if you must submit your research plans through an IRB. This can often be done online. Depending on the nature and scope of your research, though, the processes of outlining the parameters of your research for review may be quite labor-intensive and time-consuming. You should familiarize yourself with the protocol for your particular academic institution. An online search for "institutional review board" and the name of your school should get you started. (For more information, see "The IRB Process and Use of Human Subjects" in Chapter 8.)

Insider's View
Physiologist Paige Geiger on the Integrity of Scientific Writing

COURTESY OF PAIGE GEIGER

"A biomedical scientist performs basic research on questions that have relevance to human health and disease, biological processes, and systems. We design scientific studies to answer a particular research question and then report our results in the form of a manuscript for publication. Good science is only as good as the research study design itself. We value innovation, ideas, accurate interpretation of data, and scientific integrity. There is an honor system to science that the results are accurate and true as reported. Manuscripts are peer-reviewed, and there is inherent trust and belief in this system."

Connect 9.4   Freewriting about an Experiment

Building on your research question and hypothesis from Connect 9.3, imagine how you might learn more about your subject as a natural scientist. Freewrite for five minutes about how you could collect data that would test your hypothesis. As you write, consider feasible methods that you could follow soon, as well as methods that might extend beyond the current semester but that you could develop into a larger project for later use in your undergraduate studies. Consider whether an experiment or a systematic observation would be more useful. Most important, use your imagination and have fun.

Values Underlying Writing in the Natural Sciences

After observing and describing, speculating and hypothesizing, and conducting an experimental study or systematic observation, scientists move toward publishing the results of their research. This is the final step of the scientific method and the final stage of the scientific writing process that we introduced at the beginning of the chapter: scientists explain their results by reporting their data and discussing their implications. There are multiple forms through which scientists report their findings, and these often depend on the target audience. For instance, scientists presenting their research results at an academic conference for the consideration of their peers might report results in the form of a poster presentation. Research results can also be presented in the form of an academic journal article. Scientists who want to present their results to a more general audience, though, might issue a press release.

No matter the differences in genre and disciplinary focus, a set of core values connects writing in the natural sciences. These values shared among members of the scientific community have an impact on the communication practices and writing conventions of natural science fields. We'll discuss these values first and then, in the pages that follow, point out how they are reflected in Structure, Language, and Reference (SLR).

Objectivity

As we noted earlier, *objectivity* (or neutrality) in observation and experimentation is essential to the research that scientists do. Most researchers in the natural sciences believe that bias undermines the reliability of research results. When scientists report their results, therefore, they often use rhetorical strategies to bolster the appearance of objectivity in their work. Examples include the use of scientific jargon and an IMRaD organization that mirrors the scientific method process.

Replicability

Like objectivity, the replicability of research methods and findings is important to the production and continuation of scientific inquiry. Imagine that a scientific report reveals the discovery that eating an orange every day could help prevent the onset of Alzheimer's disease. This sounds great, right? But how would the larger scientific community go about verifying such a finding? Multiple studies would likely be undertaken in an attempt to replicate the original study's finding. If the finding couldn't be replicated by carefully following the research procedures outlined in the original study, then that discovery wouldn't contribute much, if anything at all, to ongoing research on Alzheimer's disease precisely because the finding's veracity couldn't be confirmed. Examples of rhetorical strategies linked to replicability include meticulous detail and precision with language.

Recency

Scientific research is an ongoing process wherein individual studies or research projects contribute bits of information that help fill in a larger picture or research question. As research builds, earlier studies and projects become the bases for additional questioning and research. As in other fields, like the social sciences, it's important that scientific researchers remain current on the developments in research in their respective fields of study. To ensure that their work demonstrates recency—that is, it is current and draws on knowledge of other recent work—researchers in the sciences select references and use documentation styles that highlight recent publication dates.

Cooperation and Collaboration

Unlike the clichéd image of the solitary scientist spending hours alone in a laboratory, most scientists would probably tell you that research in their fields takes place in a highly cooperative and collaborative manner. In fact, large networks of researchers in any particular area often comprise smaller networks of scholars who are similarly focused on certain aspects of a larger research question. These networks may work together to refine their research goals in light of the work of others in the network, and researchers are constantly sharing—through publication of reports, team researching, and scholarly conferences—the results of their work. In the humanities, where ideas are a reflection of the individuals who present them, researchers and writers often direct commentary toward individuals for their ideas when there's cause for disagreement or dissatisfaction with other researchers' ideas. Conventionally, however, science researchers treat others in their field more indirectly when objections to their research or findings come up. Instead of linking research problems to individuals, scientists generally direct their dissatisfaction with others' work at problems in the research process or design. This approach highlights the importance of cooperation and collaboration as shared values of members of the scientific community.

Structural Conventions in the Natural Sciences

As we examine structural conventions—that is, conventions governing how writing is organized—keep in mind that your goal is not to master every type of writing in the natural sciences. Instead, your goal should be to understand how scientific values inform scientific writing conventions.

IMRaD Format

Research studies in the natural sciences typically follow the IMRaD (Introduction, Methods, Results, and Discussion) format. The structure of IMRaD parallels the ordered processes of the scientific writing process: observe and describe, speculate, experiment, and report. This reporting structure under-scores the importance of objectivity because it reflects the prescribed steps of the scientific method, which is itself a research process that scientists follow to reduce or eliminate bias.

- The *Introduction* is where researchers describe what they have observed and how it relates to their speculations and hypotheses, and it is also where they report what is already known about a phenomenon or what is relevant in the current scholarship for their own research. Hypothesis statements predict the outcome of a research study, but the very nature of a prediction leaves open the possibility of other outcomes. By opening this "space" of possibility, scientists acknowledge that other researchers could potentially find results that differ from their own. In this way, scientists confirm the importance of replicability to their inquiry process.

- In the *Methods* section, researchers thoroughly explain the precise procedures they used to collect data and why they chose those methods. They may discuss how the data were interpreted or analyzed.

- The *Results* and *Discussion* sections report new information about the data the researchers gathered and their explanations and interpretations of what those results might mean. The Discussion section might also include suggestions for future research, demonstrating how research in the sciences is always building upon prior research.

For an example of a science paper in IMRaD format, see Insider Example: Student Lab Report, which begins on page 248. Also see Chapter 8, "IMRaD Format," for an extended discussion with examples.

Other Structural Conventions

● **Titles**   Scientists tend to give their reports very clear titles, reflecting the value of objectivity. Rarely will you find a "creative" or rhetorical title in science writing. Instead, scientists prefer descriptive titles or titles that say exactly what the reports are about rather than titles that play with language (as in the humanities).

● **Presentation of Researchers' Names**   As you examine published research reports, you will find that very often they provide a list, prominently, of the names of individuals who contributed to the research and to the reporting of that research. This information usually appears at the top of reports just after the title, and it may also identify the researchers' institutional and/or organizational affiliations. Names typically appear in an order that identifies principal researchers first. Naming all the members of a research team acknowledges the highly cooperative nature of the researching processes that many scientists undertake.

Observing Structural Features in the Natural Sciences

Although we've discussed a number of structural expectations for writing in the natural sciences, we'd like to stress again that these expectations are conventional. As such, you'll likely encounter studies in the natural sciences that rely on only a few of these structural features or that alter the conventional expectations in light of the researchers' particular aims. Find a scholarly article from the natural sciences, either from Part Three or your own research, and examine it in terms of these structural features. If the article deviates from the conventions we've described, what might be the writer's reasons?

- **IMRaD Format**   Does the report have a section labeled "Introduction" where the researchers describe what they have observed and how it relates to their speculations and hypotheses? Is there a "Methods" section that thoroughly explains the precise procedures they used to collect data? Are "Results" discussed and data presented? Is there a "Discussion" section that explains the significance of the researchers' findings and that includes suggestions for future research?

- **Title**   Does the title contain key words that highlight important components of the study?

- **Authors' Names**   Does the article list a team of people as study authors? Are there institutions included with their names? Does it appear that there are principal researchers who are listed first?

Language Conventions in the Natural Sciences

The way natural scientists use language reflects their emphasis on objectivity, replicability, cooperation, and collaboration.

Jargon

The word *jargon* often has negative connotations, but **jargon** is simply the specialized vocabulary used by a particular community of scholars. For example, a scientific researcher might refer to a particular rose as *Rosa spinosissima* rather than by a common name that could vary from region to region. By using the Latin name, the writer also positions the plant in terms of its genus (*Rosa*) and species (*spinosissima*), which indicates how the plant is both similar to and distinct from other plants. The use of jargon in this instance is actually clarifying for the intended audience of other botanists. Using jargon is a means of communicating with precision, and precision in language is fundamental to objective expression.

Numbers and Other Details

Scientific reports are often filled with charts and figures, and these are often filled with numbers. Scientists prefer to communicate in numbers because unlike words, which can inadvertently convey the wrong meaning, numbers are more fixed in terms of their ability to communicate specific meaning. Consider the difference between describing a tree as "tall" and giving a tree's height in feet and inches. This represents the difference between communicating somewhat qualitatively and entirely quantitatively. The preference for communicating in numbers, or quantitatively, enables members of the scientific community to reduce, as much as possible, the use of words. As writers use fewer words and more numbers in scientific reports, the reports appear to be more objective. One of the conventional expectations for scientific writing involves the level of detail and specificity, particularly in certain areas of research reporting (e.g., Methods sections). Scientists report their research methods in meticulous detail to ensure that others can replicate their results. This is how scientific knowledge builds. Verification through repeated testing and retesting of results establishes the relative value of particular research findings. It's not surprising, then, that the Methods sections of scientific research reports are typically highly detailed and specific.

Active and Passive Voice

As we discussed in Chapter 8, writers in the social sciences and natural sciences often prefer the **passive voice** because it can foster a sense that researchers are acting objectively or with neutrality. With the passive voice, the focus is on the study's subjects; the researchers are not visible as the subjects of sentences. This does not mean that scientists never use *we* or *I* in their writing; sometimes it is helpful for clarity. Consider these two sentences from an article in the journal *NeuroImage*:

Active Voice   In the present study, we extended a previous study (Shah et al., 2013) and investigated the cerebral representation maps of expert writers, comparing them to inexperienced writers.

Passive Voice   All of the participants were asked about their experience and practice of creative writing.

Connect 9.6   **Observing Language Features in the Natural Sciences**

Continue your examination of the article you selected for Connect 9.5, using the questions below as a guide. If the article deviates from the conventions we've described, what might be the writer's reasons?

- **Jargon**   Does the writer use specialized vocabulary to communicate with precision?
- **Numbers and Other Details**   Approximately what percent of the data is communicated quantitatively, rather than through words? Is there a high level of detail and specificity so that others could replicate the results?
- **Active and Passive Voice**   How often do the authors use *we* or *I*? Is there a section of the paper where they use the passive voice exclusively?

Reference Conventions in the Natural Sciences

Scientists often cite the work of others when establishing a context for their own research. Their use of recent sources reflects the value of recency, and it indicates that they are advancing the conversation around this research area. Most scholars in the natural sciences follow the documentation style of the American Psychological Association (APA) or the Council of Science Editors (CSE) when crediting their sources. These documentation styles highlight the publication year by including it as part of the in-text citation, as in the following citation in APA style:

> A team working in Guangxi, China, discovered a new species of Gesneriacaeae, *Primulina titan*, that resembles *P. hunanensis* but can be distinguished by a combination of morphological characteristics of leaf, bract, corolla, stamen and pistil (Xin et al., 2020).

This citation would be the same in CSE style, except that the comma after the authors names would not be used. For a discussion of the elements of citations and References lists, see "American Psychological Association (APA) Style" and "Council of Science Editors (CSE) Style" in the Appendix.

Insider's View
Conservation Biologist Michelle LaRue on Learning Science Writing Conventions

COURTESY OF MICHELLE LARUE

"I learned the conventions of science writing through literature review, imitation, and a lot of practice: this often included pages and pages of feedback from advisors and colleagues. Further, reading wildlife and modeling articles helped me focus on the tone, writing style, and format expected for each journal. After that, it was all about practicing my writing skills.

"I also learned the KISS principle during my undergraduate career: Keep It Simple, Stupid. This mantra reminds me to revise my writing so it's clear, concise, and informative. It is my opinion that science writing can be inherently difficult to understand, so it's important to keep the message clear and straightforward.

"I find that as I progress and hone my writing and research skills, sitting down to write gets easier, and I have been able to move up in the caliber of journal in which I publish papers. Writing is a skill that is never perfected; striving for the next best journal keeps me focused on improvement."

Conclude your examination of the article you selected for Connect 9.5. Can you identify the documentation style? If you are having difficulty, go back to the original journal and see if you can find the reference style required for the publication. What type of information is valued?

Genres: Observation Logbook

An observation logbook is a place for researchers to keep systematic notes on their object of study. It provides an organized space to focus, record, and reflect on observations made over a series of hours, days, or weeks. Students may be asked to provide their logbooks as part of an assignment in a natural sciences course. Often the logbook is accompanied by a narrative that describes and speculates on the observation as a whole.

What Is the Rhetorical Context for This Genre?

Systematic and carefully recorded observations can lay a solid foundation for further exploration of a subject. These observations might take place as an initial step in the scientific writing process, or they might be part of the data collection that occurs when testing a hypothesis. The observation logbook is a foundational part of the research process that precedes the construction of a formal lab report. As a student, your audience is your instructor. As a researcher, typically your audience would be people who are collaborating with you in some way on the project. Observation logbooks are usually not published.

Sometimes observation logbooks include speculation in addition to description, but the two types of writing should be clearly distinguished by headings to ensure that the more objective observations are not confused with any speculation. Speculation, you'll remember, occurs at the stage of formulating research questions and a hypothesis.

Strategies for Working with an Observation Logbook

● **Determine your subject, purpose, and method.**   Even if your subject is determined by your instructor, you may be able to find a focus for your study that aligns with your own interests and curiosity. Decide what kind of changes or behaviors you wish to observe and what you hope to learn through your observations. This information will not only inform your methods of observation and how often you will observe, but it will also provide the basis for the introduction section of your final logbook.

● **Decide how to record and organize your observations.** Because the logbook is meant to help you collect evidence through systematic observation, consider creating a series of questions or a list of data points that you will focus on in each session. Put this in a format and medium that will be easy for you to fill out. Consider whether a multimodal data collection process that includes digital photos and video-recorded evidence would be right for your project. Decide how many entries you will need based on how frequently you plan to observe, and be sure to have a place to record the date (and time, if applicable).

● **Observe and describe.** Keep accurate and detailed notes of your subject and methods. Write your notes in a form that can be shared with others either after each session or at the end of your entire observation period. This might also include converting data into charts or graphs, as in the Insider Example that begins on page 230. At the end of the entire period of observation, review your notes and draw conclusions:

- What did you learn about your object of study?
- What claims can you now make regarding your object of study?
- What evidence could you use from your observational logbook to support those claims?

● **Speculate.** Keep track of the questions that occur to you during your observations. What is surprising or puzzling? Are you observing changes that point to a hypothesis?

● **Remember SLR as you prepare your logbook for an audience.** The Writing Project that follows suggests a structure for sharing your completed observation logbook with others. Apply what you've learned in this chapter about the values of objectivity and replicability as you draft each section of your logbook. Focus on clearly describing and summarizing your observations in the first draft and creating the types of visuals (tables, graphs, diagrams, etc.) that show change over time. Use the revision stage to further clarify your points. When you proofread, be sure to check that you have not introduced any errors when transferring the data from your notes to your visuals.

Writing Project   **Observation Logbook**

Your goal in this writing project is to share your observation logbook with an audience. You'll describe the purpose of your study, detail your observations for each session, summarize your overall observations, speculate about the meaning or significance of what you observed, and propose a hypothesis for further research.

THE INTRODUCTION

The opening of your observation should introduce what you are studying, how you plan to conduct your study, and what you hope to learn. It can be written in the future tense, assuming that you've written the introduction before beginning your observations.

THE LOG

Provide an entry for each session, describing your observations in accurate detail for a reader. Include visuals such as photographs, tables, and charts if such visuals would clearly communicate your observations.

THE NARRATIVE

In the narrative that follows the log, include two sections: a description of your object of study and speculation about your observations. In the Description section, refrain from explaining or speculating about behavior; simply write the observations that are most important to give a clear picture of what you studied and how you studied it. Make use of time measurements and physical measurements such as weight, size, and distance. In the Speculation section, theorize about why certain behaviors emerged in your object of study. You might begin by deciding which behaviors most surprised you or seem most interesting to you. You might also use the Speculation section as a place to begin thinking about future questions that could be explored as a follow-up to your observations.

....

Insider Example
Student Observation Logbook

In the following observation logbook, written using APA style conventions, student Kedric Lemon catalogs his observations concerning the efficiency of several types of batteries over a five-day period. His observations form the basis for his experimental study, which appears later in the chapter (see Insider Example: Student Lab Report, pp. 248–57). You'll notice that he carefully separates his observations and description from any speculation about why he observed what he did. ▶

1

**Comparing the Efficiency of Various Batteries
Being Used over Time**

Kedric Lemon

North Carolina State University

Professor Matthew Chu

November 4, 2020

Comparing the Efficiency of Various Batteries
Being Used over Time

Logbook

Introduction

Establishes the purpose of the study and outlines an observational protocol

    The purpose of this study is to see if some batteries can hold their charge for longer periods of time than others. Also, this observational study will determine if there is an overwhelming difference between generic brand and the top name-brand batteries, or if people are really just paying for the name. I will perform this study by first recording all of the batteries' initial voltages, and then each day I will allow each of the batteries to go on for an hour and a half and then again check the voltage. It is important that I test the voltage immediately after the batteries come out of the flashlight. Otherwise, results could vary. Before putting in the second set of batteries, I will allow the flashlight to cool down for an hour because after being in use for an hour and a half they are likely hot, and I am unsure if this can affect how fast the other batteries will be consumed. I will look first at how much charge was lost over the duration that they were used in the flashlight. Then I will compare them to one another to determine which one has lost the most over a day, and second, which of the batteries still holds the highest voltage. I hypothesize that the Duracell battery will decrease at the slowest rate and that it will have the highest initial voltage.

Outlines methods

Establishes a hypothesis

Friday, October 11, 2020

Begins a report on systematic observation of the phenomenon

    The initial voltages of all three types of batteries (with the two batteries in each flashlight averaged) are as follows:

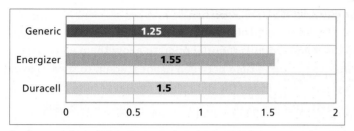

So from these initial observations the Energizer battery has the highest initial voltage.

After running all of the batteries for an hour and a half, the batteries had the following voltages:

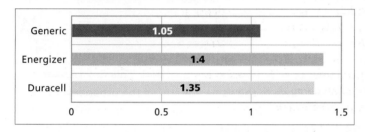

Energizer and Duracell both appear to be decreasing at approximately the same rates thus far in the observation, whereas the generic brand has already dropped much faster than the other two types of batteries. This observation raises the question: What is the composition of the Duracell and Energizer batteries that allows them to hold a better initial charge than the generic brand of batteries?

Observations leading to questions

Sunday, October 13, 2020

The three sets of batteries were placed into the flashlight, in the same order as the trial prior, to allow them all to have close to the same time between usages, again to try and avoid any variables. Today the data show similar results after all of the batteries ran in the flashlight for an hour and a half:

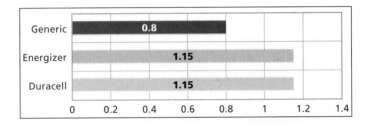

The generic brand of batteries did not decrease as significantly as it did after the first trial. This day the generic brand lost close to the same voltage as the other two types of batteries. The Energizer and Duracell had the same voltages.

Tuesday, October 15, 2020

On this day of observation the batteries were again placed into the flashlights for the trial time. The data for this day are as follows:

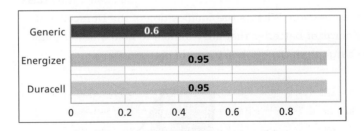

As in the preceding trial, the generic brand decreased by an amount similar to the other two batteries. Also, the generic brand's intensity has begun to decrease. However, both the other two batteries still give off a strong light intensity. This observation raises the question: At what voltage does the light

Provides evidence of the researcher's attempt to remain systematic in his observations

Student's observations continue to raise questions.

intensity begin to waver? Another question is: Will the other two batteries begin to have lower light intensity at approximately the same voltage as the generic, or will they continue to have a stronger light intensity for longer? The figures below show the change of light intensity of the generic brand of batteries from the beginning until this day's observation.

Figure 1. Before　　　　　*Figure 2.* After

Thursday, October 17, 2020

The voltage readings for the batteries on this fourth day of observation are as follows:

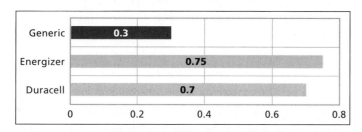

The generic brand is losing even more intensity when it is in the flashlight. It is obvious that it is getting near the end of its battery charge. Today was also the biggest decrease in charge for the generic brand of batteries. This is interesting because it is actually producing less light than before, so why does it lose more voltage toward the end of its life? Another observation is that again the Energizer brand holds more voltages than the Duracell. There is still no change in light intensity for the two name brands.

Saturday, October 19, 2020

The voltage readings for the batteries on the final day of observation are as follows:

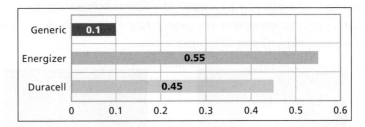

Today the generic battery hardly produced any light out of the flashlight by the end of the time period, although it still didn't drop to 0 voltage, so there are clearly still some electrons flowing in the current throughout the battery. Also, the Duracell battery has clearly dropped well below the Energizer now. The Duracell has shown a slight decrease in the light intensity compared to when the observational study first started. So what is the composition of the Energizer battery that makes it outlast the Duracell battery?

Narrative

Description

Five days of observations were conducted over an eight-day period. It did not matter what day of the week these observations were made nor the conditions of the environment around the object of study at the time of the observations. The only thing that was constant environmentally for all of the batteries in the study was the temperature because more heat results in higher kinetic energy, which causes electrons to move faster. From the battery types available in this area, the following were chosen for the study: Duracell, Energizer, and a generic brand from Walmart. Before the first observation, each battery was tested with the voltmeter to determine its initial charge. This established which battery was the most powerful and provided a baseline from which to measure change over time.

> The narrative description provides a summary of the student's systematic observation.

Each of these battery types was tested for the same amount of time for each day that they were observed. Because the flashlight took two batteries to operate, the voltages of each set of batteries were averaged, but the voltage of these batteries was determined to be very similar over the course of the observation. This similarity is a result of the entire circuit acting at the same time, causing equal electron transfer between the two batteries to occur, thus causing them to have equal voltages.

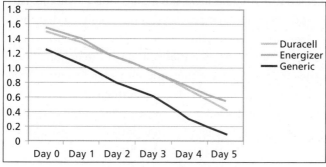

Final Graph from Five Days of Observations

The graph above shows the change in voltage over five days of observation. Duracell and Energizer were very similar to each other, with Energizer performing slightly higher than the Duracell brand. The generic had a lower initial voltage than the other two batteries and continued to decrease at a faster rate than the other two batteries. The graph also illustrates how quickly the generic brand lost its voltage toward the end of its life, whereas the other two batteries seemed to continue to decrease at approximately the same rate throughout.

Speculation

My initial hypothesis that the Duracell battery would decrease at the slowest rate was not supported by the data. An explanation for the strong performance of the Energizer battery is that the manufacturer combines lithium with the copper tip

Evaluates initial hypothesis (speculation) in light of the data

on the cathode; this allows for a longer battery life than with a copper tip alone, as in the Duracell battery. The generic brand has a carbon and copper tip, which is not as effective as copper and lithium or copper alone. Also, the cathodes and anodes of the generic batteries may not be as professionally manufactured as the other two types of batteries. All of these differences could explain why there is a higher voltage density in the Energizer battery than in the other two batteries.

The data do not support my other hypothesis, that the Duracell battery would have the highest initial voltage. An explanation for the Energizer's stronger results is that the Energizer batteries contain alkaline metals, while the Duracell batteries do not. The low initial voltage of the generic brand of batteries may be because they are not packed as well. It takes special equipment to make all the electrons store properly, and the equipment used is not as powerful as the ones that Duracell and Energizer use for their batteries. These factors may account for why there is such a major difference in the rates at which the batteries lose their charge.

For further research into this topic I would recommend using a larger sample, because I used only two batteries for each type of battery. Also, I would recommend gathering data on the new rechargeable batteries, which are a popular option for consumers. A future experiment might also extend the time that the flashlight is left on, because others have observed that Duracell does better than Energizer over continuous usage.

Another interesting question to explore is which battery is the most cost-effective. Does the consumer still save money by buying the generic brand if it needs to be replaced sooner? A future experiment could attempt to quantify the answer to this question.

Further speculates about factors that contributed to rejection of the hypothesis

Provides suggestions for future research on the subject

Genres: Research Proposal

The research proposal is one of the most common genres of academic writing in the natural sciences. It provides a description and rationale for a research project before the work of executing the research begins.

What Is the Rhetorical Context for This Genre?

Professional scholars use the research proposal to plan out complex studies, to formulate their thoughts, and to submit their research designs to institutional review boards or to grant-funding agencies. The ability to secure grant funding (i.e., to write an effective research proposal and connect it to a realistic, clear budget) is a highly sought-after skill in a job candidate for many academic, government, and private industry positions. Because the research proposal is such an important vehicle for securing the funding and materials necessary to conduct research, much of the work of science could not get done without it.

Strategies for Writing a Research Proposal

A research proposal is an advanced genre of academic writing that requires practice and knowledge of the conventions expected by the institution you are writing for. As an undergraduate student, you can begin the process of developing familiarity with this genre.

● **Review the scholarly literature on your topic.** Using the research techniques discussed in Chapter 5, investigate what work has already been done on your topic and make sure that your proposed research project fills a gap in the scholarship. You will use your findings in the introduction of your proposal to make an argument for the need for your research. This literature review also serves to demonstrate your knowledge of other scholars' research and to build your credibility as a researcher. See Chapter 8 for more on writing a literature review.

● **Think about your audience as you explain your proposed methods.** You will likely collaborate with other students or your teacher as you develop a plan for testing your hypothesis. When it is time to put your plan in writing, describe your process in enough detail so that readers will be able to replicate your methods on their own. Make it clear what kind of data you will be collecting at each stage of the process. Check that you have covered when, where, and why as well as how you will be proceeding.

● **Remember SLR as you draft.** The Writing Project that follows suggests a structure for your research proposal. Apply what you've learned in this chapter about the values of objectivity, replicability, and recency as you draft each section. Use the revision stage to further clarify your points. When you proofread, be sure to check that you have not introduced any inaccuracies.

Writing Project   **Research Proposal**

Your goal in this project is to share your plans for a research project with an audience. You will describe the purpose of your proposed research and situate it in the context of other research and then explain your hypothesis and how you plan to test it.

THE TITLE PAGE

The title page should include (1) the title of your proposal, (2) your name and the names of any co-authors/researchers, and (3) the name of your academic institution. Your instructor may require additional information such as a running header, date, or author's note. Be sure to ask your instructor what documentation and formatting style to use and what information is required in any specific writing context.

THE INTRODUCTION AND LITERATURE REVIEW

Use the Introduction section to explain the topic and purpose of the proposed research. Be sure to include your research question and/or your proposed hypothesis. Additionally, your Introduction should contextualize your research by reviewing scholarly articles related to your topic and showing how your proposed research fills a gap in what is already known about the topic. Specifically, the Introduction should explain how other researchers have approached your topic (or a closely related one) in the past, with attention to the major overlapping findings in that research.

METHODS

The Methods section of your research proposal should explain exactly what you will do to test your hypothesis (or answer your research question) and how you will do it. It differs from the Methods section of a lab report in several ways: (1) it should be written in the future tense, and (2) it should include more detail about your plans. Further, the Methods section should address how long your study will take and should specify how you will collect data (in a step-by-step descriptive manner).

DOCUMENTATION

The References list for a research proposal is essentially the same as the References list for a lab report or any other academic project. You will need to include the full citation information for any work you used in your literature review or in planning or researching your topic.

....

Insider Example
Professional Research Proposal

In the following example of a professional research proposal by Gary Ritchison, a biologist at Eastern Kentucky University, note how the Introduction section begins with a brief introduction to the topic (par. 1) and then proceeds to review the relevant literature on the topic (pars. 1 and 2). As you read, consider how a potential funding entity would likely view both the content and the form in which that content is presented. Also note that the References list is titled "Literature Cited." Minor variations like this are common from discipline to discipline and in various contexts. Here, Ritchison has followed CSE style conventions in his proposal. ▶

Hunting Behavior, Territory Quality, and Individual
Quality of American Kestrels (*Falco sparverius*)

Gary Ritchison

Department of Biological Sciences
Eastern Kentucky University

Introduction

American Kestrels (*Falco sparverius*) are widely distributed throughout North America. In Kentucky, these falcons are permanent residents and are most abundant in rural farmland, where they hunt over fields and pastures (Palmer-Ball 1996). Although primarily sit-and-wait predators, hunting from elevated perches and scanning the surrounding areas for prey, kestrels also hunt while hovering (Balgooyen 1976). Kellner (1985) reported that nearly 20% of all attacks observed in central Kentucky were made while kestrels were hovering. Habitats used by hunting kestrels in central Kentucky include mowed and unmowed fields, cropland, pastures, and plowed fields (Kellner 1985).

Several investigators have suggested that male and female American Kestrels may exhibit differences in habitat use during the non-breeding period, with males typically found in areas with greater numbers of trees, such as wooded pastures, and females in open fields and pastures (Stinson et al. 1981; Bohall-Wood and Collopy 1986). However, Smallwood (1988) suggested that, when available, male and female kestrels in south-central Florida established winter territories in the same type of habitat. Differential habitat use occurred only because migratory female kestrels usually arrived on wintering areas before males and, therefore, were more likely to establish territories in the better-quality, more open habitats before males arrived (Smallwood 1988).

In central Kentucky, many American Kestrels are residents. As a result, male and female kestrels would likely have equal opportunity to establish winter territories in the higher-quality, open habitats. If so, habitat segregation should be less apparent in central Kentucky than in areas further south, where wintering populations of kestrels are

---

Establishes the topic and provides background information on American Kestrels

Reveals evidence of a review of previous scholarship

Establishes a local context for research

largely migratory. In addition, territory quality should be correlated with individual quality because higher-quality resident kestrels should be able to defend higher-quality territories.

The objectives of my proposed study of American Kestrels will be to examine possible relationships among and between hunting behavior, territory quality, and individual quality in male and female American Kestrels. The results of this study will provide important information about habitat and perch selection by American Kestrels in central Kentucky in addition to the possible role of individual quality on hunting behavior and habitat use.

> Reveals research purposes and identifies significance of the proposed research

Methods

Field work will take place from 15 October 2000 through 15 May 2001 at the Blue Grass Army Depot, Madison Co., Kentucky. During the study period, I will search for American Kestrels throughout accessible portions of the depot. Searches will be conducted on foot as well by automobile.

An attempt will be made to capture all kestrels observed using bal-chatri traps baited with mice. Once captured, kestrels will be banded with a numbered aluminum band plus a unique combination of colored plastic bands to permit individual identification. For each captured individual, I will take standard morphological measurements (wing chord, tarsus length, tail length, and mass). In addition, 8 to 10 feathers will be plucked from the head, breast, back, and wing, respectively. Plumage in these areas is either reddish or bluish, and the quality of such colors is known to be correlated with individual quality (Hill 1991, 1992; Keyser 1998). Variation in the color and intensity of plumage will be determined using a reflectance spectrometer (Ocean Optics S2000 fiber optic spectrometer, Dunedin, FL), and

> This section provides a highly detailed description of proposed research procedures, or methods.

these values will be used as a measure of individual quality. To confirm that plumage color and intensity are dependent on condition, we will use tail feather growth rates as a measure of nutritional condition during molt. At the time of capture, the outermost tail feathers will be removed and the mean width of daily growth bars, which is correlated with nutritional condition (Hill and Montgomerie 1994), will be determined.

Each focal American Kestrel (N = at least 14;7 males and 7 females) will be observed at least once a week. Observations will be made at various times during the day, with observation periods typically 1 to 3 hours in duration. During focal bird observations, individuals will be monitored using binoculars and spotting scopes. Information will be recorded on a portable tape recorder for later transcription. During each observation, I will record all attacks and whether attacks were initiated from a perch or while hovering. For perches, I will note the time a kestrel lands on a perch and the time until the kestrel either initiates an attack or leaves for another perch (giving up time). If an attack is made, I will note attack distances (the distance from a perch to the point where a prey item was attacked) and outcome (successful or not). If successful, an attempt will be made to identify the prey (to the lowest taxonomic category possible).

The activity budgets of kestrels will also be determined by observing the frequency and duration of kestrel behaviors during randomly selected 20-min observation periods (i.e., a randomly selected period during the 1- to 3-hour observation period). During these 20-minute periods, the frequency of occurrence of each of the following behaviors will be recorded: capturing prey, preening, engaging in nonpreening comfort movements (including

References established methods, or those used by other researchers, to support his own method design scratching, stretching wing or tail, shaking body plumage, cleaning foot with bill, and yawning), vocalizing, and flying. The context in which flight occurs, including pounces on prey, and the duration of flights and of preening bouts will also be recorded.

Territories will be delineated by noting the locations of focal kestrels, and the vegetation in each kestrel's winter territory will be characterized following the methods of Smallwood (1987). Possible relationships among hunting behavior (mode of attack, perch time, attack distance and outcome [successful or unsuccessful], and type of prey attacked), territory vegetation, time budgets, sex, and individual quality will be examined. All analyses will be conducted using the Statistical Analysis System (SAS Institute 1989).

Literature Cited

Balgooyen TG. 1976. Behavior and ecology of the American Kestrel in the Sierra Nevada of California. Univ Calif Publ Zool 103:1–83.

Bohall-Wood P, Collopy MW. 1986. Abundance and habitat selection of two American Kestrel subspecies in north-central Florida. Auk 103:557–563.

Craighead JJ, Craighead FC Jr. 1956. Hawks, owls, and wildlife. Harrisburg (PA): Stackpole.

Hill GE. 1991. Plumage coloration is a sexually selected indicator of male quality. Nature 350:337–339.

Hill GE. 1992. Proximate basis of variation in carotenoid pigmentation in male House Finches. Auk 109:1–12.

Hill GE, Montgomerie R. 1994. Plumage colour signals nutritional condition in the House Finch. Proc R Soc Lond B Biol Sci 258:47–52.

Kellner CJ. 1985. A comparative analysis of the foraging behavior of male and female American Kestrels in central Kentucky [master's thesis]. [Richmond (KY)]: Eastern Kentucky University.

Keyser AJ. 1998. Is structural color a reliable signal of quality in Blue Grosbeaks? [master's thesis]. [Auburn (AL)]: Auburn University.

Mengel RM. 1965. The birds of Kentucky. Lawrence (KS): Allen Press. (American Ornithologists' Union monograph; 3).

Palmer-Ball B. 1996. The Kentucky breeding bird atlas. Lexington (KY): Univ. Press of Kentucky.

SAS Institute. 1989. SAS user's guide: statistics. Cary (NC): SAS Institute.

Smallwood JA. 1987. Sexual segregation by habitat in American Kestrels wintering in southcentral Florida: vegetative structure and responses of differential prey availability. Condor 89:842–849.

Smallwood JA. 1988. The relationship of vegetative cover to daily rhythms of prey consumption by American Kestrels wintering in southcentral Florida. J Raptor Res 22:77–80.

Stinson CH, Crawford DL, Lauthner J. 1981. Sex differences in winter habitat of American Kestrels in Georgia. J. Field Ornithol 52:29–35.

Genres: Lab Reports

Lab reports offer a written account of the purpose, methods, results, and meaning of an experiment or systematic observation.

What Is the Rhetorical Context for This Genre?

Lab reports are the formal reporting mechanism for research in the sciences. When scientists publish an article that reports the results of a research study, it is generally in the form of a lab report. The audience for the report is usually other scientists, who would be reading to see what the report's findings contribute to their understanding of the research topic.

If a group of researchers writes a research proposal before writing a lab report, they've already completed the first two sections of the lab report and only need to revise the report to reflect what they actually accomplished in the study (instead of what they planned to do). The Results and Discussion sections report new information about the data they gathered and what they offer as explanations and interpretations of what those results might mean. The Discussion section might also include suggestions for future research, demonstrating how research in the sciences is always building upon prior research.

Strategies for Composing a Lab Report

Like the research proposal, the lab report is a professional genre that you learn through studying the work of others and practicing in your courses. Lab reports usually follow the IMRaD format.

- **Revise your research proposal.** If you wrote a research proposal prior to conducting your lab work, you already have the basis for the Introduction and Methods sections of your lab report. You'd only need to revise the report to reflect what you actually accomplished in the study (instead of what you planned to do). If you did not do a research proposal, review the strategies provided in "Genres: Research Proposal" on page 239.

- **Consider visuals that will communicate your findings.** Do you have a large quantity of data that you can organize into types and categories? If so, consider using a table. Are you showing a change over time that would be more clearly illustrated with a graph? Would a photograph or short video support your description of a process or a phenomenon? Does the subject of your inquiry have parts that could be labeled in an illustration? Think of visuals as a powerful way to communicate information, rather than decorative additions.

- **Remember SLR as you draft.** The Writing Project that follows suggests a structure for your research proposal. Apply what you've learned in this chapter about the values of objectivity, replicability, and recency as you draft each section. Use the revision stage to further clarify your points. When you proofread, be sure to check that you have not introduced any inaccuracies.

Writing Project Lab Report

For this writing project, you will report results from either experimentation or systematic observation. Your research could take place in an actual laboratory setting, or it could just as easily take place in the wider environment around you. Regardless, be sure to check with your instructor about whether your lab report should be based on formal observation or experimentation. Since lab reports use IMRaD organizational format, your report should include the following sections: Introduction, Methods, Results, and Discussion.

THE INTRODUCTION

In the Introduction, establish the topic and purpose of your project. Be sure to include your research question and/or your proposed hypothesis. Additionally, your Introduction should contextualize your research by reviewing scholarly articles related to your topic and showing how your proposed research fills a gap in what is already known about the topic. Specifically, the Introduction should explain how other researchers have approached your topic (or a closely related one) in the past, with attention to the major overlapping findings in that research.

METHODS

The Methods section should explain how you tested your hypothesis (or answered your research question). It should specify the details of your process in a step-by-step descriptive manner that could be replicated by another scientist.

RESULTS AND DISCUSSION

The Results and Discussion sections report new information about the data you gathered and your explanations and interpretations of what those results might mean. The Discussion section might also include suggestions for future research, demonstrating how research in the sciences is always building upon prior research.

Insider Example

Student Lab Report

In the following sample lab report, Kedric Lemon revisits the question of which battery type is most effective. He draws on the information gathered in his observation logbook (pp. 230–38) to design a research study that allows him to conduct further investigation to answer his research question. ▶

**Which Type of Battery Is the Most Effective
When Energy Is Drawn Rapidly?**

Kedric Lemon
North Carolina State University
Professor Matthew Chu
November 4, 2020

The researcher provides a descriptive, non-rhetorical title.

**Which Type of Battery Is the Most Effective
When Energy Is Drawn Rapidly?**

Introduction

Batteries power many of the products that we use every day, from the TV remote to the car we drive to work. AA batteries are one of the most widely used battery types, but which of these AA batteries is the most effective? Almeida, Xará, Delgado, and Costa (2006) tested five different types of batteries in a study similar to mine. They allowed each of the batteries to run the product for an hour. The product they were powering alternated from open to closed circuit, so the batteries went from not giving off energy to giving off energy very quickly. The researchers then measured the pulse of the battery to determine the charge. The pulse test is a very effective way of reading the battery because it is closed circuit, meaning it doesn't run the battery to find the voltage, and it is highly accurate. They found that the Energizer battery had the largest amount of pulses after the experiment. The Energizer had on average 20 more pulses than the Duracell battery, giving the Energizer battery approximately a half hour longer in battery life when being used rapidly. Booth (1999) also performed a battery experiment using the pulse test. Unlike the experiment performed by Almeida et al., Booth's experiment involved allowing the batteries to constantly give off energy for two hours, and then measuring the pulse. My observational study is closer to Booth's because the product I used, a flashlight, was constantly drawing energy from the battery. Booth found that the Duracell battery had over 40 more pulses per minute than the Energizer battery, which means that the battery could last for an hour longer than the Energizer battery and was therefore more effective.

In today's market, rechargeable batteries are becoming increasing popular. Zucker (2005) compared 16 different types

---

The report follows the conventional IMRaD format.

The researcher establishes a focus for his research by positing a research question.

Reviews previous research, and connects that research to the current research project

of rechargeable batteries. Most of these batteries were Nickel Metal Hydride, but some were the more traditional rechargeable AA battery, the Nickel Cadmium. Zucker looked at how these batteries fared on their second charge after being discharged as closely as possible to empty; rechargeable batteries are not allowed to go to 0 volts because then they cannot be recharged. Zucker found that all but four of the batteries came back up to at least 70% of their initial charge, two of which did not even recharge at all. The two most effective rechargeable batteries were Duracell and Energizer, which both came back to 86% of the first charge. However, the Energizer rechargeable battery had the higher initial charge, so Zucker concluded that the Energizer battery was the most effective rechargeable battery. Yu, Lai, Yan, and Wu (1999) looked at the capacity of three different Nickel Metal Hydride (NiMH) rechargeable batteries. They first took three different types of NiMH batteries and found the electrical capacity through a voltmeter. After, they measured the volume of each of the batteries to discover where it fell in the AA battery range of 600 to 660 mAh/cm3. They used this to test the efficiency of the NiMH batteries, as there are slightly different chemical compositions inside the batteries. In the end they concluded that the NiMH battery from the Duracell brand was the most efficient.

Li, Daniel, and Wood (2011) looked at the improvements being made to lithium ion AA batteries. Lithium ion AA batteries are extremely powerful and have been studied by many researchers. Li et al. tested the voltage of the lithium ion AA rechargeable battery and found that the starting voltage was on average 3.2 volts. That is more than the average onetime-use AA battery. They further found that what makes modern lithium ion batteries so much more powerful are the cathodes, which are composed of materials that significantly increase the rate of reactions.

Continues review of previous scholarship on this topic

4

The objective of this study is to determine which brand of regular AA batteries is the most efficient and to compare a generic rechargeable battery to these regular AA batteries. While my initial research question concerned the effectiveness of batteries over extended usage, for my final study I wanted to look at how batteries reacted when they were being used very quickly. Two research questions drove this study: Which type of battery is the most effective for rapid uses? How do regular AA batteries compare to a generic AA rechargeable battery? My hypothesis for this experiment is that the Energizer battery will be the most effective battery when energy is being taken from the battery rapidly.

Method

Observation Logbook

In my observation logbook I looked at how different types of batteries compared when they were being tested through a flashlight. The batteries I observed were Duracell, Energizer, and a generic brand. Each set of batteries was placed in a flashlight that ran for one continuous hour. After the hour was up, the voltage was tested with a voltmeter. This process was repeated four times, for a total of five days of observations. The batteries were stored at a consistent temperature over the course of the study because temperature affects kinetic energy. The flashlight remained off for one hour between each test so it could cool down.

[Sidebar notes:]

Establishes specific research questions on the basis of previous observations

Hypothesis

Reports on research previously conducted

For the follow-up study, I looked at another aspect of battery performance—how batteries compare when they are being used in quick bursts, rapidly changing from using no energy to using a lot of energy. In addition, I added a rechargeable battery to the study. A strobe light was used instead of a flashlight because a strobe light quickly turns on and off automatically. The batteries were attached to a voltmeter immediately after they were taken out of the strobe light. Each set of batteries was in the strobe light for 20 minutes.

Variables that remained constant for this experiment were the temperature of the room as well as the temperature of the strobe light. For this reason I allowed the strobe light a 30-minute cooldown before I put the next set of batteries into it.

Limitations

Because of budget constraints, the sample size was small. A larger sample size would correct for variations among individual batteries within a brand; data from many batteries would have been averaged. Another limitation of the study was imprecise data, due to a low-quality voltmeter and lack of access to a thermocouple to verify the data. Because the voltmeter was not finely calibrated, the data might not have been completely accurate. With a thermocouple, the temperature of the battery could have been measured and the voltage located on a graph provided by a secondary source. Lack of access to a pulse test reader was another limitation; such an instrument can estimate battery life with high precision.

Results

My results from my logbook provided me with primarily quantitative data. For each of the types of batteries I found these results:

> Provides a detailed account of research procedures

> The researcher uses technical language, or jargon.

> Outlines the major findings of the study. A number of results are also presented visually, in the form of graphs and figures.

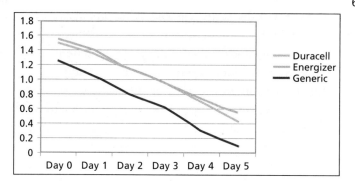

6

The researcher frequently presents results in tables and charts.

The Energizer battery started off with the largest initial charge of 1.55 volts. On average the Energizer battery lost .16 volts for every hour. The Duracell battery had an initial charge of 1.5 volts and lost an average of .18 volts per hour. Last, the generic brand of battery had an initial voltage of 1.25 volts and lost on average .23 volts every hour.

In this experiment the Energizer battery again had the highest starting charge and highest ending charge. The Duracell AA battery was close behind the Energizer. The generic brand of batteries came next, followed by the rechargeable battery.

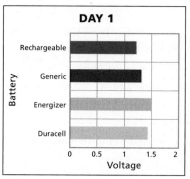

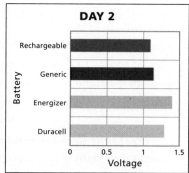

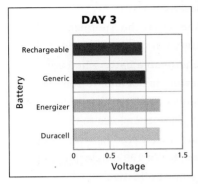

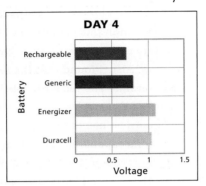

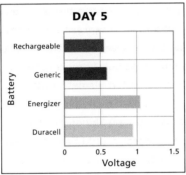

This experiment showed similar results to what I had found in my logbook. The Duracell and Energizer batteries were both very similar, while the generic brand lagged behind.

Battery	Initial voltage (volts)	Final voltage (volts)	Average volts lost (volts/20 min)
Energizer	1.60	1.10	0.10
Duracell	1.55	0.95	0.12
Generic	1.40	0.60	0.16
Rechargeable	1.20	0.55	0.13

The table shows that the Energizer battery had the best results in all categories.

Discussion

Through this experiment I found that the Energizer battery is the most effective battery when used in rapid bursts. Also, I found that the rechargeable battery had very bad ratings. The rechargeable battery is not able to commit as many of its chemicals to solely providing the maximum amount of energy; it has to provide some of the chemicals to the battery's capabilities of recharging. Other studies with similar methods (Booth 1999; Yu, Lai, Yan, & Wu 1999) determined that the Duracell battery was the most effective.

If I had had more days to conduct this experiment, I could have more accurately represented the usefulness of the rechargeable battery, because after it exhausted its first charge it came back completely recharged for the next day. A longer testing period would also allow the batteries to drain more completely, and data could be gathered on how the regular batteries acted near the end of their charge. An area of study for further research would be to compare different types of rechargeable batteries.

If the experiment had a longer overall duration or if the strobe light had been left on for a longer time, it is likely that the rechargeable battery would be ahead of the generic battery in terms of the average voltage lost. It is also likely that the gap would have been larger between the Duracell battery and the Energizer battery because looking at my results from the observation logbook shows that the Energizer battery does a lot better than the Duracell battery toward the end of its life. It appears the Duracell battery does not handle the rapid uses as well as the extended uses.

These results show that the Energizer battery is the most effective battery for rapid use and, from my observation logbook, the most effective for extended use. The value of the rechargeable battery is inconclusive because the data

Provides an overview of the implications of major findings in light of previous scholarship on the rechargeable battery do not take into account its sole advantage, recharging. It would also be interesting to see how the Duracell and Energizer rechargeable batteries compare to their regular batteries.

References

Almeida, M. F., Xará, S. M., Delgado, J., & Costa, C. A. (2006). Characterization of spent AA household alkaline batteries. *Waste Management, 26*(5), 466–476. https://doi.org/10.1016/j.wasman.2005.04.005

Booth, S. A. (1999). High-drain alkaline AA-batteries. *Popular Electronics, 16*(1), 5.

Li, J., Daniel, C., & Wood, D. (2011). Materials processing for lithium-ion batteries. *Journal of Power Sources, 196*(5), 2452–2460. https://doi.org/10.1016/j.jpowsour.2010.11.001

Yu, C. Z., Lai, W. H., Yan, G. J., & Wu, J. Y. (1999). Study of preparation technology for high performance AA size Ni–MH batteries. *Journal of Alloys and Compounds, 293*(1–2), 784–787. https://doi.org/10.1016/S0925-8388(99)00463-6

Zucker, P. (2005). AA batteries tested: Rechargeable batteries. *Australian PC User, 17*(6), 51.

Provides a list of sources used in the construction of the lab report

- **Systematic observation plays a critical role in the natural sciences.** The disciplines of the natural sciences rely on methods of observation to generate and answer research questions about how and why natural phenomena act as they do.

- **Many natural scientists work in interdisciplinary fields of study.** These fields, such as biochemistry and biophysics, combine subject matter and methods from more than one field to address research questions.

- **Scientists typically conduct research according to the steps of the scientific method:** observe, ask a research question, formulate a hypothesis, test the hypothesis through experimentation, and explain results.

- **The scientific writing process follows logically from the steps of the scientific method:** observe and describe, speculate, experiment, and report.

- **To test their hypotheses, or their proposed answers to research questions, natural scientists may use multiple methods.** Two common methods are systematic observation and experimentation.

- **Scientific research proposals are typically vetted by institutional review boards (IRB).** Committees that review research proposals are charged with the task of examining all elements of a scientific study to ensure that it treats subjects equitably and ethically.

- **Conventional rhetorical features of the scientific community reflect the shared values of the community's members.** Some of these values are objectivity, replicability, recency, and cooperation and collaboration.

- **Members of the scientific community frequently produce a number of genres.** These include the observation logbook, the research proposal, and the lab report.

Reading and Writing in the Applied Fields

This chapter offers a basic introduction to a handful of the many applied fields that students often encounter or choose to study as part of their college experience. In some cases, one or more of these applied fields may correspond to your intended major(s) or to selected areas of focus for your intended career. Throughout the chapter, we explore some of the kinds of writing that commonly occur in these fields and that are regularly produced by both students and professionals working in these fields. Because the applied fields vary so much, and since it would be impossible to generalize conventional expectations for communication across these diverse fields, our aim here is not to teach you to become an expert researcher or communicator in these fields. Instead, our purpose is to highlight a rhetorical approach to these fields that would be helpful for any student attempting to acclimate to one or more of the diverse communities of the applied fields and their expectations.

Applied fields are areas of academic study that focus on the production of practical knowledge and that share a core mission of preparing students for specific careers. Often, such preparation includes hands-on training. The applied fields that we will look at in this chapter are nursing, teaching, business, law, engineering, and information technology. A list of some additional applied fields appears below.

ANDREA TSURUMI

Some Applied Fields

Accounting	Journalism
Architecture	Manufacturing technology
Aviation technology	Physical education
Counseling	Social work
Cybersecurity	Software development
Forensics	Sports psychology
Hospitality management	Statistics

As you might expect, research that occurs in the applied fields is quite varied. These variations among the fields are often reflected in the kinds of questions each field asks and attempts to answer, the forms of evidence it relies on, the data-collection methods it employs, and the ways it reports findings from research to differing audiences. Nevertheless, research in the applied fields typically attempts to solve problems. An automotive engineering team, for example, might start with a problem like consumers' reluctance to buy an all-electric vehicle. To address the issue, the engineering team would first attempt to define the scope of the problem. Why does the problem exist? What are the factors contributing to consumers' reluctance to buy an all-electric vehicle? Once the problem has been identified and clearly defined, the team of researchers can then begin to explore possible solutions.

Examples of large-scale problems that require practical applications of research include issues such as racial inequality in the American criminal justice system, the lack of clean drinking water in some nonindustrialized nations and U.S. cities, obesity and heart disease, and ways to provide outstanding public education to children with special needs. These are all real-world problems scholars and practitioners in the applied fields are working to solve this very moment.

Professionals in applied fields often work in collaboration with one another, or in teams, to complete research and other projects, and professors who teach in these areas frequently assign tasks that require interaction and cooperation among a group of students to create a product or to solve a problem. In the field of business management, for example, teams of professionals often must work together to market a new product. Solid communication and interpersonal skills are necessary for a team to manage a budget, design a marketing or advertising campaign, and engage with a client successfully all at the same time. As such, the ability to work cooperatively — to demonstrate effective interpersonal and team communication skills — is highly valued among professionals in the applied fields. You shouldn't be surprised, then, if you're one day applying for a job in an applied field and an interviewer asks you to share a little about your previous experiences working in teams to successfully complete a project. As you learn more about the applied fields examined in this chapter, take care to note those writing tasks completed by teams, or those moments when cooperation among professionals working in a particular field is highlighted by the content of the genres we explore.

Connect 10.1   **Considering Additional Applied Fields**

Visit your college or university's website, and locate a listing of the majors or concentrations offered in any academic department. In light of the definition of an *applied field* proposed above, consider whether any of the majors or →

concentrations identified for that particular discipline could be described as applied fields. Additionally, spend some time considering your own major or potential area of concentration: Are you studying an applied field? Are there areas of study within your major or concentration that could be considered applied fields? If so, what are they, and why would you consider them applied fields?

Rhetoric and the Applied Fields

Because applied fields are centrally focused on preparing professionals who will work in those fields, students are often asked to engage audiences associated with the work they'll do in those fields after graduation. Imagine that you've just graduated from college with a degree in business management and have secured a job as a marketing director for a business. What kinds of writing do you expect to encounter in this new position? What audiences do you expect to be writing for? You may well be asked to prepare business analyses or market reports. You may be asked to involve yourself in new product management or even the advertising campaign for a product. All these activities, which call for different kinds of writing, will require you to manage information and to shape your communication of that information into texts that are designed specifically for other professionals in your field—such as boards of directors, financial officers, or advertising executives. As a student in the applied field of business management, you therefore need to become familiar with the audiences, genres, conventions, and other expectations for writing specific to your career path that extend beyond academic audiences. Being mindful of the rhetorical situation in which you must communicate with other professionals is essential to your potential success as a writer in an applied field.

As with more traditional academic writing, we recommend that you analyze carefully any writing situation you encounter in an applied field. You might begin by responding to the following questions:

1. **Who is my audience?** Unlike the audience for a lab report for a chemistry class or the audience for an interpretation of a poem in a literature class, your audience for writing in an applied field is just as likely to be non-academic as academic. Certainly, the writing most students will do in their actual careers will be aimed at other professionals in their field, not researchers or professors in a university. In addition to understanding exactly who your audience is, you'll want to be sure to consider the specific needs of your target audience.

2. **In light of my purpose and my audience's needs, is there an appropriate genre I should rely on to communicate my information?** As in the more traditional academic disciplines, there are many genres through which professionals in applied fields communicate. Based on an analysis of your rhetorical

situation, and keeping your purpose for writing in mind, you'll want to consider whether the information you have to share should be reported in a specific genre: Should you write a memorandum, a marketing proposal, or an executive summary, for instance? Answering this question can help you determine if there is an appropriate form, or genre, through which to communicate your information.

3. **Are there additional conventional expectations I should consider for the kind of writing task I need to complete?** Beyond simply identifying an appropriate genre, answering this question can help you determine how to shape the information you need to communicate to your target audience. If the writing task requires a particular genre, then you're likely to rely on features that conventionally appear as part of that genre. Of course, there are many good reasons to communicate information in other ways. In these situations, we recommend that you carefully consider the appropriateness of the structural, language, and reference features you employ.

In the sections that follow, we offer brief introductions to some applied fields of study and provide examples of genres that students and professionals working in these fields often produce. We explore expectations for these genres by highlighting conventional structure, language, and reference features that writers in these fields frequently employ.

Health Fields

One of the fastest-growing segments of the U.S. economy is related to health services. As the population of the country ages, and as science and medicine come together to lengthen average life spans, it's not surprising that health professionals of all sorts, including those with various levels of training and expertise in providing emotional, mental, and physical health services, are in high demand.

Along with this increased demand and the continued development of the medical arts as a result of scientific discoveries and technological advances, it's also not surprising that the allied health fields are constantly expanding and evolving to meet the needs of patients. The Association of Schools of Allied Health Professionals defines *allied health* as "those health professions that are distinct from medicine and nursing." Allied health professionals typically work in a highly cooperative manner with other professionals, including medical doctors and nurses, to provide various forms of direct and indirect care to patients. In fact, allied health professionals regularly have a role to play in the prevention, diagnosis, treatment, and recovery from illness for most patients. A small sampling of the many diverse allied health fields includes the following:

- Medical assistant
- Nutritionist
- Occupational therapist

- Phlebotomist
- Physical therapist
- Physician assistant
- Radiographer
- Respiratory therapist
- Speech pathologist

Most of us have had experiences with nurses, who, along with physicians and other health professionals, serve on the front lines of preventing and treating illness in our society. In addition to their hands-on engagement with individuals in clinical and community settings, nurses spend a good deal of their time writing—whether documenting their observations about patients in medical charts, preparing orders for medical procedures, designing care plans, or communicating with patients. A student of nursing might encounter any number of additional forms of writing tasks, including nursing care plans for individuals, reviews of literature, and community or public health assessment papers, just to name a few. Each of these forms of communication requires that nurses be especially attuned to the needs of various audiences. A nurse communicating with a patient, for example, might have to translate medical jargon so that the individual can fully understand his or her treatment. Alternatively, a nurse who is producing a care plan for a patient would likely need to craft the document such that other nurses and medical professionals could follow methodically the assessments and recommendations for care. Some nurses, especially those who undertake advanced study or who

Insider's View
Janna Dieckmann on Research in Nursing

COURTESY OF JANNA DIECKMANN

"Research in nursing is varied, including quantitative research into health and illness patterns, as well as intervention to maximize health and reduce illness. Qualitative research varies widely, including research in the history of nursing, which is my focus. There is a wide variety of types of writing demanded in a nursing program. It is so varied that many connections are possible. Cross-discipline collaborations among faculty of various professional schools are valued at many academic institutions today. One of my colleagues conducted research on rats. Another looked at sleep patterns in older adults as a basis for understanding dementia onset. One public health nursing colleague conducts research on out-of-work women, and another examines cross-cultural competence. These interests speak to our reasons for becoming nurses—our seeking out of real life, of direct experience, of being right there with people, and of understanding others and their worlds."

prepare others to become nurses, often design, implement, or participate in research studies.

● **Discharge Instructions**   If you've ever been hospitalized, then you probably remember the experience quite vividly. It's likely that you interacted with a nurse, who perhaps assessed your health upon arrival. You were also likely cared for by a nurse, or a particular group of nurses, during your stay. Nurses also often play an integral role in a patient's discharge from a hospital. Typically, before a patient is released from a hospital, a nurse explains to the patient (and perhaps a family member or two, or another intended primary caregiver) and provides in written form a set of instructions for aftercare. This constitutes the discharge instructions.

This document, or series of documents, includes instructions for how to care for oneself at home. The instructions may focus on managing diet and medications, as well as caring for other needs, such as post-operative bandaging procedures. They may also include exercise or diet management plans recommended for long-term recovery and health maintenance. These plans may include seeing an allied health professional such as a physical or occupational therapist. Often presented in a series of bulleted items or statements, these lists are usually highly generic; that is, the same instructions frequently apply for patients with the same or similar health conditions. For this reason, discharge instruction forms may include spaces for nurses or other healthcare professionals to write in more specific information relating to a patient's individual circumstances. As well, discharge instructions frequently include information about a patient's follow-up care with his or her doctor or primary caregiver. This could take the form of a future appointment time or directions to call for a follow-up appointment or to consult with another physician. An additional conventional element of discharge instructions is a list of signs of a medical emergency and directions concerning when and how to seek medical attention immediately, should certain signs or symptoms appear in the patient. Finally, discharge instructions are typically signed and dated by a physician or nurse, and they are sometimes signed by the patient as well.

Many patients are in unclear states of mind or are extremely vulnerable at the time of release from a hospital, so nurses who provide and explain discharge instructions to patients are highly skilled at assessing patients' understanding of these instructions.

....

Insider Example
Discharge Instructions

The following text is an example of a typical set of discharge instructions. As you read the document, consider areas in the instructions that you think a nurse would be more likely to stress to a patient in a discharge meeting: What would a nurse cover quickly? What would a nurse want to communicate most clearly to a patient?   ▶

FIRST HOSPITAL
Where Care Comes First

Patient's Name:	John Q. Patient
Healthcare Provider's Name:	First Hospital
Department:	Cardiology
Phone:	617-555-1212
Date:	Thursday, May 8, 2021
Notes:	**Nurses can write personalized notes to the patient here.**

Discharge Instructions for Heart Attack

A heart attack occurs when blood flow to the heart muscle is interrupted. This deprives the heart muscle of oxygen, causing tissue damage or tissue death. Common treatments include lifestyle changes, oxygen, medicines, and surgery.

Steps to Take

Home Care

- Rest until your doctor says it is okay to return to work or other activities.
- Take all medicines as prescribed by your doctor. Beta-blockers, ACE inhibitors, and antiplatelet therapy are often recommended.
- Attend a cardiac rehabilitation program if recommended by your doctor.

Diet
Eat a heart-healthy diet:

- Limit your intake of fat, cholesterol, and sodium. Foods such as ice cream, cheese, baked goods, and red meat are not the best choices.
- Increase your intake of whole grains, fish, fruits, vegetables, and nuts.
- Discuss supplements with your doctor.

Your doctor may refer you to a dietician to advise you on meal planning.

Physical Activity
The American Heart Association recommends at least 30 minutes of exercise daily, or at least 3–4 times per week, for

---

Provides identifying information about the patient, as well as name and contact information of healthcare provider

Much of the information provided in discharge instructions is generic, so nurses can provide "personalized notes" here.

Provides a brief overview of the patient's medical issue treated by the healthcare provider

Provides specific instructions for the patient to follow upon release from the medical facility

Note that each of these directions begins with a verb, stressing the importance of taking the action indicated.

patients who have had a heart attack. Your doctor will let you know when you are ready to begin regular exercise.

- Ask your doctor when you will be able to return to work.
- Ask your doctor when you may resume sexual activity.
- Do not drive unless your doctor has given you permission to do so.

Medications

The following medicines may be prescribed to prevent you from having another heart attack:

- Aspirin, which has been shown to decrease the risk of heart attacks
  - Certain painkillers, such as ibuprofen, when taken together with aspirin, may put you at high risk for gastrointestinal bleeding and also reduce the effectiveness of aspirin.
- Clopidogrel or prasugrel
  - Avoid omeprazole or esomeprazole if you take clopidogrel. They may make clopidogrel not work. Ask your doctor for other drug choices.
- ACE inhibitors
- Nitroglycerin
- Beta-blockers or calcium channel blockers
- Cholesterol-lowering medicines
- Blood pressure medicines
- Pain medicines
- Anti-anxiety or antidepressant medicines

If you are taking medicines, follow these general guidelines:

- Take your medicine as directed. Do not change the amount or the schedule.
- Do not stop taking them without talking to your doctor.
- Do not share them.
- Ask what the results and side effects are. Report them to your doctor.
- Some drugs can be dangerous when mixed. Talk to a doctor or pharmacist if you are taking more than one drug. This includes over-the-counter medicine and herbal or dietary supplements.
- Plan ahead for refills so you do not run out.

Lifestyle Changes and Prevention

Together, you and your doctor will plan proper lifestyle changes that will aid in your recovery. Some things to keep in mind to recover and prevent another heart attack include:

Note that specific directions are listed in a series of bulleted sections. Bulleted lists make the information easier to read and follow.

Directions are provided in as few words as possible.

- If you smoke, talk to your doctor about ways to help you quit. There are many options to choose from, like using nicotine replacement products, taking prescription medicines to ease cravings and withdrawal symptoms, participating in smoking cessation classes, or doing an online self-help program.
- Have your cholesterol checked regularly.
- Get regular medical check-ups.
- Control your blood pressure.
- Eat a healthful diet, one that is low in saturated fat and rich in whole grains, fruits, and vegetables.
- Have a regular, low-impact exercise program.
- Maintain a healthy weight.
- Manage stress through activities such as yoga, meditation, and counseling.
- If you have diabetes, maintain good control of your condition.

Follow-Up

Since your recovery needs to be monitored, be sure to keep all appointments and have exams done regularly as directed by your doctor. In addition, some people have feelings of depression or anxiety after a heart attack. To get the help you need, be sure to discuss these feelings with your doctor.

Schedule a follow-up appointment as directed by your doctor.

Provides directions for how to "follow up" with medical provider(s)

Call for Medical Help Right Away If Any of the Following Occurs

Call for medical help right away if you have symptoms of another heart attack, including:

- Chest pain, which may feel like a crushing weight on your chest
- A sense of fullness, squeezing, or pressure in the chest
- Anxiety, especially feeling a sense of doom or panic without apparent reason
- Rapid, irregular heartbeat
- Pain, tingling, or numbness in the left shoulder and arm, the neck or jaw, or the right arm
- Sweating
- Nausea or vomiting
- Indigestion or heartburn
- Lightheadedness, weakness, or fainting
- Shortness of breath
- Abdominal pain

If you think you have an emergency, call for medical help right away.

Identifies emergency indicators

Education

When your teachers tell you that writing is important, they're probably conveying a belief based on their own experiences. Professional educators do a lot of writing. As students, you're aware of many contexts in which teachers

Insider's View
Vice Chancellor Bruce Moses on Writing as an Administrator

COURTESY OF BRUCE MOSES

"In my college administrative role, I typically engage in two types of writing, expository and persuasive (argumentative) writing. College administrators spend a significant amount of time investigating ideas, collecting and evaluating evidence that supports these ideas, and presenting innovations to their colleagues through expository writing. The exploration of these ideas requires an extensive amount of research to build a strong case based on logic, facts, peer-based examples, and expert opinions. Typically, innovative ideas are met with scrutiny, which requires presenting multiple arguments to convince the audience that your idea is a logical option. The culture of higher education institutions necessitates that the narrative presents appropriate contextualized evidence, consideration of alternative views, and incorporates inclusive voices from across the college.

"My experience with persuasive writing often involves responding to outside agencies that have standards, regulations, and laws the college has an external accountability to meet. It is similar to writing a law brief. In most cases, the content contains issues that the reader can dispute if the facts of the matter and argument do not significantly meet the minimum threshold of the standard, regulation, and law. My goals are to be short in content, concise, and to provide data or evidence that supports my argument or synopsis."

write on a daily basis. They have project assignment sheets to design, papers to comment on and grade, websites to design, and e-mails to answer, just to name a few. However, educators also spend a great deal of time planning classes and designing lesson plans. Though students rarely see these written products, they are essential, if challenging and time-consuming, endeavors for teachers.

● **Lesson Plan** When designing a lesson plan, teachers must consider many factors, including their goals and objectives for student learning, the materials needed to execute a lesson, the activities students will participate in as part of a lesson, and the methods they'll use to assess student learning. Among other considerations, teachers must also make sure their lesson plans help them meet prescribed curricular mandates.

....

Insider Example
Student Lesson Plan

The following lesson plan for a tenth-grade English class was designed by Myra Moses, who at the time of writing the plan was a doctoral candidate in education. In this plan, Moses begins by identifying the state-mandated curricular standards the lesson addresses. She then identifies the broader goals of her lesson plan before establishing the more specific objectives, or exactly what students will do to reach the broader learning goals. As you read, notice that all the plan's statements of objectives begin with a verb, as they identify actions students will take to demonstrate their learning. The plan ends by explaining the classroom activities the teacher will use to facilitate learning and by identifying the methods the instructor will use to assess student learning. These structural moves are conventional for the genre of a lesson plan.

Educational Standard ➤ Goals ➤ Objectives ➤ Materials ➤ Classroom Activities ➤ Assessment

▶

Lesson Plan

Overview and Purpose

This lesson is part of a unit on Homer's *Odyssey*. Prior to this lesson students will have had a lesson on Greek cultural and social values during the time of Homer, and they will have read the *Odyssey*. In the lesson, students will analyze passages from the *Odyssey* to examine the author's and characters' points of view. Students will participate in whole class discussion, work in small groups, and work individually to identify and evaluate point of view.

Education Standards Addressed

This lesson addresses the following objectives from the NC Standard Course of Study for Language Arts: English II:

1.02 Respond reflectively (through small group discussion, class discussion, journal entry, essay, letter, dialogue) to written and visual texts by:
- relating personal knowledge to textual information or class discussion.
- showing an awareness of one's own culture as well as the cultures of others.
- exhibiting an awareness of culture in which text is set or in which text was written.

1.03 Demonstrate the ability to read, listen to, and view a variety of increasingly complex print and non-print expressive texts appropriate to grade level and course literary focus, by:
- identifying and analyzing text components (such as organizational structures, story elements, organizational features) and evaluating their impact on the text.
- providing textual evidence to support understanding of and reader's response to text.
- making inferences, predicting, and drawing conclusions based on text.
- identifying and analyzing personal, social, historical, or cultural influences, contexts, or biases.

5.01 Read and analyze selected works of world literature by:
- understanding the importance of cultural and historical impact on literary texts.

Identifies the state-mandated curricular elements, or the educational objectives, the lesson addresses. Notice that these are quite broad in scope.

Goals

1. To teach students how to identify and evaluate an author's point of view and purpose by examining the characters' point of view
2. To teach students to critically examine alternate points of view

Teacher identifies specific goals for the lesson. These goals fit well within the broader state-mandated curricular standards.

Objectives

Students will:

1. Identify point of view in a story by examining the text and evaluating how the main character views his/her world at different points in the story.
2. Demonstrate that they understand point of view by using examples and evidence from the text to support what they state is the character's point of view.
3. Apply their knowledge and understanding of point of view by taking a passage from the text and rewriting it from a supporting character's point of view.
4. Evaluate the rationality of a character's point of view by measuring it against additional information gathered from the text, or their own life experience.

Objectives identify what students will do as part of the lesson. Notice that the statements of objectives begin with verbs.

Materials, Resources

- Copies of *The Odyssey*
- DVD with video clips from television and/or movies
- Flip chart paper
- Markers
- Directions and rubric for individual assignment

Identifies materials needed for the lesson

Activities

Session 1

1. Review information from previous lesson about popular cultural and social views held during Homer's time (e.g., Greek law of hospitality). This would be a combination of a quiz and whole class discussion.
2. Teacher-led class discussion defining and examining point of view by viewing clips from popular television shows and movies.
3. Teacher-led discussion of 1 example from *The Odyssey*. E.g., examine Odysseus's point of view when he violates Greek law of hospitality during his encounter with the Cyclops, Polyphemus. Examine this encounter through

Outlines classroom procedures for the two-day lesson plan

the lens of what Homer might be saying about the value Greeks placed on hospitality.

4. In small groups the students will choose 3 places in the epic and evaluate Odysseus's point of view. Students will then determine what Odysseus's point of view might reflect about Homer's point of view and purpose for that part of the epic.

5. Groups will begin to create a visual using flip chart paper and markers to represent their interpretations of Odysseus's point of view to reflect about Homer's point of view and purpose.

Session 2

1. Groups will complete visual.
2. Groups will present their work to the rest of the class.
3. The class will discuss possible alternate interpretations of Homer's point of view and purpose.
4. Class will review aspects of point of view based on information teacher provided at the beginning of the class.
5. Beginning during class and finishing for homework, students will individually take one passage from the epic that was not discussed by their groups and do the following:
   - write a brief description of a main character's point of view
   - write a response to prompts that guide students in evaluating the rationality of the main character's point of view based on information gathered from the text, or the students' own life experience
   - rewrite the passage from a supporting character's point of view

Assessment

Identifies how the teacher will assess students' mastery of the concepts and material covered in the lesson

- Evaluate students' understanding of Greek cultural/social values from Homer's time through the quiz.
- Evaluate group's understanding of point of view by examining the visual product—this artifact will not be graded, but oral feedback will be provided that should help the students in completing the independent assignment.
- Evaluate the written, individual assignment.

Business

Communication in businesses takes many forms, and professionals writing in business settings may spend substantial amounts of time drafting e-mails and memos, or writing letters and proposals. In some instances, businesses may hire individuals solely for their expertise in business communication practices. Such individuals are highly skilled in the analysis and practice of business communication, and their education and training are often aimed at these purposes. Still, if your experiences lead you to employment in a business setting, you're likely to face the task of communicating in one or more of the genres frequently used in those settings. It's no surprise, then, that schools of business, which prepare students to work in companies and corporations, often require their students to take classes that foster an understanding of the vehicles of communication common to the business setting. In the following section, we provide some introductory context and an annotated example of a business memorandum, a common genre of communication in the business community.

● **Memorandum** The memorandum, or memo, is a specialized form of communication used within businesses to make announcements and to share information among colleagues and employees. Although memos serve a range of purposes, like sharing information, providing directives, or even arguing a particular position, they are not generally used to communicate with outside parties, like other companies or clients. While they may range in length from a couple of paragraphs to multiple pages, they're typically highly structured according to conventional expectations. In fact, you'd be hard-pressed to find an example of a professional memo that didn't follow the conventional format for identifying the writer, the audience, the central subject matter, and the date of production in the header. Also, information in memos typically appears in a block format, and the content is often developed from a clear, centralized purpose that is revealed early on in the memo itself.

....

Insider Example

Student Memorandum

The following is an example of a memo produced by a student in a professional writing class. His purpose for writing was to share his assessment of the advantages and drawbacks of a particular company he's interested in working for in the future. As you read, notice how the information in the opening paragraphs forecasts the memo's content and how the memo summarizes its contents in the concluding passages. We've highlighted a number of the other conventional expectations for the memo that you'll want to notice. ▶

MEMO

To: Jamie Larsen
          Professor, North Carolina State University
From: James Blackwell
          Biological Engineering, North Carolina State University
Date: September 2, 2014
Subject: Investigative Report on Hazen and Sawyer

I plan on one day using my knowledge gained in biological engineering to help alleviate the growing environmental problems that our society faces. Hazen and Sawyer is a well-known environmental engineering firm. However, I need to research the firm's background in order to decide if it would be a suitable place for me to work. Consequently, I decided to research the following areas of Hazen and Sawyer engineering firm:

- Current and Past Projects
- Opportunities for Employment and Advancement
- Work Environment

The purpose of this report is to present you with my findings on Hazen and Sawyer, so that you may assist me in writing an application letter that proves my skills and knowledge are worthy of an employment opportunity.

Current and Past Projects

Founded in 1951, Hazen and Sawyer has had a long history of providing clean drinking water and minimizing the effects of water pollution. The company has undertaken many projects in the United States as well as internationally. One of its first projects was improving the infrastructure of Monrovia, Liberia, in 1952. I am interested in using my knowledge of environmental problems to promote sustainability. Designing sustainable solutions for its clients is one of the firm's main goals. Hazen and Sawyer is currently engaged in a project to provide water infrastructure to over one million people in Jordan. Supplying clean drinking water is a problem that is continuously growing, and I hope to work on a similar project someday.

Opportunities for Employment and Advancement

Hazen and Sawyer has over forty offices worldwide, with regional offices in Raleigh, NC, Cincinnati, OH, Dallas, TX, Hollywood, FL, Los Angeles, CA, and its headquarters in New York City. The company currently has over thirty job openings at offices across the United States. I would like to live in the

The writer uses conventional formatting in the To, From, Date, and Subject lines.

Paragraphs are blocked and single-spaced.

Reasons for the student's interest in this company are bulleted and become the developed sections in the remainder of the memo. Important information is often bulleted in memos.

The memo announces its purpose clearly, forecasting the content to follow.

Headers are used to break up the content in memos. In this instance, the student uses headers that correspond to the areas of interest in the company he is exploring for potential employment.

The writer relies on formal language, evidenced here by avoiding contractions.

Raleigh area following graduation, so having a regional office here in Raleigh greatly helps my chances of finding a local job with the company. Hazen and Sawyer also has offices in Greensboro and Charlotte, which also helps my chances of finding a job in North Carolina. I am interested in finding a job dealing with stream restoration, and the Raleigh office currently has an opening for a Stream Restoration Designer. The position requires experience with AutoCAD and GIS, and I have used both of these programs in my Biological Engineering courses.

In addition to numerous job openings, Hazen and Sawyer also offers opportunities for professional development within the company. The Pathway Program for Professional Development is designed to keep employees up-to-date on topics in their fields and also stay educated to meet license requirements in different states. Even if I found a job at the Raleigh office, I would most likely have to travel out of state to work on projects, so this program could be very beneficial. I am seeking to work with a company that promotes continuous professional growth, so this program makes me very interested in Hazen and Sawyer.

Work Environment

Hazen and Sawyer supports innovation and creativity, and at the same time tries to limit bureaucracy. I am seeking a company that will allow me to be creative and assist with projects while not being in charge initially. As I gain experience and learn on the job, I hope to move into positions with greater responsibility. The firm offers a mentoring program that places newly hired engineers with someone more experienced. This program would help me adapt to the company and provide guidance as I gain professional experience. I hope to eventually receive my Professional Engineering license, so working under a professional engineer with years of experience would be a great opportunity for me. Hazen and Sawyer supports positive relationships among its employees, by engaging them in social outings such as sporting events, parties, picnics, and other activities.

References

Hazen and Sawyer—Environmental Engineers and Scientists. Web. 2 Sept. 2014. <http://www.hazenandsawyer.com/home/>.

Notice the organizational pattern employed in the body paragraphs. The writer begins by describing potential employer and then relates that information to his particular needs, desires, or circumstances.

References are usually indicated in an attachment.

Connect 10.4   **Considering Audience Values for a Business Memo**

Business memos are typically addressed to a specific audience, most often made up of business professionals. Study the sample student memo on pages 274–76 carefully and write a one-paragraph description of its intended audience. As part of your response, answer the following questions about the audience:

- Who is the intended audience for the memo? How do you know who the intended audience is?

- What does the audience need to learn from the memo? How do you know what the intended audience needs to learn?

- What does the memo's intended audience value, based on their position or role? How does the memo address or connect to those values?

Criminal Justice and Law

Millions of people are employed in the areas of law and criminal justice in the United States. When we encounter the terms *law* and *criminal justice*, the image of a lawyer, or attorney, often comes to mind first. No doubt, attorneys make vital contributions to almost every aspect of our lives; their work helps us to understand, to enforce, and even to change our policies, procedures, and laws, whether they are civil or criminal in nature. Though attorneys make a significant contribution to our system of governance, they actually represent only a fraction of the vast number of professionals who work in the U.S. criminal justice system.

If you've ever watched a crime show on television, then you've likely been exposed to some of the many areas of training and expertise that make up the U.S. criminal justice system. Professionals who work in the fields of criminal justice are responsible for enforcing our laws and ensuring the safety of our communities. They are also responsible for such jobs as investigating crime scenes, staffing our jails and prisons, and providing essential services to victims of crimes and to those charged with or convicted of a crime. Careers in the fields of criminal justice range from forensic technician to parole officer to corrections counselor. While each of these career paths requires a different level of training and expertise, and many colleges and universities offer specific plans of study that culminate in certification or licensure in these diverse areas, they are unified by a commitment to the just treatment of all individuals under the law.

As criminologist Michelle Richter notes in her "Insider's View," there are various reasons that might compel an individual to choose a career in criminal justice, and there are various constituencies to whom differing careers in the fields of criminal justice must deliver support and services. Here's a small sampling of the many career paths available to those interested in the field of criminal justice:

- Bailiff
- Correctional officer
- Corrections counselor
- Court reporter
- Emergency management director
- Fire inspector
- Forensic science technician
- Legal secretary
- Paralegal
- Police detective
- Sheriff and deputy sheriff

Insider's View
Criminologist Michelle Richter on Choosing a Career in Criminal Justice

"Motivation can be really critical. . . . If you want to work with people, it gets really complex. Do you want to work with law-abiding citizens or folks who have not been convicted of anything? Or do you want to work with the offender population? Do you want to work with the victim population? If you're looking at offenders, do you want to work with adults? Juveniles? Men, women, the elderly, the disabled, the mentally disabled? Most of the time students go into criminal justice, criminology, and forensics to understand a particular type of behavior, or to make the world a better place, or to make it safer, or something has happened to them in the past, and they want to make sure nobody ever has to go through that again. So there's a wide variety of reasons for being here."

Most of us probably have clichéd understandings of the law at work. Many of these likely originated from television shows and movies. In these scenarios, there's almost always lots of drama as the lawyers battle in court, parse witnesses' words, and attempt to sway a judge or jury to their side of a case.

In real life, the practice of law may not always be quite as dramatic or enthralling as it appears on the screen. In fact, many lawyers rarely, or maybe never, appear in court. A criminal defense attorney may regularly appear before a judge or jury in a courtroom setting, but a corporate lawyer may spend the majority of her time drafting and analyzing business contracts. This difference is directly related to the field of law an individual specializes in, be it criminal law, family law, tax law, or environmental law, just to name a few.

Regardless of an attorney's chosen specialization, though, the study of law remains fundamentally concerned with debates over the interpretation of language. This is because the various rules that govern our lives—statutes, ordinances, regulations, and laws, for example—are all constructed in language. As you surely recognize, language can be quite slippery, and rules can often be interpreted in many different ways. We need only briefly to consider current debates over free speech issues or the "right to bear arms" or marriage equality to understand how complicated the business of interpreting laws can become. In the United States, the U.S. Supreme Court holds the authority to provide the final interpretation on the meaning of disputed laws. However, there are lots of legal interpretations and arguments that lower courts must make on a daily basis, and only a tiny portion of cases are ever heard by the U.S. Supreme Court.

As in the other applied fields, there are many common forms of communication in the various fields of law, as lawyers must regularly communicate with different kinds of stakeholders, including clients, other lawyers, judges, and law enforcement officials. For this reason, individuals working in the legal professions are generally expert at composing e-mail messages, memos, letters to clients, and legal briefs, among other genres. The following example of an e-mail communication from an attorney provides a glimpse into one type of writing through which lawyers frequently communicate.

● **E-Mail Correspondence**   As you might expect, technological advances can have a profound impact on the communication practices of professionals. There may always be a place for hard copies of documents, but e-mail communication has no doubt replaced many of the letters that used to pass between parties via the U.S. Postal Service. Like most professionals these days, those employed in the legal fields often spend a lot of time communicating with stakeholders via e-mail. These professionals carefully assess each rhetorical situation for which an e-mail communication is necessary, both (1) to make sure the ideas they share with stakeholders (the explanations of legal procedures, or legal options, or applicable precedents, etc.) are accurate, and (2) to make sure they communicate those ideas in an appropriate fashion (with the appropriate tone, clarity, precision, etc.).

Insider Example

E-Mail Correspondence from Attorney

The following example is an e-mail sent from a practicing lawyer to a client. In this instance, the lawyer offers legal advice concerning a possible donation from a party to a foundation. As you read the lawyer's description of the documents attached to his e-mail correspondence with the client, pay attention to the ways the attorney demonstrates an acute awareness of his audience, both in terms of the actual legal advice he provides and in terms of the structure and language of his message. ▶

Establishes the level of familiarity and tone

Provides transactional advice, explaining what procedure needs to occur between the two parties involved: a donor and a receiving foundation

Provides additional advice to protect the interests of the parties in the event that either party decides to back out of the transaction

Explains more specific details included in the attached legal documents to protect the interests of the Foundation

Communicates a willingness to continue the relationship with the client

Provides standard identification and contact information for communication between and among professionals

Dear _____

As promised, here are two documents related to the proposed gift of the ABC property to the XYZ Foundation (the "Foundation"). The first document summarizes the recommended due diligence steps (including the creation of a limited liability company) that should take place prior to the acceptance of the property, accompanied by estimated costs associated with each such step. The second document contains a draft "pre-acceptance" agreement that the Foundation could use to recover its documented costs in the event that either the donor or the Foundation backs out of a gift agreement following the due diligence process.

You will note that we have limited the Foundation's ability to recover costs in the event that the Foundation is the party that "pulls the plug." In such a scenario, the Foundation could recover costs only if it reasonably determines that either (i) the property would create a risk of material exposure to environmentally related liabilities or (ii) the remediation of environmental issues would impose material costs on the Foundation. We realize that even in light of this limiting language, the agreement represents a fairly aggressive approach with the donor, and we will be glad to work with you if you wish to take a softer stance.

Please don't hesitate to call me with any questions, concerns, or critiques. As always, we appreciate the opportunity to serve you in furthering the Foundation's good work.

Best regards,

Joe

Joseph E. Miller, Jr.
Partner

joe.miller@FaegreBD.com
Direct: +1 317 237 1415
FaegreBD.com Download vCard
FAEGRE BAKER DANIELS LLP
300 N. Meridian Street
Suite 2700
Indianapolis, IN 46204, USA

Engineering

Engineers shape our daily lives in countless ways. Nearly everything we might purchase at a store has been shaped by one or more engineers, who design, develop, and deliver products that make our lives better. Their influence is evident in the roads we drive on, in the design and construction of the buildings in which we learn and work, and in the technologies we employ on a daily basis. *Engineering* is a broad term used to describe various applied fields of study that rely on mathematical and scientific concepts to analyze, design, model, and/or develop structures for practical purposes. Some fields of engineering include:

- Chemical engineering
- Civil engineering
- Computer engineering
- Electrical engineering
- Mechanical engineering
- Nuclear engineering

In addition to being skilled in science and mathematics, engineers typically are highly adept at teamwork: they work with others to identify problems, propose solutions, and develop tools or systems to respond to those problems. For example, it would likely take a rather large team of engineers with varying backgrounds and expertise to diagnose a flaw in the design of an airplane, to offer a new design in response, and to test the new design for safety and reliability. The work of engineers also requires a substantial amount of writing.

MICHAEL GIERDOWSKI

"Many of my day-to-day activities involve completing forms to document the need for training and the generation of training materials such as lesson plans (typically PowerPoint), lab guides, and qualification guides for the conduct of on-the-job training. Much of my actual *writing* experience comes from developing these materials. Our training materials must be written at the right level of detail to (1) ensure the trainees get the knowledge they need from the training and (2) provide assurance that the same training can be reproduced the next time it is taught. It needs to contain the appropriate level of detail about a subject, rather than just a prompt to discuss a broad subject."

● **PowerPoint Training Slides**   One form of communication engineers often engage in involves the training of others. Imagine, for instance, that you're a lead engineer at a nuclear power plant, and you are tasked with the job of training a group of newly hired engineers in the technical operations of the plant. Likely as not, you would have to produce a substantial amount of training material. In the Insider Example below, we offer a look at such training materials, which often take the form of PowerPoint slides. As you study the slides, pay attention to evidence that points to an audience of trainees.

Insider Example

PowerPoint Slides

The slides and accompanying script in this Insider Example illustrate one of the many types of texts that engineers produce.

Notice when the slides rely on images to convey information in a concise form.

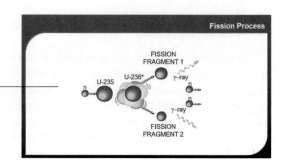

- A U-235 nucleus absorbs a neutron, resulting in U-236* in the "excited state," indicated by the asterisk.
- A fraction of a second later, the nucleus splits into 2 new nuclei, or fission fragments, emitting 2 or 3 neutrons and gamma rays.
- A self-sustaining chain reaction occurs when enough neutrons produced from fission events go on to produce more fissions.
- Once the chain reaction is self-sustaining, the reactor is critical.

Notice that each slide has a title that indicates its topic.

Notice the use of bulleted lists in a number of slides. These lists indicate important ideas or concepts to be discussed during the presenter's remarks.

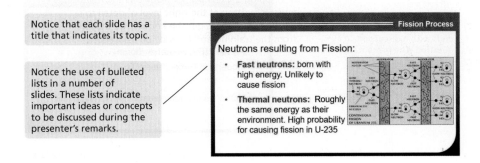

- These 2 terms are related to the amount of energy a neutron has:
  - **Fast neutrons** are born with a large amount of energy and are unlikely to cause fission. As they travel through the moderator (water), they slow down, or thermalize.
  - **Thermal neutrons** are at roughly the same energy as their environment.
- The majority of fission-induced neutrons are born fast.
- Reactor coolant acts as a moderator to "thermalize" fast neutrons.
- As the fast neutrons collide with hydrogen atoms in H_2O, they transfer energy to the water molecules, which thermalizes the neutrons.

Notice that each slide contains a relatively small amount of information. Most of the content of the presentation appears in the notes, which are discussion points for the presenter to raise.

Reactivity

$$\rho = 1 - \frac{1}{K_{eff}}$$

- For a critical reactor $\rho = 0$
- For a supercritical reactor $\rho > 0$
- For a subcritical reactor $\rho < 0$

- Recall the definitions of reactivity.
- The relationship between ρ and $K_{eff} \rightarrow \rho = 1 - 1/K_{eff}$
- For a critical reactor $\rho = 0$
- For a supercritical reactor $\rho > 0$
- For a subcritical reactor $\rho < 0$

Notice that the final slide ends with a discussion question. The presentation is designed to end with a discussion between the presenter and those attending the presentation.

Factors Affecting Reactivity

- Fuel
- Control Rods
- Poisons (FP, Burnable, Boron)
- Moderator Temperature (T_{AVG})

Which ones can Maintenance personnel affect?

- All of these factors affect the overall "net" core reactivity.
- The fuel represents positive reactivity because more fuel means more fissions, and more neutrons. This reactivity decreases over core life as fuel is "burned" up.
- Control rods add negative reactivity because they absorb neutrons, preventing them from being absorbed by the fuel. Neutrons absorbed by the control rods are considered leakage in the 6-factor formula. This reactivity decreases (gets less negative) slightly over the life of the control rod.
- Poisons built into the fuel, FPs (fission products) and boron dissolved in the moderator also absorb neutrons and add negative reactivity. These are accounted for in the thermal utilization factor.
- Because the moderator is what thermalizes the neutrons, it adds positive reactivity. Because of what's physically happening in the moderator, its density affects reactivity. As temperature decreases, the density increases, which results in more collisions. This results in less leakage out of the core and an increase in thermal neutrons, which adds positive reactivity.

Information Technology

Professionals in information technology (IT) are interested in how to store, retrieve, manipulate, and transmit data through technology. Usually IT professionals are working with computer technology, but they might also work with other kinds of technology used to share information. People who work in IT can be found in all kinds of businesses and other establishments because information is shared via technology in nearly every possible occupation and profession. IT professionals work at the school that you attend, and they also work at companies and organizations all over the world.

The broad field of IT contains many different areas of specialization, including the following:

- Cyber- and network security
- Data management
- Data analytics
- Systems technology and administration
- Entrepreneurship
- Software development
- Web design and application development

Understanding how to communicate detailed information to a broad range of audiences is a foundation of successful communication in IT. An IT professional might have to communicate the same information both to people who understand and have specialized knowledge of a system and also to people who do not have that specialized knowledge but need to understand the broader implications of what the IT professional is recommending or building. Sometimes an IT professional's writing is almost like a translation. It is essential that the IT professional have both a high level of expertise in his or her area of specialization as well as effective communication strategies to explain that work to clients, colleagues, and management. In the following Insider's View, Tom Tolleson explains why it is important to communicate effectively to avoid misunderstandings that lead to wasted energy and effort.

TOM TOLLESON

"I communicate to groups with a fairly wide range of technical skill. I have to provide the context in which complex behaviors occur and explain the impact. Sometimes I need to provide options for a strategy based on the situation. The feedback that computer technicians often receive is 'What are the details?'—usually followed by 'That's too many details.' My solution for this is to provide a sort of inverted-pyramid style of writing where I give a non-technical summary of the issue in the first paragraph followed by an increasing level of details in subsequent paragraphs (usually preceded by a warning that a dive into data is imminent).

"The only thing that matters is if the audience can understand what I'm communicating. Misunderstandings can result in lot of time and effort being wasted, not to mention frustration. Because electronic media is so integral to my work, I find that succinct writing based on a thoughtful understanding of another person's role, context, and technical understanding is much more helpful than robust and properly formatted writing. I save that for presentations, papers, and documentation."

Insider Example
Student Summary of Shift Operations

In the following Insider Example, student Chrischale Panditharathne explains and analyzes a programming process in the computer language C. She uses technical language to explain the process and provides step-by-step instructions for how to conduct a shift operation. Pay attention to the structure, language, and referencing conventions that she uses in her analysis. ▶

Chrischale Panditharathne

Professor Thomas

November 18, 2017

Shift Operations in C

Among the other bitwise operations available in C, such as AND, OR, XOR, and NOT, there is also one called the shift operation. The bitwise shift allows you to shift a binary value to the right or left by a desired number of bits. However, because each bit pattern is required to have a certain size (for instance, 32 bit or 64 bit), the shift operation also adds bits to either end of the existing bit pattern when the excess bits after the shift are dropped off. Think of this as a pipe, closed loosely at either end, filled with water. If someone wanted to have new water in the pipe, one would open the bottom end and the water near the bottom would empty. You close the pipe when you've emptied enough. However, as a rule the pipe must always be full, so you add more water in from the top to ensure it remains full. Another, albeit less practical way to do it would be to pump in water from the bottom and have the excess spill out from the top. The type of water one would pump in to replace the water lost changes according to which side it was emptied from in the first place.

This is how bit shifting works. Bits are pushed from the right or left and replaced with either 1s or zeros depending on the type of shift and the Most Significant Bit in the bit pattern.

The ability to perform shifts ensures you can keep your code portable between compilers, and therefore between machines, since compilation format depends on the compiler itself, and not the particular machine the code is running on.

C allows programmers to perform three kinds of shifts on binary bit patterns. The type of shift only differs by the direction in which it is shifted and which bit, 0 or 1, is used to fill in the gaps once the existing bit pattern is pushed left or right.

C is a computing language. Like English and other spoken languages, computing languages have their own rules and syntax.

Chrischale uses an analogy to help clarify a complex technical topic.

1. **Logical Left Shift** ($\ll$).

   The most straightforward of shifts, the left shift is always logical and simply shifts bits to the left and fills in the rest of the space with 0s.

   For example, let's say bit pattern x = 01100010

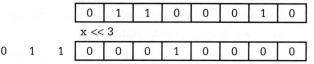

0	1	1	0	0	0	1	0

   x $\ll$ 3

   0   1   1
0	0	0	1	0	0	0	0

   Zeros are pushed in to replace the three bits that were pushed out the left end. The logical left shift is basically equivalent to multiplying a number by 2.

2. **Logical Right Shift** ($\gg$).

   The logical right shift is similar to the logical left shift, and it shifts bits to the right, filling the gaps with 0s.

   For example, let's say bit pattern x = 01100010

0	1	1	0	0	0	1	0

   x $\gg$ 3

0	0	0	0	1	1	0	0
   0   1   0

   Zeros are pushed in to replace the three bits that were pushed out the right end.

3. **Arithmetic Right Shift** ($\gg$).

   The arithmetic right shift is a little more complicated but is the most commonly used. It too shifts the bit pattern to the right, but instead of always filling the gaps with 0s, it will fill them with the most significant bit. This is useful when we want to preserve the sign of the bit pattern we are dealing with.

Binary code is a computer language that sends commands to the machine using combinations of 1s and 0s.

For example, let's say bit pattern x = 11100010

1	1	1	0	0	0	1	0

x >> 3

1	1	1	1	1	1	0	0	0	1	0

Most Significant Bit is pushed in to replace the three bits that were pushed out the right end.

The issue with having two kinds of right shifts is that you could use either arithmetic or logical right shift, and the code would still work. This is problematic because if one compiler assumes right shifts to be logical and the other assumes right shifts to be arithmetic, then there could be grave consequences in bit manipulation and calculations. Little mistakes like this are what cause losses of millions in real-world projects, so it is crucial to understand the difference.

Therefore, the convention in C is to use the arithmetic right shift if the integer is signed, that is, the integer value represents only positive numbers, or logical shift if the integer is unsigned, that is, the integer could be both positive and negative. This only applies to C, however. In other programming languages the convention is similar but with additional rules as to how and when each shift is applied.

Writing Project   **Genre Analysis of Writing in an Applied Field**

In this chapter, you've read about some of the conventions of writing in the applied fields. You might be interested in a field that's not represented in this chapter, though. For this assignment, you will conduct research to discover more about the kinds of writing that are common within a particular applied field—ideally, one you're interested in. You might conduct either primary or secondary research to respond to this assignment. However, you should focus on collecting examples of the kinds of writing done in the field. Consider the following steps to complete this assignment:

1. Collect examples of the kinds of writing done in the field.

2. Describe the different genres and how they relate to the work of that applied field.

3. Look for comparisons and contrasts across those genres. Do any commonalities point to conventions shared across genres? Are there differences that are important to notice? What do the patterns across the genres tell you about the work and values of that applied field?

Variation: Imagine that your audience is a group of incoming students interested in the same field of study you've researched for this project. Your task is to write a guide for those students about the conventions of writing expected in this applied field. Depending on what you have found, you may need to identify what conventions are appropriate for specific genres of writing.

Insider Example

Student Genre Analysis of Electrical and Computer Engineering Standards

In this Insider Example, Reece Neff, a first-year writing student, responds to an assignment that asked him to describe some of the conventional rhetorical features of a genre of writing specific to his intended field of study, computer engineering. In his response, Reece identifies some of the structural, reference, and language features characteristic of the Institute of Electrical and Electronics Engineers (IEEE) Standards and suggests that professionals' use of these features highlights some of the values shared by members of the computer engineering community. ▶

Reece Neff

English 101 – 051

Prof. Roy Stamper

May 4, 2017

Project Five

Electrical and Computer Engineering Standards:

A Rhetorical Analysis

Electrical and Computer Engineering (ECE) is a field that deals with improving circuits, transistors, and computer hardware/software to make life easier for those using those devices. Professionals in this field typically research and design innovative ways to use electronic components. In this field, ECE professionals typically write standards for their company or organization. Standards are crucial for product manufacturing in that company or organization because this provides continuity across all the designs, and this allows for the designs to work together easier for anyone designing a new method/process/product. "IEEE Standard for Floating-Point Arithmetic" by Institute of Electrical and Electronics Engineers Computer Society (IEEE) is an example of a standard widely used by ECE professionals who follow the IEEE standards. This standard contains instructions for how ECE professionals should write and process bits in low-level programming. This standard also contains similar conventional features across other standards written by ECE professionals. "Introducing Students to Disciplinary Genres: The Role of the General Composition Course" by P. Linton et al. asserts that these conventional features can be classified into three distinct categories: structure, which controls the argument's progression; reference, which is the way that the writer uses outside work; and language, which covers basic sentence structure. This standard utilizes many conventional features of structure, reference, and language, and analysis of

Reece provides a brief introduction to the field of study.

Reece describes the specific genre, along with the specific example of this genre, on which his analysis focuses.

Reece asserts a thesis that identifies the categories of rhetorical features he'll describe. He also points to a larger purpose in his analysis, which is to demonstrate that the rhetorical features he'll describe reflect values held by members of this professional community.

these features reveals the values of ECE professionals: easily referenceable material and collaboration.

One category of conventional features that Linton et al. define is structure. They state that these conventions "control the flow of the argument and, more importantly, determine the kinds of cues available to readers" (66). One convention of structure found in IEEE's standard is headings and subheadings that promote the value of easily referenceable information within the ECE community. For example, IEEE includes "Floating-point formats" (6) with multiple subheadings such as "Binary interchange format encodings" (9) and "Decimal interchange format encodings" (10). IEEE then goes on to explain each of the subheadings. Another example of this is IEEE's heading "Operations" (17), going into more detail with the subheadings "Quiet-computational operations" (23) and "Signaling-computational operations" (24), and finally explaining what each of those subheadings is. This detailed organization allows the ECE professionals that are designing something to quickly and easily reference the material that they are trying to find. Their time is valuable, so they cannot waste it trying to find information buried deep within a text—they need a reliable way to easily and quickly find that information. This adds to the value of easily referenceable information that ECE professionals need when viewing standards as they try to design new methods or products.

Another convention of structure that IEEE uses in its standard is the inclusion of a definitions section, which improves readability, thus promoting the value of collaboration. IEEE inserts a "Definitions, abbreviations, and acronyms" (3) section and provides definitions such as ". . . **applicable attribute:** The value of an attribute governing a particular . . ." (3) and ". . . **arithmetic format:** A floating-point format that

---

Reece introduces a category of conventions he'll address first, structural conventions.

One structural feature he'll look at is the use of headings and subheadings.

Provides examples from the genre

Explains what the use of headings and subheadings might suggest about the values of this community

can be used to represent . . ." (3). These definitions provide the reader interpretations of each word the writer(s) agreed with. This way, everyone is on the same page in terms of understanding what each word means, leaving less room for misinterpretation among the ECE community. IEEE's improvement of readability by including a definitions section promotes collaboration between ECE professionals because they will be able to interpret the standard more effectively.

The second category of conventional features, reference, aims to "establish standard ways of addressing the work of other scholars; they encode the formal or public relationships among members of the discourse community" (Linton et al., 66). A convention of reference that IEEE uses in its standard is the inclusion of an informative bibliography which promotes the value of collaboration between ECE professionals. IEEE adds a bibliography at the end, stating "(informative)" (53), meaning they did not reference this material in the text. This bibliography is purely meant to expand the reader's knowledge on this topic by looking at other sources that use this standard. In the bibliography, IEEE states at the beginning "The following documents might be helpful to the reader" and then includes a myriad of documents related to this standard. The inclusion of an informative bibliography such as this one allows the reader to expand his/her knowledge on the usage of this standard and to show other works by ECE professionals. Because of this, IEEE's inclusion of an informative bibliography promotes the value of collaboration between ECE professionals.

Another convention of reference that IEEE utilizes is the inclusion of revisions, which also promotes the value of collaboration between ECE professionals. IEEE includes a parenthetical if their standard is a revision of an older standard. In this standard, this is located in the top right

Reece introduces a second category of conventional features he'll examine, reference.

Describes how references appear in the genre

Provides a rationale for the use of these reference features that is grounded in the community's shared belief or goals

hand of the title page stating "**IEEE Std 754™-2008** (Revision of IEEE Std 654-1985)" (IEEE i). This revision parenthetical shows that this standard was revised from the previous 1984 standard of floating-point arithmetic. The parenthetical allows readers to go back to the original document and review changes between the two. IEEE's inclusion of a revision parenthetical promotes the value of collaboration between ECE professionals because this shows (subjective) improvement on a previous document.

The final category of conventional features that Linton et al. define is language, which "guide[s] phrasing at the sentence level" (66) and "reflect[s] characteristic choices of syntax and diction" (66). A convention of language that IEEE uses in its standard is the inclusion of bullet points, which increases readability, promoting the value of easily referenceable information within the ECE community. Going more in detail from the headings and subheadings, IEEE includes bullet points to help explain each topic in the subheadings. An example of this includes an example in the "Formats" overview of "Floating-point formats" where IEEE states "Five basic formats are defined in this clause:

- Three binary formats, with encodings in lengths of 32, 64, and 128 bits.
- Two decimal formats, with encodings in lengths of 64 and 128 bits" (6).

Another example of IEEE's use of bullet points can be seen in the "Infinity arithmetic" subheading where IEEE defines "The exceptions that do pertain to infinities are signaled only when

- ∞ is an invalid operand (see Figure E-7: IEEE 7, Level 2)
- ∞ is created from finite operands by overflow (see Figure E-7: IEEE 7, Level 4) or division by zero (see Figure E-7: IEEE 7, Level 3)
- remainder (subnormal, ∞) signals underflow" (34).

The use of these bullet points allows IEEE to condense their information into smaller and concise chunks. This makes it easier for ECE professionals to reference and use the information found within the standard. Because of this, IEEE's use of bullet points promotes the value of easily referenceable information.

Provides a rationale for the use of bullet points that is grounded in the community's values or beliefs

Another convention of language that IEEE uses is the inclusion of diagrams and tables, making them easier to read, promoting the value of collaboration between ECE professionals. IEEE includes tables and diagrams such as:

Level 1	$\{-\infty \dots \ 0 \ \dots +\infty\}$	Extended real numbers.
many-to-one ↓	*rounding*	↑ projection (except for NaN)
Level 2	$\{-\infty \dots -0\} \cup \{+0 \dots +\infty\} \cup$ NaN	Floating-point data—an algebraically closed system.
one-to-many ↓	*representation specification*	↑ many-to-one
Level 3	*(sign, exponent, significand)* $\cup \{-\infty, +\infty\} \cup$ qNaN $\cup$ sNaN	Representations of floating-point data.
one-to-many ↓	*encoding for representations of floating-point data*	↑ many-to-one
Level 4	**0111000...**	Bit strings.

Figure E-7. IEEE 7, Levels 1-4.

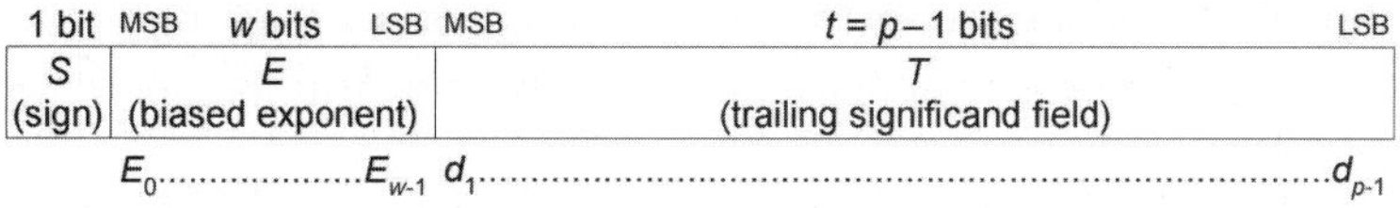

1 bit MSB	w bits LSB	MSB	$t = p-1$ bits	LSB
S (sign)	E (biased exponent)		T (trailing significand field)	

$E_0 \dots\dots\dots\dots E_{w-1}$ $d_1 \dots\dots\dots\dots\dots\dots\dots\dots\dots\dots\dots\dots\dots\dots\dots\dots d_{p-1}$

Figure E-8. IEEE 9

The inclusion of tables and diagrams makes interpretation easier with some of the concepts that the standards are trying to describe. Without trying to explain something in hundreds of words, IEEE inserts a table or diagram to describe a topic easier and reduce misinterpretation of it. Increased proper interpretation of the standard makes it easier for ECE professionals to collaborate with each other without any conflicts with the interpretation of this standard. Thus, IEEE's

In this conclusion to his analysis, Reece reiterates his position that the rhetorical features identified highlight values shared among members of this applied field community.

Identifies another conventional feature of the genre that was not present in the text he analyzed

inclusion of tables and diagrams promotes the value of collaboration between ECE professionals.

The analysis of IEEE's standard shows many kinds of conventional features as illustrated by Linton et al. — structure, reference, and language. The analysis of this standard shows that the use of these conventions reflects the values of ECE professionals in being easily referenceable, and collaborative. One feature that could not be explored were normative references because as they were present in many other standards published by ECE professionals, they were not present in this standard. This analysis hopes to help students further increase their understanding of ECE standards in the applied field and to spur further analysis of different genres of writing in the applied fields.

Works Cited

Institute of Electrical and Electronics Engineers Computer Society. "IEEE Standard for Floating-Point Arithmetic." The Institute of Electrical and Electronics Engineers, Inc., 2008. doi: 10.1109/IEEESTD.2008.4610935

Linton, Patricia, et al. "Introducing Students to Disciplinary Discourse: The Role of the General Composition Course." *Language and Learning across the Disciplines*, vol. 1, no. 2, 1994, pp. 63–78.

tip sheet

Reading and Writing in the Applied Fields

- **The applied fields focus on the practical application of knowledge and career preparation.** Many applied fields also focus on problem-solving as part of the practical application of knowledge.

- **When beginning a writing task in applied fields, carefully analyze the rhetorical situation.** Consider your purpose and your audience carefully, and assess the appropriateness of responding in a particular genre.

- **Much of the writing in applied fields follows conventional expectations for structure, language, and reference appropriate to the fields.** Regardless of your writing task, you should be aware of these conventional expectations.

- **Students and professionals in applied fields often communicate information through field-specific genres.** Nurses, for example, often construct discharge directions, just as students and professionals in the fields of law often compose legal briefs.

Introduction to Documentation Styles

You've likely had some experience with citing sources in academic writing, both as a reader and as a writer. Many students come to writing classes in college with experience only in MLA format, the citation style of the Modern Language Association. The student research paper at the end of Chapter 7 is written in MLA style, which is the most commonly required citation style in English classes. Although MLA is the citation style with which English and writing teachers are usually most familiar, it is not the only one used in academic writing—not by a long shot.

Some students don't realize that other citation styles exist, and they're often surprised when they encounter different styles in other classes. Our goal in this appendix is to help you understand (1) why and when academic writers cite sources and (2) how different citation styles represent the values and conventions of different academic disciplines. This appendix also provides brief guides to MLA, APA (American Psychological Association), and CSE (Council of Science Editors) styles—three styles that are illustrated in student papers found in Part Two of this book. Near the end of this appendix, you'll find a table with other citation styles commonly used in different disciplines, including some of the applied fields discussed in Chapter 10.

Why Cite?

There are several reasons why academic writers cite sources that they draw upon. The first is an ethical reason: academic research and writing privilege the discovery of new knowledge, and it is important to give credit to scholars who discover new ideas and establish important claims in their fields of study. Additionally, academic writers cite sources to provide a "breadcrumb trail" to show how they developed their current research projects. Source citations show what prior work writers are building on and how their research contributes to that body of knowledge. If some of the sources are well respected, that ethos helps to support the writers' research as well. It demonstrates that the writers have done their homework; they know what has already been discovered, and they are contributing to an ongoing conversation.

These two values of academic writing—the necessity of crediting the person or persons who discover new knowledge, and the importance of understanding prior work that has led to a specific research project—shape the choices that academic writers make when citing sources. Anytime you quote, summarize, or paraphrase the work of someone else in academic writing, you must give credit to that person's work. *How* academic writers cite those sources, though, differs according to their academic discipline and writing situation.

Disciplinary Documentation Styles

Citation styles reflect the values of specific disciplines, just like other conventions of academic writing that we've discussed in this book. When you compare the similarities and differences in citation styles, you might notice that some conventions of particular citation styles that seemed random before suddenly have meaning. For example, if we compare the ways that authors and publication dates are listed in MLA, APA, and CSE styles, we'll notice some distinctions that reflect the values of those disciplines:

MLA	Greenwell, Amanda M. "Rhetorical Reading Guides, Readerly Experiences, and WID in the Writing Center." *WLN: A Journal of Writing Center Scholarship*, vol. 41, no. 7–8, Mar.–Apr. 2017, pp. 9–16.	• Author's full name • Year of publication listed near the end
APA	Greenwell, A. (March–April 2017). Rhetorical reading guides, readerly experiences, and WID in the writing center. *WLN: A Journal of Writing Center Scholarship, 41*(7–8), 9–16.	• Only author's last name included in full • Year included toward the beginning, in a place of importance
CSE	Greenwell A. 2017 Mar–Apr. Rhetorical reading guides, readerly experiences, and WID in the writing center. WLN. 41(7–8):9–16.	• Only last name given in full, and first and middle initials are not separated from last name by any punctuation. • Year also has a place of prominence and isn't distinguished from the name at all, emphasizing that timeliness is as important as the name of the author.

MLA lists the author's full name at the beginning of the citation, emphasizing the importance of the author. Date of publication is one of the last items in the citation, reflecting that a publication's currency is often not as important in the humanities as it is in other disciplines. By contrast, APA and CSE list the date of publication near the beginning of the citation in a place of prominence.

Interestingly, CSE does not use any unique punctuation to distinguish the author from the date other than separating them by a period, reflecting that they are of almost equal importance.

Citation styles reflect the values of the respective disciplines. In a very real sense, citation styles are rhetorically constructed: they are developed, revised, updated, and used in ways that reflect the purpose and audience for citing sources in different disciplines. Some rules in documentation styles don't seem to have a clear reason, though, and this is why it's important to know how to verify the rules of a certain system. Our goal is to help you understand, on a rhetorical level, the way three common citation styles work. Memorizing these styles is not always the most productive endeavor, as the styles change over time. Really understanding how they work will be much more useful to you long term.

Modern Language Association (MLA) Style

What Is Unique about MLA Style?

MLA style is generally followed by researchers in the disciplines of the humanities such as foreign languages and English. One of the unique aspects of MLA style, when compared with other styles, is that the page numbers of quoted, summarized, or paraphrased information are included in in-text citations. While other styles sometimes also include page numbers (especially for exact quotations), the use of page numbers in MLA allows readers to go back to find the original language of the referenced passage. In the disciplines that follow MLA style, the way in which something is phrased is often quite important, and readers might want to review the original source to assess how you are using evidence to support your argument.

We offer some basic guidelines here for using MLA style, but you can learn more about the style guides published by the Modern Language Association, including the *MLA Handbook*, at www.mla.org. For an example of MLA paper format, see the Insider Example in Chapter 7.

In-Text Citations in MLA Style

When sources are cited in the text, MLA style calls for a parenthetical reference at the end of a sentence or, if multiple sources are cited in a single sentence, at the end of the information being cited. The page number(s) of the reference appear in parentheses with no other punctuation, and then the end-of-sentence punctuation appears after the parenthetical reference. The source author's name is either included in a signal phrase or within the parentheses.

> According to Döring and Wansink, the frequency with which customers ordered dessert at restaurants can be correlated with the BMI of the waitstaff (198).

The frequency with which customers ordered dessert at restaurants can be correlated with the BMI of the waitstaff (Döring and Wansink 198).

Works Cited Citations in MLA Style

The citations list at the end of an academic paper in MLA style is called a Works Cited page. Citations are listed on the Works Cited page in alphabetical order by the authors' last names (or by title for works with no authors).

> Döring, Tim, and Brian Wansink. "The Waiter's Weight." *Environment and Behavior*, vol. 49, no. 2, 2017, pp. 192–214.

1. **Author** Author's name is listed first, with the last name preceding the first name and any middle initials. The first name is spelled out and followed by a comma, and then the second author is listed with the first name preceding the last name. For three or more authors, use "et al." after the first author's name.

2. **Title of Source** Article titles and book chapters are given in quotation marks. All words in the title are capitalized except for articles, prepositions, coordinating conjunctions, and the *to* in infinitives (unless they are the first words). Include a period after the title, inside the last quotation mark.

3. **Title of Container Where the Source Was Found** Book, journal, magazine, and newspaper titles appear in italics. A comma follows the title.

4. **Other Contributors** If the container has editors, translators, or other contributors, those would be listed directly after the title of the container.

5. **Version** If the source is an edition or specific version of a text, that information would be listed next.

6. **Number** For a journal, the volume number follows the title of the journal, preceded by the abbreviation "vol." If the journal has an issue number, that would then be listed after the volume number, preceded by the abbreviation "no." Use commas to separate the volume, issue number, and any information that follows.

7. **Publisher** If a specific publisher is listed, give the name of the publisher next.

8. **Publication Date** The year of publication is listed next, followed by a comma. For journals, include the month and/or season before the year.

9. **Location** Inclusive page numbers are provided in the MLA citation of a journal article, preceded by "pp." and followed by a period. If you are citing an online source, give a permalink or DOI (digital object identifier) if a source has one. If a source does not have a permalink or DOI, provide the full URL. (Unless you want a live link, you may omit the protocol, such as "http://".)

Citing Different Types of Sources in MLA Style

Comparison of different kinds of sources in MLA style

Type of Source	Example of Works Cited Entry	Notes
Book	Davies, Alice, and Kathryn Tollervey. *The Style of Coworking: Contemporary Shared Workspaces.* Prestel Verlag, 2013.	When more than one author is listed, only the first author's name is reversed in MLA style.
Book Chapter	Ludvigsen, Sten, and Hans Christian Arnseth. "Computer-Supported Collaborative Learning." *Technology Enhanced Learning*, edited by Erik Duval et al., Springer International, 2017, pp. 47–58.	Be sure to list both the book chapter and the title of the book when citing a chapter from an edited collection.
Scholarly Journal Article	Waldock, Jeff, et al. "The Role of Informal Learning Spaces in Enhancing Student Engagement with Mathematical Sciences." *The Journal of Mathematical Education in Science and Technology*, vol. 48, no. 4, 2017, pp. 587–602. *Taylor Francis Online*, https://doi.org/10.1080 /0020739X.2016.1262470.	If more than two authors are listed, use *et al.* after the first author's name. If the source was found in an online database, list the database or website as a second, external, container.
Magazine or Newspaper Article	Goel, Vindu. "Office Space Is Hard to Find for Newcomers." *The New York Times*, 2 Apr. 2015, p. F2.	Periodical articles can differ in print and online, so be sure to cite the correct version of the article.
Website	Goodloe, Amy. "TIPS—Composing and Framing Video Interviews." *Digital Writing 101*, 2017, digitalwriting101.net/content /composing-and-framing-video-interviews/.	If a permalink or DOI is not available for online sources, include the exact URL for the source as the location, excluding http:// or https://, unless you want to provide a live link.
Website with No Individual Author Listed	Sage One. "Eight Ideas for Designing a More Collaborative Workspace." *Microsoft for Work*, Microsoft Corporation, 10 Jul. 2014, blogs .microsoft.com/work/2014/07/10/eight-ideas-for -designing-a-more-collaborative-workspace.	When no author is listed, you can begin the citation with the title of the article or site. If an organization or some other entity is sponsoring the article (as in this case), that can be listed as the author.

SAMPLE MLA WORKS CITED PAGE

Running Head 7

Works Cited

Davies, Alice, and Kathryn Tollervey. *The Style of Coworking: Contemporary Shared Workspaces*. Prestel Verlag, 2013.

Goel, Vindu. "Office Space Is Hard to Find for Newcomers." *The New York Times*, 2 Apr. 2015, p. F2.

Goodloe, Amy. "TIPS — Composing and Framing Video Interviews." *Digital Writing 101*, 2017, digitalwriting101 .net/content/composing-and-framing-video-interviews/.

Ludvigsen, Sten, and Hans Christian Arnseth. "Computer-Supported Collaborative Learning." *Technology Enhanced Learning*, edited by Erik Duval et al., Springer International, 2017, pp. 47–58.

Sage One. "Eight Ideas for Designing a More Collaborative Workspace." *Microsoft for Work*, Microsoft Corporation, 10 Jul. 2014, blogs.microsoft.com/work/2014/07/10/ eight-ideas-for-designing-a-more-collaborative-workspace.

Waldock, Jeff, et al. "The Role of Informal Learning Spaces in Enhancing Student Engagement with Mathematical Sciences." *The Journal of Mathematical Education in Science and Technology*, vol. 48, no. 4, 2017, pp. 587–602. *Taylor Francis Online*, https://doi.org/10.1080/0020739X .2016.1262470.

American Psychological Association (APA) Style

What Is Unique about APA Style?

Researchers in many areas of the social sciences and related fields generally follow APA documentation procedures. Although you'll encounter page numbers in the in-text citations for direct quotations in APA documents, you're less likely to find direct quotations overall. Generally, researchers in the social sciences are less interested in the specific language or words used to report research findings than they are in the results or conclusions. Therefore, social science researchers are more likely to paraphrase information from sources than to quote information.

Additionally, in-text documentation in the APA system requires that you include the date of publication for research. This is a striking distinction from the MLA system. Social science research that was conducted fifty years ago may not be as useful as research conducted two years ago, so it's important to cite the date of the source in the text of your argument. Imagine how different the results would be for a study of the effects of violence in video games on youth twenty years ago versus a study conducted last year. Findings from twenty years ago probably have very little bearing on the world of today and would not reflect the same video game content as today's games. Including the date of research publication as part of the in-text citation allows readers to quickly evaluate the currency, and therefore the appropriateness, of the research you reference. Learn more about the *Publication Manual of the American Psychological Association* at www.apastyle.org. For an example of APA paper format, see the Insider Examples in Chapter 8.

In-Text Citations in APA Style

When sources are cited in the text, APA style calls for a parenthetical reference at the end of a sentence or at the end of the information being cited (if in the middle of a sentence). The author's name and the year of publication are included in parentheses, separated by a comma, and then the end-of-sentence punctuation appears after the parenthetical reference. Page numbers are included for summaries and paraphrases from long sources such as books and for direct quotations.

> The frequency with which customers ordered dessert at restaurants can be correlated with the BMI of the waitstaff (Döring & Wansink, 2017).

Often, the author's name is mentioned in the sentence, and then the year is listed in parentheses right after the author's name.

> According to Döring and Wansink (2017), the frequency with which customers ordered dessert at restaurants can be correlated with the BMI of the waitstaff.

References Page Citations in APA Style

The citations list at the end of an academic paper in APA style is called a References page. Citations are listed on the References page in alphabetical order by the authors' last names.

> Döring, T., & Wansink, B. (2017). The waiter's weight. *Environment and Behavior, 49*(2), 192–214.

1. The author's name is listed first, with the last name preceding first and middle initials. Only the last name is spelled out, and the initials are followed by periods. With two or more authors, separate the names with commas. Include names for up to twenty authors, with an ampersand (&) before the last author's name.

2. The date of publication directly follows the name, listed in parentheses and followed by a period outside the parentheses. For books, give the year. For other types of publications, give the month and day of posting or publication, if available.

3. Article titles and book chapters are listed with no punctuation other than a period at the end. Only the first word in the title and any proper nouns are capitalized. If there is a colon in the title, the first word after the colon should also be capitalized.

4. Journal titles appear in italics, and all words are capitalized except articles and prepositions (unless they are longer than four letters or are the first words). A comma follows a journal title.

5. The volume number follows the title, also in italics. If there is an issue number, it is listed in parentheses immediately following the volume number, but not in italics. This is followed by a comma.

6. Inclusive page numbers appear at the end, followed by a period.

Citing Different Types of Sources in APA Style

Comparison of different kinds of sources in APA style

Type of Source	Example of References Page Entry	Notes
Book	Davies, A., & Tollervey, K. (2013). *The style of coworking: Contemporary shared workspaces.* Prestel Verlag.	In APA, multiple authors are linked with an ampersand (&).
Book Chapter	Ludvigsen, S., & Arnseth, H. C. (2017). Computer-supported collaborative learning. In E. Duval, M. Sharples, & R. Sutherland (Eds.), *Technology enhanced learning* (pp. 47–58). Springer International Publishing.	Be sure to list both the book chapter and the title of the book when citing a chapter from an edited collection.
Scholarly Journal Article	Waldock, J., Rowlett, P., Cornock, C., Robinson, M., & Bartholomew, H. (2017). The role of informal learning spaces in enhancing student engagement with mathematical sciences. *The Journal of Mathematical Education in Science and Technology, 48*(4), 587–602. https://doi.org/10.1080/0020739X.2016.1262470	In APA, the journal number is italicized with the journal title, but the issue number (in parentheses) is not. Include the DOI (digital object identifier) if the source has one.
Magazine or Newspaper Article	Goel, V. (2015, April 2). Office space is hard to find for newcomers. *The New York Times*, F2.	Periodical articles can differ in print and online, so be sure to cite where you found your version of the article.
Website	Goodloe, A. (2017). TIPS—composing and framing video interviews. *Digital Writing 101.* digitalwriting101.net/content/composing-and-framing-video-interviews/	
Website with No Individual Author Listed	Sage One. (2014, July 10). Eight ideas for designing a more collaborative workspace [Web log post]. Microsoft. http://blogs.microsoft.com/	When no author is listed for a web-based source, you can begin the citation with the title of the article or site. If an organization or some other entity is sponsoring the article (as in this case), that can be listed as author.

SAMPLE APA REFERENCES PAGE

7

References

Davies, A., & Tollervey, K. (2013). *The style of coworking: Contemporary shared workspaces*. Prestel Verlag.

Goel, V. (2015, April 2). Office space is hard to find for newcomers. *The New York Times*, F2.

Goodloe, A. (2017). TIPS—composing and framing video interviews. *Digital Writing 101*. digitalwriting101. net/content/composing-and-framing-video-interviews/

Ludvigsen, S., & Arnseth, H. C. (2017). Computer-supported collaborative learning. In E. Duval, M. Sharples, & R. Sutherland (Eds.), *Technology enhanced learning* (pp. 47–58). Springer International Publishing.

Sage One. (2014, July 10). Eight ideas for designing a more collaborative workspace [Web log post]. Microsoft. http:// blogs.microsoft.com/

Waldock, J., Rowlett, P., Cornock, C., Robinson, M., & Bartholomew, H. (2017). The role of informal learning spaces in enhancing student engagement with mathematical sciences. *The Journal of Mathematical Education in Science and Technology*, *48*(4), 587–602. https://doi.org/10.1080/ 0020739X.2016.1262470

Council of Science Editors (CSE) Style

What Is Unique about CSE Style?

As the name suggests, the CSE documentation system is most prevalent among disciplines of the natural sciences, although many of the applied fields of the sciences, like engineering and medicine, rely on their own documentation systems. As with the other systems described here, CSE requires writers to document all materials derived from sources. Unlike MLA or APA, however, CSE allows multiple methods for in-text citations, corresponding to alternative forms of the reference page at the end of research reports. The three styles—**Citation-Sequence**, **Citation-Name**, and **Name-Year**—are used by different publications. In this book, we introduce you to the Name-Year system.

For more detailed information on CSE documentation, you can consult the latest edition of *Scientific Style and Format: The CSE Manual for Authors, Editors, and Publishers*, and you can learn more about the Council of Science Editors at its website: http://www.councilscienceeditors.org. For an example of CSE paper format, see the Insider Example: Professional Research Proposal in Chapter 9.

In-Text Citations in CSE Style

When sources are cited in the text, CSE style calls for a parenthetical reference directly following the relevant information. The author's name and the year of publication are included in parentheses with no other punctuation.

> The frequency with which customers ordered dessert at restaurants can be correlated with the BMI of the waitstaff (Döring and Wansink 2017).

References Page Citations in CSE Style

The citations list at the end of an academic paper in CSE style is called a References page. Citations are listed on the References page in alphabetical order by the authors' last names.

> Döring T, Wansink B. 2017. The waiter's weight. Envir and Behav. 49:192–214.

1. The author's name is listed first, with the full last name preceding the first and middle initials. No punctuation separates elements of the name.
2. The year directly follows the name, followed by a period.
3. Article titles and book chapters are listed with no punctuation other than a period at the end. Only the first word in the title and any proper nouns

are capitalized. If there is a colon in the title, the first word after the colon should not be capitalized.

4. Journal titles are often abbreviated, and all words are capitalized. A period follows the journal title.

5. The volume number follows the title. If there is an issue number, it is listed in parentheses following the volume number, but not in italics. This is followed by a colon. No space appears after the colon.

6. Inclusive page numbers appear at the end, followed by a period.

Citing Different Types of Sources in CSE Style

Comparison of different kinds of sources in CSE style

Type of Source	Example of References Page Entry	Notes
Book	Davies A, Tollervey K. 2013. The style of coworking: contemporary shared workspaces. Munich (Germany): Prestel Verlag. 159 p.	Listing the number of pages is optional in CSE, but useful.
Book Chapter	Ludvigsen S, Arnseth HC. 2017. Computer-supported collaborative learning. In: Duval E, Sharples M, Sutherland R, editors. Technology enhanced learning. Gewerbestrasse (Switzerland): Springer International Publishing. p. 47–58.	
Scholarly Journal Article	Waldock J, Rowlett P, Cornock C, Robinson M, Bartholomew, H. 2017. The role of informal learning spaces in enhancing student engagement with mathematical sciences. Journ of Math Ed in Sci and Tech. 48(4):587–602.	Some journal titles in CSE are abbreviated.
Magazine or Newspaper Article	Goel V. 2015 Apr 2. Office space is hard to find for newcomers. New York Times (National Ed.). Sect. F:2 (col. 1).	
Website	Goodloe A. 2017. Tips — composing and framing video interviews. Digital Writing 101; [accessed 2018 Jan 10]. http://digitalwriting101 .net/content/composing-and-framing-video -interviews/.	CSE calls for the exact URL and an access date for web-based sources.
Website with No Individual Author Listed	Sage One. 2014. Eight ideas for designing a more collaborative workspace [blog]. Microsoft at Work. [accessed 2015 Apr 2]. Available from http://blogs.microsoft.com/work/2014/07/10 /eight-ideas-for-designing-a-more -collaborative-workspace/.	

SAMPLE CSE REFERENCES PAGE

References

Davies A, Tollervey K. 2013. The style of coworking: contemporary shared workspaces. Munich (Germany): Prestel Verlag. 159 p.

Goel V. 2015 Apr 2. Office space is hard to find for newcomers. New York Times (National Ed.). Sect. F:2 (col. 1).

Goodloe A. 2017. Tips—composing and framing video interviews. Digital Writing 101; [accessed 2018 Jan 10]. http://digitalwriting101.net/content/composing-and-framing-video-interviews/.

Ludvigsen S, Arnseth HC. 2017. Computer-supported collaborative learning. In: Duval E, Sharples M, Sutherland R, editors. Technology enhanced learning. Gewerbestrasse (Switzerland): Springer International Publishing. p. 47–58.

Sage One. 2014. Eight ideas for designing a more collaborative workspace [blog]. Microsoft at Work. [accessed 2015 Apr 2]. Available from http://blogs.microsoft.com/work/2014/07/10/eight-ideas-for-designing-a-more-collaborative-workspace/.

Waldock J, Rowlett P, Cornock C, Robinson M, Bartholomew H. 2017. The role of informal learning spaces in enhancing student engagement with mathematical sciences. Journ of Math Ed in Sci and Tech. 48(4):587–602.

Other Common Documentation Styles

Many disciplines have their own documentation styles, and some are used more commonly than others. The following chart lists a few of the most popular.

Name of Citation Style	Disciplines	Website
American Chemical Society (ACS)	Chemistry and Physical Sciences	http://pubs.acs.org/series/styleguide
American Institute of Physics (AIP)	Physics	http://publishing.aip.org/authors
American Mathematical Society (AMS)	Mathematics	http://www.ams.org/publications/authors
American Medical Association (AMA)	Medicine	http://www.amamanualofstyle.com/
American Political Science Association (APSA)	Political Science	http://www.apsanet.org/Portals/54/files/APSAStyleManual2006.pdf
American Sociological Association (ASA)	Sociology	http://www.asanet.org/documents/teaching/pdfs/Quick_Tips_for_ASA_Style.pdf
Associated Press Stylebook (AP Style)	Journalism	https://www.apstylebook.com/
Bluebook Style	Law and Legal Studies	https://www.legalbluebook.com/
Chicago Manual of Style (CMoS)	History and other humanities disciplines	http://www.chicagomanualofstyle.org/
Institute of Electrical and Electronics Engineers (IEEE)	Engineering	https://www.ieee.org/documents/style_manual.pdf
Linguistic Society of America (LSA)	Linguistics	http://www.linguisticsociety.org/files/style-sheet.pdf
Modern Humanities Research Association (MHRA)	Humanities	http://www.mhra.org.uk/Publications/Books/StyleGuide/StyleGuideV3.pdf

Tracking Research

There are many useful, free digital tools online that can help you track your research and sources. Three of the best are personalized research-tracking tools and social applications that enable you to find additional resources through other users of the application:

- **Diigo (https://www.diigo.com/)** Diigo is a social bookmarking application that solves two dilemmas faced by many writers. First, you can access all of the bookmarks that you save in a browser on multiple devices. Additionally, you can tag your sources and share them with others. That means you can search using tags (not very different from searching with key words in a database) and find other sources that users of Diigo have tagged with the same words and phrases that you have chosen.

- **Zotero (https://www.zotero.org/)** Zotero is a robust research tool that helps you organize, cite, and share sources with others. You can install Zotero into your web browser and quickly save and annotate sources that you're looking at online. Zotero can help you generate citations, annotated bibliographies, and reference lists from the sources that you have saved.

- **Mendeley (http://www.mendeley.com/)** Similar to Zotero, Mendeley is a free reference manager and academic social network that allows you to read and annotate PDFs on any device.

Your school may also have licenses for proprietary tools such as RefWorks and EndNote, which are very useful research-tracking applications. Most of these applications can help you generate citations and reference lists as well. However, you need to understand how a documentation style works in order to check what is generated from any citation builder. For example, if you save the title of a journal article as "Increased pizza consumption leads to temporary euphoria but higher long-term cholesterol levels," a citation builder will not automatically change the capitalization if you need to generate a citation in MLA format. You have to be smarter than the application you use.

Glossary

academic disciplines Areas of teaching, research, and inquiry within higher education.

active voice A sentence structure in which the subject of the sentence is the agent—the person or thing doing the action.

annotated bibliography List of citations formatted in a consistent documentation style that includes summaries of source material.

applied fields Academic disciplines that are generally focused on practical application.

argument The process of making a logical case for a particular position, interpretation, or conclusion.

audience The recipient or consumer of a piece of writing.

author The person who produced a piece of writing.

claims Arguable assertions that are supported with evidence from research.

closed-ended question A question that can be answered by *yes* or *no*.

close reading The careful observation of a text in the pursuit of understanding and engaging with it fully.

content/form-response grid An organizational format used to generate ideas when interpreting a text.

conventions In the context of academic writing, the customs associated with how to organize findings, use language, and cite sources.

counterarguments The objections of those who might disagree with you.

disciplinary discourse Writing or speaking that is specific to different disciplines.

discourse communities Groups that share common values and similar communication practices, both socially and professionally.

ethos An appeal based on credibility or character.

freewriting Writing in a free-flow form, typically for a set amount of time.

genres Approaches to writing situations that share some common features, or conventions, relating to form and content.

hedging The action of adding qualifiers to a sentence to limit the scope of a claim in a way that allows for other possibilities.

humanities Academic disciplines that ask questions about the human condition using methods of inquiry based on analysis, interpretation, and speculation.

hypothesis A proposed explanation or conclusion that is usually either confirmed or denied following examination.

idea mapping A brainstorming technique that creates a visual representation of ideas and their connections.

interdisciplinary field An area of study in which different disciplinary perspectives or methods are combined into one.

jargon A specialized vocabulary used by a particular community.

listing A brainstorming technique to help generate and record ideas, often in response to a prompt.

literacy narrative A reflective genre that examines how someone has developed reading and writing skills over time.

logos An appeal based on elements of logic and reason.

natural sciences Academic disciplines that ask questions about the natural world using methods of inquiry based on experimentation and quantifiable data.

open-ended question A question that provokes a fuller response beyond *yes* or *no*.

paraphrasing Translating the author's words and sentence structure into your own.

passive voice A sentence structure that eliminates or subordinates mention of the agent.

pathos An appeal based on emotions.

peer review The process of evaluating a peer's writing during the drafting phase to provide feedback.

plagiarism Failure to attribute source material to its original author.

popular sources Research produced for a general, public audience.

prewriting/invention The step in the writing process that involves brainstorming and organizing ideas.

primary audience The targeted recipient or consumer of a piece of writing.

primary sources Direct, first-hand evidence that helps support arguments.

purpose A reason for producing a piece of writing.

quoting Directly pulling the words of a source verbatim.

rebuttal A measured response to a counterargument that strengthens your own position.

research questions A question or set of questions that requires further investigation in order to answer.

revision Making content-level and organizational changes to a piece of writing.

revision plan A list of the big-picture changes the writer would like to make.

rhetoric The study of how language is used to communicate.

rhetorical analysis Close, critical reading of a text or image, examining the elements of author, audience, topic, and purpose.

rhetorical appeals Persuasive strategies within a piece of writing, including ethos, logos, and pathos.

rhetorical context Considerations of author, audience, topic, and purpose that are fundamental to each writing situation.

scholarly sources Research produced for an audience of other academics.

search terms Key words and phrases used to differentiate and locate specific research materials.

secondary audience An implied recipient who may be interested in a piece of writing.

secondary sources Evidence that offers commentary, description, or analysis of primary sources.

social sciences Academic disciplines that ask questions about human behavior and society using methods of inquiry based on theory building or empirical research.

structure, language, and reference (SLR) Categories that offer a guideline for analyzing the conventions of genres at a deeper level.

summarizing Condensing a piece of writing to its main ideas.

text Any object that can be "read" and transmits some kind of informative message.

thesis statement The central claim of an argument.

topic The subject of the writing.

transitional words or phrases Language used to signify shifts between and among the different parts of a text.

writing process The steps and methods used to produce a piece of writing.

Acknowledgments

Index

argument, 315
    analysis of, 59–65
    appeals to ethos, logos, and pathos, 49–50
    assumptions, understanding, 56–57
    claims, making, 48–51
    controversial issue, example of, 93–99
    counterarguments, anticipating, 57–59
    defined, 48
    evidence to support reasons, 53–56, 60
    position, qualifying, 58
    proofs and appeals, 49–50
    reasons, developing, 52–53
    simple and complex thesis statements,
        52–53
    statistical data and research findings, 54–55
    thesis-driven, in the humanities, 139
    thesis statement, forming, 50–51
Aristotle, 49–50
artistic proofs, 49–50
artistic texts, 147
Associated Press Stylebook (AP Style), 312
assumptions, understanding, 56–57
audience, 315
    in the applied fields, 261–62
    as element of rhetorical contexts, 34, 38, 42
    for press release, 104
    primary and secondary, 34–35
    and reading rhetorically, 38
    rhetorical contexts and, 34, 39, 42
author, 315
    as element of rhetorical contexts, 34, 38, 42
    reading rhetorically, 38
    and rhetorical context, 34, 39, 42

B

Bahls, Patrick (mathematics), on genres and
        the writing process, 17
bias, avoiding, 170, 216, 224
bibliography, annotated, 315
    in academic research, 88–89
    in literature review, 187
Bieda, Michaela (student), "My Journey to Writing,"
        29–32
Bluebook style, 312
Bonghi, Max (student), "Writing about Love:
        Comparing Language Differences in Two
        Scholarly Articles," 113–16
Bose, Dev (disability writing studies scholar), on
        reflection and accessible design, 25
Brotherton, Mike (astronomy), 103–4
    on audience for a press release, 105–6

on conventions of science journal articles, 111
on counterarguments, 58
"Hubble Space Telescope Spies Galaxy/Black Hole
        Evolution in Action," 104–5
"A Spectacular Poststarburst Quasar," 109–10
on writing for different audiences, 104
on writing in the sciences, 103–4
Bush, George H. W., "Letter to Saddam Hussein,"
        42–44
business writing memorandum, 273–77

C

characters, in student essay, 31
charts, tables, and figures, 177–79, 225–26
Chicago Manual of Style (CMS), 151–52, 312
Chopin, Kate, "The Story of an Hour," 136–38
citations, 150–51, 299–300
claims, 48, 315
    hedging, 148, 182–83
    making, 50–51
close-ended question, 315
close reading, 133, 315
    analyzing a short story, 136–39
    content/form-response grid, 134–35
    in the humanities, 126–27
    responding to others' interpretations, 139
    sample annotation and content/form-response
        grids, 134–35
    strategies for, 133–39
cluster mapping, 17
colleges and universities
    expectations of writing skills, 2
    mission or values statements, 3–4
    purpose of, 3–4
    resources at your school, 4
comics, close reading of, 127–32
communication skills, 25, 38, 260
"Comparing the Efficiency of Various Batteries Being
        Used over Time" (Lemon), 230–38
composing, discovering ideas through, 16–17
content/form-response grid, 134–35, 315
control group, 220
conventions, 315
    language
        active and passive voice, 167–68, 182
        in different disciplines, 108
        in the humanities, 146–48
        in the natural sciences, 225–26
        in the social sciences, 182
    references
        in the humanities, 150–52

in the natural sciences, 227
in the social sciences, 223
structural
in the humanities, 139–46
in the natural sciences, 223–25
in the social sciences, 171–79
cooperation and collaboration, 223
in the applied fields, 260
other researchers, treatment of, 224
Council of Science Editors (CSE), 88, 227
citing different types of sources in, 310
in-text citations, 309
reference page citations in, 309–10
sample references page, 311
unique features of, 309
Council of Writing Program Administrators (CWPA)
outcomes, common, of first-year writing course,
9–10
selected goals for writing process, 15–16
counterarguments, 315
anticipating, 57–59
criminal justice and law
careers in, 277–79
e-mail correspondence, 279–80
cultural literacy, 28–29

D

debatable subject in academic research, 58
debate. *See* argument
descriptive and rhetorical language
in the humanities, 147
in the natural sciences, 217
detail, sensory, 27, 31
dialogue, 30
Dieckmann, Janna (nursing), on areas of research in
nursing, 263
Diigo, social bookmarking application,
312–13
disciplinary discourse, 102, 315
discourse communities, 102, 315
"Diversifying Design: Understanding Multilingual
Perceptions of Learning in a Flexible
Classroom" (Gierdowski and Miller-Cochran),
211–12
documentation
American Psychological Association (APA),
87, 300–301
avoiding plagiarism, 85–86
Chicago Manual of Style, 151–52, 312
Council of Science Editors, 88, 300–301
in the humanities, 151–52

Modern Language Association (MLA), 86–87,
300–301
in the natural sciences, 227
in the social sciences, 170, 183–85
understanding documentation systems, 86–89
drafting, 18–19

E

EbscoHOST, 77–78
editing/proofreading, 17
education
lesson plan, 269–73
written products of educators, 269
"Effects of Sleep Deprivation: A Literature Review"
(O'Brien), 191–98
e-mail correspondence, 13, 279–80
engineering, 281–85
PowerPoint training slides, 282–84
ethos, appeals to, 49–50, 54, 62, 63, 315
"Evaluating Hydration Levels in High School Athletes"
(Gomperts), 93–99
"Evaluation of the Attribution Theory" (Kapadia),
201–9
evidence to support reasons, 53–56, 60
expert testimony, 54

F

feedback, giving and acting on, 19–23
five-paragraph essay, 144–45
focus/stance, establishing, 150–51
freewriting, 16, 315

G

Garrigan, Shelley (Spanish language and literature), on
learning disciplinary conventions, 140
Geiger, Paige (molecular and integrative physiology) on
the integrity of scientific writing, 221
genre analysis, of writing in applied field, 290–96
genres, 315
in the academic disciplines, 102, 106–7
analyzing, 103
choosing, in the applied fields, 261–64
defined, 106
in the humanities, 152–61
in the natural sciences, 228–57
of reflective writing, 25
in the social sciences, 185–212
understanding, 35–37

Gierdowski, Dana, and Susan Miller-Cochran, "Diversifying Design: Understanding Multilingual Perceptions of Learning in a Flexible Classroom," 211–12

Gierdowski, Mike (engineer), on professional writing, 282

Gilbert, Matthew Sakiestewa (history), on research in American Indian studies, 124

Gomperts, Jack (student), "Evaluating Hydration Levels in High School Athletes," 93–99

Google and identifying search terms, 74–77

graphs, 178

H

"Happiness in Everyday Life: The Uses of Experience Sampling," excerpts from Csikszentmihalyi and Hunter, 186, 189

health fields
   allied health professions, 262–63
   discharge instructions, 264–68
   nursing, 263–64
   writing for, in the applied fields, 262–64

hedging, 148, 182–83, 315

"Hubble Space Telescope Spies Galaxy/Black Hole Evolution in Action" (Brotherton), 104–5

humanities, 122–61, 315
   American Council of Learned Societies, 122
   asking "why," 140–42
   conventions of writing
      learning from peer and others' writings, 139–40
      open-ended questions, 142
      paragraphs and transitions, 145–46
      research questions, developing, 140–42
      thesis statements, 140–44
      titles and subtitles, 146
      why, what, and *how* questions, 140–42
   documentation of sources, 151–52
   engaging with theory, 126–27
   genres of writing in
      artistic texts, 147
      textual interpretation, 152–61
   language conventions, 146–49
      active voice *versus* passive voice, 147–48
      descriptive and rhetorical language, 147
      hedging of claims, 148
   references conventions, 150–52
      Chicago Manual of Style (CMS), 151–52
      focus/stance, establishing, 150–51
      introduction and citations in, 150–51
      Modern Language Association (MLA), 151–52

other scholars, incorporating works of, 150–51
      values reflected in citations, 150–51
   research in
      close reading, 133–39
      content/form-response grid, 134–35
      images, observing and interpreting, 125
      interpretations, responding to, 139
      role of theory in, 125–26
      texts as primary source for, 123
   scholars in, 6, 7
   structural conventions, 139–46
   texts, 123

"Hunting Behavior, Territory Quality, and Individual Quality of American Kestrels (*Falco sparverius*)" (Ritchison), 240–46

hypotheses, 315
   defined, 51
   in the natural sciences, 218–19, 220
   in the social sciences, 164–65

I

ideas
   discovering through composing, 16–17
   main idea, 26
   mapping, 17, 315
   tools for composing/invention, 16–17

images, observing and interpreting, 125

inartistic proofs in argument, 49, 50

information technology
   areas of specialization, 285
   shift operations, summary, 286–89

Institute of Electrical and Electronics Engineers (IEEE), 312

institutional review board (IRB), 170, 220–21

interdisciplinary fields, 214, 315

Introduction, Methods, Results, and Discussion (IMRaD) format, 107, 172–79, 210, 223–24, 247

"I" point of view, 26, 27, 29

issues or topics
   controversial, developing a supported, 92–99
   as element of rhetorical writing, 34, 38, 42
   and rhetorical context, 34, 39, 42

J

Jackson, Karen Keaton (writing studies)
   on accidental plagiarism, 85
   on considering purpose and audience, 34

natural sciences, 214–58, 316
 bias, eliminating, 216, 224
 conventions of writing in
  active and passive voice, 226
  charts and figures, 225–26
  cooperation and collaboration, 224
  documentation, 227
  jargon in research writing, 225
  numbers, 225–26
  precision in writing, 222
  recency, 223
  replicability, 222
 descriptive writing, 217
 designing a research study, 219–20
 genres of writing
  Introduction, Methods, Results and Discussion
   (IMRaD) format, 223–24
  lab reports, 247–58
  observation logbook, 228–38
  research proposal, 239–46
 institutional review board (IRB), 220–21
 interdisciplinary fields, 214
 language, or word choice, in research papers, 225–26
 open-ended questions, 218–19, 316
 other researchers' work, treatment of, 224
 references in, 227, 240
 research in
  closed-ended questions, 218–19
  comparative experiment, 220
  control group, 220
  from description to speculation, 217–18
  designing a research study, 219–20
  hard and soft sciences, 219
  hypotheses, forming, 218–19, 220
  institutional review board (IRB), 220–21
  observation and description, 216
  open-ended questions, 218–19
  publishing, 222
  qualitative data, 219–20
  replicable and quantifiable methods, 219
  results, presenting, 222
  speculative writing, 217–18
 scholars in, 6
 scientific method, 214–15
 scientific writing process, 214–15
 structural conventions of research papers, 223–25
 titles of research papers, 224
 values underlying writing in
  cooperation and collaboration, 223
  objectivity, 222
  recency, 223
  replicability, 222
Neff, Reece (student), genre analysis, 290–96

neutrality, in the social sciences, 170
newspapers as popular sources, 79
notetaking steps, 133–34
nursing field, writing for, 263–64

O

objectivity, 170, 222
O'Brien, William (student), "Effects of Sleep
  Deprivation: A Literature Review," 191–98
observation
 in academic disciplines, 123–24
 and description, 216
 and interpretation, 123–24
 logbook, 228–38
 in natural sciences, 216
observation logbook, 228–38
 strategies for working with an, 228–29
 Writing Project, 229–38
open-ended questions, 142, 218–19
organization of writing, 108

P

Panditharathne, Chrischale (student), summary of shift
  operations, 286–89
paragraphs and transitions, 145–46
paraphrasing, 82–84, 185, 316
passive voice, 37, 182, 316
 in the natural sciences, 226
pathos, appeals to, 49–50, 60, 64, 316
peer review, 17, 19–23, 316
 responding to, feedback, 23
 of student's literacy narrative, 19–23
peer-reviewed articles, 76, 78
personal experiences, writing about, 54, 198
personal investment, in academic research, 68–69
plagiarism, 316
 avoiding, 85–86
popular sources, 316
position, qualifying, in argument, 58
poster presentation, 210–12
 strategies for designing, 210–11
 Writing Project, 211–12
PowerPoint slides, 282–84
press releases, 103–4
prewriting/invention, 16–17, 316
primary audience, 34, 316
primary sources for academic research, 71, 316
Proctor, Sian (geology), on diversity of work within a
  scientific discipline, 216
"Profile of a Writer: Benu Badhan" (Kumar), 12–14

proofs in argument, inartistic and artistic, 49–50
PsycINFO database, 77–78
Publication Manual of the American Psychological Association (APA), 87, 151, 183–85, 227, 305–8
purpose, 316
    rhetorical context and, 34, 39, 42

Q

qualitative research methods, 168–69, 219–20
quantitative research methods, 167–68, 219–20
questions
    developing research questions, 260
    why, what, and *how* questions, 140–42
quoting, 316
    in academic research, 84
    others' interpretations of texts, 126
    in the social sciences, 185
    summarizing and paraphrasing others' writing, 185

R

Ramirez, Cristina (writing studies), on writing in the humanities, 149
Rathunde, Kevin (social sciences), 166
    on having multiple perspectives on a question, 166
    "Middle School Students' Motivation and Quality of Experience: A Comparison of Montessori and Traditional School Environments," excerpts from (with Csikszentmihalyi), 167–68, 169, 173–74, 175–79, 180, 181
    on research questions, 166
Ray, Sarah (student), "Till Death Do Us Part: An Analysis of Kate Chopin's 'The Story of an Hour,'" 154–61
reading and writing rhetorically, 33, 37–41
rebuttal, 57, 58, 316
recency of research, 223
reference conventions
    American Psychological Association (APA), 151, 183–84, 305–6
    Chicago Manual of Style (CMS), 151–52, 312
    Council of Science Editors (CSE), 88, 227, 309–10
    in different disciplines, 108–9
    in the humanities, 150–52
    Modern Language Association (MLA), 151–52, 301–3
    in the natural sciences, 227
    for a research proposal, 240
    in the social sciences, 183–85, 240
    summarizing and paraphrasing others' writing, 185

reflective writing, 19, 24–25
RefWorks, research-tracking application, 313
replicability, 222
replicable and quantifiable research methods, 219
reports, lab, 247–58
research
    developing questions, in the humanities, 140–42
    in the humanities, 123–32
    in idea mapping stage, 17
    issues, researchable, 69
    in the natural sciences, 163, 181
    primary and secondary, 70–72
researchable subject in academic research, 69
research methods
    institutional review boards (IRBs) format, 170
    mixed-methodology studies, 169
    qualitative, 168–69
    quantitative, 167–68
research papers, structure of, 223–25
research process
    designing a research study, 219–20
    hypotheses, 216, 218–19, 220
    methods section, 224
    observation, 216, 228–38
    sections in, 224
    speculation, 218–19
    statistical data and findings, 54–55
    study, designing, 219–20
research proposal, 239–46
    methods section, 240
    strategies for writing a, 239
    Writing Project, 240–45
research questions, 140–42, 316
    content/form-response grid, 142
    developing, 68–70
    in the humanities, 140–42
    natural sciences, 218–19
    open-ended questions, 142
    popular sources, 79–81
    in the social sciences, 164–65
results, 175–76
review of scholarship. *See* literature review
revising, 316
    of drafts, 19
    in idea mapping stage, 17
revision plan, 23, 316
rhetoric, 316
    in the applied fields, 261–62
    principles of, for college writing, 9–10
rhetorical analysis, 42, 44–47, 103, 316
rhetorical appeals, 49–50, 316
"Rhetorical Appeals in 'Letter from Birmingham Jail'" (Ahamed), 61–66

rhetorical contexts, 34, 42, 81, 316
  to analyze academic writing, 103–5
Richter, Michelle (criminology)
  on choosing a career in criminal justice, 278
  on quantitative and qualitative research, 55
Ritchison, Gary, "Hunting Behavior, Territory Quality,
    and Individual Quality of American Kestrels
    (*Falco sparverius*)," 240–46

S

scene writing, 26–27, 29
scholarly articles and engaging with other scholars,
    150–51
scholarly sources, 79–81, 316
scientific writing process, 214–15
scope in academic research, 69
search engines, 73–76
search terms, 73–76, 316
secondary audience, 34–35, 316
secondary sources for academic research, 71–72, 316
short story, analyzing, 136–39
SLR (structure, language, and reference) for analyzing
    genres, 107–121, 316
social literacy, 28–29
social sciences, 162–213, 316
  charts and figures, 177–79
  conventions of writing
    abstracts, 180
    acknowledgments, 180
    appendices, 181
    conclusion, 180
    Introduction, Methods, Results and Discussion
      (IMRaD) format, 172–79
    references, 183–85
    structural, other, 180–81
    titles, 181
  Discussion section, 179
  genres of writing
    literature review, 185–98
    poster presentation, 210–12
    source synthesis chart, 187
    theory response essay, 198–209
  introduction to, 162–63
  language conventions
    active and passive voices, 182
    hedging, 182–83
  observing behavior, 163
  others' experiences, 200
  personal experiences, 198
  reference conventions, 183–85
    in-text documentation, 184–85

*Publication Manual of the American Psychological
    Association* (APA), 183–85
  summary and paraphrase, 185
  research in, 163–71
    bias, addressing, 170
    institutional review board (IRB) policies, 170
    methods, 166–70
    mixed-methodology studies, 169
    neutrality, 170
    qualitative research methods, 168–69
    quantitative research methods, 167–68
    questions and hypotheses, 164–65
    statisticians, role in, 167–68
    theories of human behavior and human systems, 164
    theory, role of, 163–64
  results, 175–76
  scholars in, 6
  structural conventions, 171–79
  synthesizing sources, in the social sciences,
    188–89
  titles, for articles, 181
  visual representations of data, 177–79
  writing about others' experiences, 200
  writing about personal experiences, 198
sources
  evaluating, 79–81
  citing, 299–300
  journal databases, 76–78
  peer-reviewed articles, 76, 78
  primary and secondary, 70–72
  scholarly versus popular, distinguishing between, 79–81
  searching for, 73–78
  summarizing, paraphrasing, and quoting, 81–85
  synthesizing, in the social sciences, 188–89
source synthesis chart, 187
"Spectacular Poststarburst Quasar, A" (Brotherton, Van
    Breuge, Stanford, Smith, Boyle, Miller, Shanks,
    Croom, and Filippenko), 109–10
speculative writing, 217–18
statistics
  data and research findings, 54–55
  procedures, 167–68
  role in social sciences, 167–68
Stegner, Jack (student), draft of literacy narrative, 21–23
"Story of an Hour, The" (Chopin), 136–38
Stout, Sam (student), on academic writing, 9
"Strategies of Forbidden Love: Family across Racial
    Boundaries in Nineteenth-Century North
    Carolina, The" (Milteer), 82
structure
  conventions in social sciences, 171–79
  in the humanities, 139–46
  in the natural sciences, 223–25